LOST CERTAINTIES

The old order changeth yielding place to new,
And God fulfils himself in many ways
Lest one good custom should corrupt the world.

LOST CERTAINTIES

Reflections on a lifelong journey
for
friends and fellow travellers

Essays, Talks, and Letters

by

Brian W J G Wilson

The Memoir Club

© Brian W J G Wilson 2012

First published in 2012 by
The Memoir Club
Arya House
Langley Park
Durham
DH7 9XE
Tel: 0191 373 5660
Email: memoirclub@msn.com

ISBN: 978-1-84104-540-5

Printed by Xpresslitho, Washington, Tyne & Wear

For my beloved

Sara

who has travelled with me

all the way

Contents

D. Letters and Conversations

E. Explorations - Moving Forward

F. Soundbites

G. Building Upon the Ruins

H. Bibliography

Acknowledgements

In his great poem Tennyson's Ulysses says of himself that 'I cannot rest from travel' and, a little later, that 'I am a part of all that I have met.' Given that this book is, in a sense, the story of my own travels through the realms of faith over a lifetime, I owe a debt of gratitude to all that I have met, whether friends, mentors and acquaintances on the one hand, or writers, teachers, and preachers on the other, whose words of wisdom have opened magic casements onto the perilous seas of religious and doctrinal exploration.

My debt to them all is great, and acknowledged, however inadequately, in the text of what I have written and the bibliography at the end. Where I have quoted from their work, usually briefly, I hope that it will be taken as the compliment intended and not an attempt to pass off as my own what is the work of others. My life has been spent as a working schoolmaster. Although I have read much and my temperament is mildly academic, I have never had time for original research. The loss is mine. I remain to the end a student, a seeker after truth, and a searcher who in different circumstances would fain have been a researcher.

My greatest debt is to Sara, my wife. She is my most perceptive critic and nothing I write for sermons, speeches, or books is allowed to pass without her *imprimatur*. But cursed as I am with a profound lack of self-belief, she has also always been the source of great encouragement to me, to believe that what I have written is worth saying and may even be of help to others travelling a similar road. In a very real sense she has travelled with me all the way. My children too have cheered me from the sidelines and encouraged me by their interest. In all my family I have been quite singularly blessed.

Beyond that, Don McClen and John Churcher have both read the earlier drafts of this book. Their critical comments and detailed suggestions have greatly helped to improve the original. They too have urged me onwards - Don in our now massive correspondence spanning more than a decade, and John in his letters, sermons, website, and leadership of PCN-B (the Progressive Christianity Network of Britain), have both fortified me greatly in the struggle to find and keep a faith that is 'fit for purpose' for the new century. (I hate that cliché, but it works).

Teaching is a great career. Where else can you be paid to read, think, argue, and talk with civilised colleagues, who will keep your education going for the rest of your life? Or be required to argue with young, fresh minds, whose directness of comment and criticism will keep your own mind sharp and your certainties healthily challenged almost to the end of your days? Many of those whose letters and questions have provoked much of the material of this book were former colleagues with whom I have stayed in touch. Many, like me, were concerned by the failure of the leadership of our church to lead its hungry sheep to the green pastures needed to keep the Faith alive. As Milton, an earlier alumnus of my own Cambridge college, was to lament in the 17th century, 'The hungry sheep look up and are not fed.' I salute them all and list a number of them (including more clergy that might have been expected) among the mentors acknowledged in my chapter, Three Wise Men.

At the more technical level, my thanks are also due to the artist, Emma Hales, for offering me no less than three original works, two paintings and a photograph, to choose from for the cover of this book. All three spoke to me of wanderings and lost certainties. The pictures now hang on my walls, and on her advice the photograph was used for the cover. It speaks to me of a child lost (like many believers) upon an empty shore, against a blank horizon, with behind him the 'melancholy, long withdrawing roar' of a retreating sea (of faith?), an empty fishing net (is it not time to let our religious nets down on the other side of the boat?), and the lack of any adult near at hand to help (least of all the church, which suffers from arrested development and has failed to rise to adulthood). Others may find their own additional implications from the image.

Lynn Davidson and Leanne Garbutt of the Memoir Club have been superbly patient executors of an author's doubtless sometimes tiresome whims in turning typescript into book. It is the second time I have cast myself upon their mercies and been rewarded with (I think) an excellent result. I thank them and their supporting staff most warmly.

Introduction

I have been blessed over the years with a number of friends whose commitment to the Anglican faith, in which we were all raised, has been (like mine) much eroded, and whose disenchantment with the failure of those in authority or leadership roles in our Church to reinterpret the faith for a modern age has been similar to mine. We have not left the Church; rather we feel that the Church has abandoned us. Some of us still strive to remain within its embrace; others have lapsed into atheism or indifference. We have often exchanged letters (and e-mails); some have even asked me for my ideas or opinions on the subject. In retirement I have much enjoyed the challenge of trying to set out where I stand, and why, on a number of related issues. Some have been generous enough to tell me that they have found my 'essays' helpful. This volume is for them.

I have been much struck also, in my membership of PCN (the Progressive Christianity Network), to find how many retired clergy within its membership seem to feel that in their thinking they, too, have left the church behind. They have found it a real liberation to be able to say what they really think, now that they have passed beyond the control of their bishops, the church authorities, and their usually all too conservative congregations. I have also been quite surprised to find that the older generation seems less frightened of new ideas and more willing to be radical in its thinking than much of the younger generation, where it is not indifferent to religion altogether. But too often my children's generation seem to have found that the church has little or nothing to say to them. They remain benevolently disposed, but unpersuaded by the teaching of a church to which they still nominally belong.

By about 1980, nearly twenty years after the publication of John Robinson's *Honest to God*, nothing much seemed to have changed. By then I was already finding myself at odds with conventional theology. The literal interpretation of the Bible, the Church's reluctance to acknowledge that science had revolutionised our understanding of the universe, and scholarship our understanding of the Bible, its failure to promulgate or encourage an up to date view of scripture, and its failure to explore new ways of expressing its ancient truths - all these I found increasingly difficult to reconcile with the fruits of my own reading and understanding. Its attitude to women, especially their ordination whether as priests or bishops, I found neither biblical nor Christian, and certainly unsupported by any rational justification that could be categorised as anything much more than residual superstition.

Now, some thirty or more years later, I am aware that deep in the forest something may be stirring; there are movements for change. But they are still relatively small and dimly discernible and, perhaps surprisingly, much of it seems to be coming from the USA, where the work of the Jesus Seminar and its associated scholars, together with The Center for Progressive Christianity, may in time prove to have been seminal in the evolution of our faith. But in the wider world, vested interest and innate conservatism, as well as rank superstition, still prevail. Growth, which church optimists boast of, seems to my perhaps jaundiced eye to be found largely in the areas where universal education remains inadequate and a simple faith, hardly distinguishable from residual superstition, survives. The charismatic churches of the more developed world also show some growth, but their activities seem to my perhaps too sceptical mind difficult to distinguish from self-induced hysterics, while the superficially successful Alpha courses offer (I suspect) only a short-term appeal to those desiring certainties through simplicity rather than painful thought, and inevitably therefore depend upon a literal-minded approach to Biblical texts, which modern scholarship has discredited. More cynically – but delightfully none the less - I am told they also represent an attractive alternative marriage-mart for the prosperous middle-class young amid the loneliness of big cities.

My regret is that traditional religion seems to be dying; belief in a God or divine force of some kind much less so. My hope is that this is the way God wants it; my suspicion is that my revered grandfather, John Gregg, Archbishop of Armagh and 'Father' of the 1958 Lambeth Conference, was probably right when he remarked to a friend that 'it may be that the true mission of the church is to disappear.' In this, as my anecdote (Ch.31, page 142) suggests, he was supported by the great Michael Ramsey, Archbishop of Canterbury.

My own conviction is that we need a new prophet and a revolution in the way we present our Christian faith. Sadly we seem to lack such figures at present, certainly in the leadership of the Anglican Communion on this side of the Atlantic. Such prophetic figures as there are have yet to find an effective forum for their ideas. But then, it has always been the fate of prophets to be despised and rejected by their contemporaries.

In April 2008 a very kind retired Bishop wrote a generous review of my recently published family Memoir, *Experience is an Arch*. Understandably he found the sections on my evolving faith less than convincing, and probably too subjective for one who, as he did, understood better than I the importance of Authority and stability in the management of any institution. My letter to him in acknowledgement of his very generous comments still seems to me to sum up better than anything else I have written why and how I have reached the position that I have.

For that reason I am using it to round off this brief introduction to my collection of essays, letters, and discussions. They offer few solutions to the dilemmas of those like me who wish to profess and call themselves Christians. But the knowledge that we are not alone in our search for something more convincing than what we are currently offered by the conventional churches offers comfort of a kind, and (as Socrates pointed out to his disciples two and half thousand years ago), a confession of ignorance is the beginning of wisdom; a conviction of certainty the surest route to perdition, since (as another wise philosopher once pointed out) the opposite of faith is not doubt, but certainty.

* * *

I very much wanted to write to you and thank you for an undeservedly generous review of my Memoir.

You could have been far more severe, and yet I could easily have forgiven you all because of your very kind reference to Mark 12.34. I wish I felt that I was as close to the Kingdom as that quotation seems to imply. At best I hope I will be received with the classic pedagogic absolution: 'he tried hard.' I like your quotation from the great Francis Bacon: as Alexander Pope also observed, 'a little learning is a dangerous thing.' I do indeed have little philosophy and wish I had read more – but I am not temperamentally suited to it. But, as with the Bible, there is a quotation for every argument. Bacon also said, 'If a man will begin with certainties, he shall end in doubts; but if he will be content with doubts, he shall end in certainties.' I only hope that my doubts will end in some sort of certainty. But I doubt it.

When I published my collected broadcasts and sermons, I felt as if I was a traitor to my inheritance (and indeed to my beloved grandfather). I gave the book the title *A Faith Unfaithful*, because I felt very much that I had indeed been unfaithful to my faith. So to find that you, my kind reviewer, could recognise the struggle for belief and the genuine desire to remain within the embrace of my mother church (I still think of myself as C of I rather than C of E) was a considerable comfort.

I derive also some comfort from grandfather's dictum that you must 'know your ground and stand your ground', though I am pretty sure that it was uttered in connection with refusing to allow the Roman Catholic Church to bully the Anglican into submission or subservience. He also said, as George Seaver (his official Biographer) recorded, that 'the basis of religious certainty is the individual consciousness .... A certainty that rests on authority only, whether the authority of a book, such as the Bible, or the authority of a body such as the Church, or the authority of a fact or of a person, may have a certain temporary value, but it is only temporary. ... We are put here to be educated and enhanced – and second hand truth will only do that in a very small degree.'

Individual consciousness and individual conscience are, I am sure, very good protestant characteristics. That is why I have always tried to think my way through to a faith that can withstand the shocks and challenges of modern insights. It is not that I believe that the intellect is the final word – it clearly is not, as even Plato observed two and a half thousand years ago. There always has to be in the end the 'leap of faith.' But a faith that is not founded upon and defended by intellectual rigour is, in my view, proof against nothing.

That really is my complaint against the Church: it has (in my view) to the point of dishonesty failed to educate its people into the changing understanding of its origins, and of the world and the cosmos which informed its first theology. As a result, those with even half a mind have simply abandoned it for an atheistic secularism or (more feebly) retreated into a fundamentalism, which spares them the thought needed to continue to work out their theological salvation. Some (and more than at first I thought) still wrestle, and certainly there are within PCN a surprising number of retired clergy, freed at last from the shackles of their (mainly very conservative) congregations – and even, perhaps, their bishops – to explore honestly the possibilities and deficiencies of the traditional faith.

I think in fact that one could argue that 'latitudinarianism,' which you clearly disapprove of, and of which I am actually happy to plead guilty, is the Church's only hope. Indeed if I were more of an historian, I could probably make a case for arguing that the Church has always to a degree been latitudinarian – certainly in its early centuries, before the creeds were imposed upon its self-serving bishops by the secular authority of Roman emperors, Theodosius being an even worse offender than Constantine. But I heard Keith Ward argue at a lecture in Oxford a few weeks ago that liberalism lies at the heart of Protestantism, and that liberalism is the only way forward. Almost by definition, to be liberal is to be latitudinarian, and when Queen Elizabeth I said that 'there is one faith – and the rest is dispute about trifles', it would be interesting to know where her definition of that 'one faith' would have rested, before correctly dismissing most of its theological squabbles as 'dispute about trifles.'

For me belief in a God is the least difficult element of a faith. How you define or describe Him is quite a different matter – Mother used the phrase 'Eternal Mind, expanding ever to elude,' and I still find it helpful. Jesus is more problematical, but even grandfather pointed out that men came to God long before Jesus appeared on earth, and that Simone Weil's description of how she came to Jesus through God (rather than vice versa) had much to commend it.

By contrast for me at least the Bible is no longer a difficulty. Few, if any, of serious academic standing in the world of theology would, I suspect, argue any longer that it is 'inerrant'– or indeed, except in the widest metaphorical sense, that it is literally the 'Word of God.' It is a great library of history, poetry, prayer, and theology – collected over a lifespan of 1000 years, more important than individual writers such as Shakespeare, Milton, Plato, Aristotle, Sophocles, Thucydides, Virgil, Dante, Julian of Norwich, TS Eliot, etc., but of similar value perhaps to the combined wisdom and insight that they represent - and no less prone to error. It is a precious book, to be treated with reverence certainly, but to be examined and studied as critically and dispassionately as any other work of literature.

Though I once contemplated the prospect, even Holy Orders (forgive me) similarly seem to me simply an administrative convenience, possibly a necessity, but that is all; and the track record of those who held such offices within the Churches collectively does little to suggest that they are repositories of divine wisdom or goodness – closer really to structures for the retention of power.

From all that you will see why I have found some sort of refuge in PCN-B, the Progressive Christianity Network of Britain – offshoot of its American counterpart, TCPC: The Center for Progressive Christianity, (there are liberals even in fundamentalist America, thank goodness!)** For PCN I recently wrote the enclosed article (*A God for the Gaps* – *See Chapter 3*), which tries to summarise reasonably succinctly the current dilemmas facing the church and how as a benevolent layman I view them. It is deeply latitudinarian, I am afraid, but within the readership it has been kindly received, and the much larger TCPC has asked for permission to re-print it.

I am certain that we need a new prophetic voice for the Christian faith; and the likes of Spong, Holloway, Borg, Crossan, (and even Cupitt, whom I do not understand), as well as the more popular writers like Karen Armstrong, are for me closer to that role than those who see themselves as defenders of the traditional faith.

I only hope that Tennyson's view of honest doubt proves in the end to be more accurate than his earlier suggestion that such doubts are devil-born. I have long loved, often quoted, and even preached on the Hebrews passage you mention, that 'faith is the substance of things hoped for...' I am certainly still hoping.

**I should perhaps have added also OCN, the Open Christianity Network, which is the Irish equivalent of these organisations. I may not have been aware of its existence when I wrote this letter.

Section A: The Problem

All the gear; no idea

The true enemy of Faith is not Doubt but Certainty

If one can define a problem clearly, one may have taken the first step towards a solution. The pieces in this section reflect my own dilemmas and those of others with whom I have corresponded. They do not define the problems of faith in a modern age; rather they describe various aspects of those problems as they affect those who are, like me, sympathetic to the Faith but troubled by the problems of belief, when that belief cannot readily be reconciled with their own rationality.

Throughout the book I must ask readers to tolerate a degree of repetition in letters and essays written on similar subjects and with similar ideas, but with different recipients.

CHAPTER ONE

Lost Certainties

The Sea of Faith
Was once, too, at the full, and round earth's shore
Lay like the folds of a bright girdle furled.
But now I only hear
Its melancholy, long withdrawing roar,
Retreating, to the breath
Of the night-wind, down the vast edges drear
And naked shingles of the world.

Ah, love, let us be true
To one another! For the world, which seems
To lie before us like a land of dreams,
So various, so beautiful, so new,
Hath neither joy, nor love, nor light,
Nor certitude, nor peace, nor help for pain.

Matthew Arnold *Dover Beach*

I wonder if any poem has more successfully captured the sense of yearning for a lost world of certainty, such as a child might feel for the comfort of the nursery or the warmth of its mother's arms, than this poem. Housman's *blue remembered hills* evoke a similar idea, but somehow the too perfect metre and deceptive simplicity of the language leave us always on the verge of sentimentality.

Into my heart an air that kills
From yon far country blows.
What are those blue remembered hills,
What spires, what farms are those?

That is the land of lost content,
I see it shining plain,
The happy highways where I went
And cannot come again.

But there too we catch something of the feeling of loss, the longing for a once-upon-a-time Garden of Eden, whose gates are now closed to us, because we too have eaten of the fruit of the tree of the knowledge of good and evil, and can never again enjoy the innocence of childhood. It has been in some such mood that I have spent well over half a lifetime trying to reconcile the crumbling certainties of a childhood faith with the ever growing certainties of the workaday world, which has come of age in terms of the knowledge of its own origins and the psychology of human thought and behaviour, which have shaped the patterns of its culture and systems of belief. Every child learns to its sorrow that Santa Claus does not exist. But that it has to learn is inevitable. Sooner or later common sense must force upon that child, even if its contemporaries (rather sooner than its parents) do not, that such a being could not possibly accomplish in a lifetime what he is supposed to accomplish in a single snow-covered night.

And yet religious belief, almost alone of mankind's cultural presuppositions, seems well nigh untouchable, retaining an inviolable quality of holy ground, not to be trespassed upon by the irreligious yokels of the modern world. Growing up, as we all know, is a painful and difficult process. The conclusion forced upon me is that religious belief appeals to some residual element of childhood to which many of us cling, long after we have reached maturity in all the other aspects of our life's span. Once we grow up, the vast majority seem to lapse into atheism, or at best a benign agnosticism, deterred by good manners, kindness, or even the fear of fanatics, from disturbing the comfort zones of those whose ideas are different. Religion alone remains the Peter Pan of human cultural development.

Like many others of my generation, I suppose, I was first set free to speculate about the foundations of my belief by John Robinson's *Honest to God*. Suddenly it was no longer blasphemous to think for myself. And then, to my surprise, my father (a surgeon, but an entirely conventional church member), discussing the Nativity story with my mother (also a surgeon) declared that he 'could not help feeling that Joseph had something to do with it.' On another occasion she herself, in a letter to me, assured me that her own generation in the 1920's had already dismissed the Virgin Birth as an impossibility. That my very conventional and church-going parents could have such thoughts was well nigh incredible to me as a late teenager, but obviously it had a bearing on my changing views.

The church, by contrast – and understandably – never pointed out to its innocent worshippers that virgin birth stories are absent from the gospels of Mark and John, that Paul in his epistles, which pre-date the gospels, shows no sign of having even heard of such stories, and that the divinity of Jesus was a matter of vigorous debate until the late 4th century in the Western Christendom, and until the 7th century in the East. In time my own reading offered me the simple explanation – the nativity stories developed relatively late in the evolving 'mythology' of the new faith, typical of the mythopoeic tendency of human memory in every age. Significant historical figures of early history, such as Alexander the Great, Julius Caesar, Augustus and succeeding Roman emperors, were all credited with semi-divine parentage. (So, I am told, was Kim Jong-Il, the recent dictator of North Korea, as part of the political cult of the Dear Leader).

It was not until nearly fifty years later that I first heard of the sack of Sepphoris by the Roman army during their suppression of the Jewish revolt, which followed the death of Herod the Great in 4 BC. The accompanying slaughter of men, the widespread pillage, and the enslavement or ill-treatment of women and children, opened up a very different picture of what may have happened in nearby Nazareth. For obvious reasons it would be something that conventional adherents of the faith would not wish or even dare to contemplate. For me it simply reinforces the humanity of Jesus, the messy (and in the light of recent history very modern) circumstances of his birth, the admirable qualities of Joseph, whether actual or legendary, as a 'just man,' who stood by the girl he loved, and broadens the rich variety of possibilities and implications suggested by the legend of his birth. The freedom to speculate, the invitation to wonder, is all part of the new freedom offered by modern scholarship. It may offend traditionalists, but for me it enhances the realism and power of the whole event.

Over the last forty or fifty years I was gradually able to discard much of the mythical apparatus which inhibits honest thought about our faith. The fact that *Honest to God* was written by a Bishop was a help, since clearly he had dared to slip the surly bonds of earthly self-interest, which had kept too many of his fellow churchmen tightly bound to the official party line, even though they knew perfectly well that modern scholarship had weakened, if not invalidated it. It seemed to me that the traditional churches had too much to lose by way of power, influence, wealth, and status to surrender easily. They have still not done so, and inevitably their congregations have declined, because (unlike Oscar Wilde, I think it was) they have not been able to 'believe half a dozen incredible things before breakfast.'

Yet in some ways mythology was the easiest and most obvious element to discard, perhaps in part because, once I had acknowledged that it was myth, it seemed perfectly acceptable (even if only out of sheer affection) to retain it for its metaphorical or symbolic meaning, in the same way as one retains the much loved stories of one's childhood. The Nativity Plays produced annually for the genuine delight of parents and families owe everything to the fact that the children manifestly believe in what they are doing; for the young the boundaries between fact and fiction are, we know, very loosely defined. The innocent re-telling of much loved stories is utterly captivating.

I feel something of the same towards science and its unveiling of the mysteries of the cosmos. After all, though currently scientists are deemed almost incapable of error, we should remember too that throughout history they have misled us with their 'legends' of creation and the universe, and their myths of the origins of matter. Even the Higgs boson as the current explanation of mass is unlikely ever to be seen, as opposed to merely measured by its effects on a photographic plate.

The merit of scientists, though, is that unlike theologians they have always been willing (indeed delighted) to be proved wrong. Wrong they have been; and will continue to be again. But no-one complains that they have seduced us through the centuries with their mythologies of creation. Yet many of their theoretical assertions sound little different from theological ones. Both depend on metaphorical analogy to some degree (such as the use of Mrs Thatcher's handbag as an illustration of the operation of the Higgs boson). And it is only some twenty years since Fred Hoyle and the Steady State theory of the universe held sway.

Much more difficult has been the sorting out of the post-mythological residue of belief which remained. It took much longer for me to discover the degree to which the Bible is in no sense an historical record, let alone the Word of God in any but a metaphorical sense. Others I am sure have preceded him, but it was the work of another Bishop, John Shelby Spong, whose books I have read over the last ten years or so, that has spelled out with brilliant lucidity and unequivocal directness, the degree to which the Biblical record is on one side a human construct, a blend of myth, legend, folk memory, midrash, and an element of historically demonstrable fact, and on the other side sometimes profound religious thought, with additional elements of poetry (some of it sublime), creative fiction, epistolary controversy, and partisan propaganda. The work of the Jesus Seminar (*The Five Gospels* and *The Acts of Jesus*) lent powerful reinforcement to this perception.

In the Bible, in fact, within one volume, we have a veritable library. Once we are aware of that, we can work out more coherently how to use its contents to reinforce whatever arguments we wish to deploy in support of our beliefs, and the degree of validity to accord to its 'evidence.' Perceptions expressed in poetry or story may well be just as true as those of recorded history (which as we know is always written by the winners), but their kind of truth is different.

But still there remains the Church, which has been going for rather longer than most human institutions. Surely somewhere within its institutional memory it must have preserved some special insight, some element of truth, some deeper understanding of the nature of the God which it proclaims? The third phase of my exploration has taken me back to my own academic discipline as a student of Greek and Latin, later specialising in ancient history, at Cambridge University during an exciting period of its Classics department.

The works of Dominic Crossan, Marcus Borg, Charles Freeman, Geza Vermes, Keith Ward, the Jesus Seminar, Raymond Brown, Burton Mack, Karen Armstrong, John Churcher, Tom Holland, and others of course, have sent me back to the very beginnings of Christianity to try to get some sense of the context within which that remarkable teacher and preacher, Jesus of Nazareth, lived out his life's destiny. Without an understanding of context (for which Crossan, Borg, Vermes, Holland, and Freeman are essential reading), we cannot possibly hope to understand what Jesus was trying to say about the human condition and the society of his day, in a way that is still relevant to us today - a point persuasively brought out in many of the Internet sermons of John Churcher, on his Permission to Speak Website, as well as in his books.

What has become increasingly clear to me is that the Church (and its creeds), like the Bible, is a human construct, and that Jesus himself stands within a long tradition of Jewish charismatics and prophets. The concepts and deeds which we think of as being specifically Christian (Son of God, Kingdom of God, Abba/Father, Miracles, Healings etc.) have been shown (persuasively to me at least) by Geza Vermes in his *Christian Beginnings* to be part and parcel of that Jewish tradition. None of this invalidates the importance of his teaching, the moral force of his example, and the undoubted effect of his mission. All of these were manifestly so powerful that over succeeding centuries his followers steadily metamorphosed him from a great prophet into the incarnation of the Divine Logos, the manifestation of God on earth, and the second member of the Holy Trinity — a concept that has proved beyond the capacity of Christian scholars to explain satisfactorily to ordinary congregations.

Jesus' mission, in fact, began as a reforming movement within Judaism; the worldwide extension of the faith after the sack of Jerusalem in 70 AD was certainly not in his original game plan, but rather the result of a degree of persecution of his followers by the Jewish establishment in Jerusalem and by conservative members of the wider Jewish community after their dispersal throughout the Roman Empire. The Jesus Seminar (*The Five Gospels* and *The Acts of Jesus*) rightly colour-coded as black the instruction in Matthew 28 to his disciples to go out and preach the gospel to the whole world. Black indicates that they 'would not include this passage in the primary data base' and that 'Jesus did not say this; it represents the perspective or content of a later or different tradition.'

Interestingly, none of Jesus' words recorded in the Gospel of St John earns the red colour-coding, which would have indicated that the Seminar believed that 'Jesus undoubtedly said this, or something very like it.' St John's Gospel is not by the Beloved Disciple; it is by another John, a meditation, dated to about 100 AD, on the meaning of the Jesus phenomenon, probably written for the guidance of the author's own community in Ephesus, sometimes called the Community of the Beloved Disciple. It would not be unreasonable to suggest, therefore, that there is a degree of partisanship or even doctrinal 'spin' within it. Its Epilogue is clearly by a different hand, added later, perhaps (it is suggested) to correct the gospel's emphasis on the insights of the Jerusalem group and to suggest a later understanding of what the resurrection really meant and how it came about. Spong's *Reclaiming the Bible for a non-Religious World* has a fascinating approach to this.

Jesus' execution was a political expedient, probably contrived by the Jewish establishment but entirely acceptable to the Roman authorities, who (Pilate least of all) will not have given a second thought to the 'human rights' of someone they thought of as a political agitator. Crucified like a common criminal, Jesus was treated like one. There was certainly no physical resurrection, almost certainly no tomb in Gethsemane (at best a common grave shared with other executed malefactors), and quite possibly no disciple even to witness the crucifixion, since they 'all forsook him and fled.' Realism suggests that the account of the whole event is legendary rather than factual – a typical foundation myth, developed from folk memory and oral transmission, as was usual in ancient society for any new city or institution. Even the Easter date has been disputed; it has been argued that autumn was a more likely time for the Passion events.

What is undeniable is that the influence of Jesus on his embryonic movement remained immensely powerful. And given mankind's propensity for myth-making, and the Jewish propensity for re-working their own history in the light of contemporary experience (Midrash), this is the likely source of the legends of his appearances, whether on the Road to Emmaus, in the garden of Gethsemane to Mary, or in the upper room. The ability to appear and disappear, and to pass through locked doors, is highly suggestive. This Recognition of Jesus in the Other, whether in community, friendship, distress, or at a meal, as in the Emmaus story, is probably the template for all the appearance stories.

I much enjoyed Richard Holloways's suggestion in his autobiographical *Leaving Alexandria* that the Jesus of Faith is rather like a strip-tease in reverse. Over centuries Jesus has become ever more clothed with the trappings of institutionalised religion and burdened with its baubles, until now he bears little resemblance to the original Jesus of Nazareth, who began as nothing more than a reformer of traditional Judaism. The Jesus of History has little to do with the later Christ of Faith, who is the creation of political and ecclesiastical squabbles in the third and fourth centuries.

After the initial panic and flight, a clear resolution developed among his followers that his teaching and example, the Jesus 'Way', must be preserved and promulgated. But at first the focus lay entirely within Judaism, and even when the teaching spread out across the Roman Empire, it was largely within the Jewish *diaspora*. Wherever he went, Paul made contact with and taught in local synagogues. The final and irrevocable break with Judaism did not come till a little before AD 100.

Initially there were probably two branches of the movement, one based in Galilee, the other in Jerusalem, both seeing themselves as groupings within the Jewish faith. Both alike believed that Jesus was the promised Messiah and that the meaning of his life could be found in the writings of the Old Testament, of which he was the fulfilment. To this end they scoured the (Jewish) scriptures, notably the Psalms and the Prophets, seeking especially to account for the apparent 'failure' of his mission, finding particular comfort in the vision of the Suffering Servant of Second Isaiah, and passages from the Psalms. The Passion story is designed around these insights. They expounded their ideas within the synagogues, adapting their story to the religious requirements and readings of the Jewish liturgical year, and their high festivals such as the Passover, Hannakah and so on. That is why we get the impression that Jesus' mission only lasted one year.

They believed, too, that they were living in the 'last days', and awaited some form of apocalyptic event, a Second Coming and Day of Judgement, for which they must prepare urgently and warn as many others as possible to do likewise. This is probably why there were no written records initially, though it is also perfectly possible that few, if any, of Jesus' original followers were literate. Certainly the gospel writers were not members of the original band of disciples.

But when the Day of Judgement did not occur, they had to think again. And as they took their teaching out to the wider Jewish communities of the Roman empire, following the sack of Jerusalem in AD 70, controversy inevitably arose, squabbles at first with the parent Jewish communities and then later among fellow Christians as to the meaning and 'theology' of Jesus' teaching. In the light of Christianity's later split from its Jewish 'mother,' (which may even be the source of the 'Son, behold thy mother legend,') and its expansion all over the Roman Empire, it became important to airbrush Roman 'guilt' in Jesus' death from the record, as far as possible. Hence the emphasis on Jewish guilt ('on our heads be it') and the positive spin applied to such favourable tales as that of the Roman soldier at the cross ('truly this was a God's son'), Herod's initial protection of John, Pilate's hand-washing, and the centurion, the like of whose faith Jesus had not seen in all Israel, etc.

Once the split from Judaism was complete, new independent Christian communities grew up. They were not necessarily seen as dangerous, nor were they always persecuted. The Younger Pliny, the Roman Governor of the province of Bithynia, a fair minded and reasonably objective witness, reported to the emperor Trajan around AD 110 that their 'guilt' amounted to no more than this: 'they had met regularly before dawn on a fixed day to chant verses alternately among themselves in honour of Christ, as if to a god, and also to bind themselves by oath, not for any criminal purpose, but to abstain from theft, robbery, and adultery, to commit no breach of trust and not to deny a deposit when called upon to restore it. After this ceremony it had been their custom to disperse and reassemble later to take food of an ordinary, harmless kind....' Though he describes it as 'a wretched cult,' it is clear that he sees no great harm in it, so long as its members will acknowledge the imperial religion, whatever other religion they belonged to. The problem was, of course, that committed Christians would not do so – and were consequently executed.

Bishops (*episkopoi* = overseers) did not emerge until around AD 100; Latin was not used in worship until as late as AD 180; Christianity was a disparate body, with far from uniform beliefs, in which 'in the late 3rd century there were for example eighty African bishops, each ruling an area little more than a village,' and its membership was probably little more than 10% of the population of the Empire, the majority of which remained pagan. Rome itself was home to a fragmented Christianity, where there was as yet no Pope, and the Bishop of Rome had problems asserting his authority, because so many church leaders were immigrants, bringing their own cultures and theologies with them. The pre-eminence of Rome was a later phenomenon, and Ignatius' list of the bishops of Rome to justify the claim to Apostolic succession and supremacy in the Church may be dismissed as a pious fiction.

The creeds are the product of the fourth century, when the Roman Emperors, Constantine and later Theodosius, imposed uniformity on a rather loose and disparate body, which argued incessantly about the divinity of Jesus Christ, the nature of God, the attractions of paganism (a much more tolerant religion than Christianity or Judaism), and Gnostic ideas, which from as early as AD 100 were beginning to influence the development of the early faith. It is worth noting, almost as a footnote, that Robert Bellah in his *Religion in Human Evolution* observes that, 'for us there is an ontological chasm between the divine and the human that simply was not there in the archaic mind … If mountains could be divinised, so could extraordinary humans, and who more likely than a king?' To which I would add, that if Augustus could be emperor and accorded divine origin as *divi filius*, Son of God, (because he was adopted by the deified Julius Caesar), it must have seemed essential for the followers of Jesus, whose kingdom they proclaimed in deliberate contrast to that of Augustus, that he too should be accorded divine origin; and so, in time his mother too became invested with supernatural qualities.

Like St Paul, neither of the two of the gospel writers, Mark and John, appear to have heard of the story of the virgin birth; and the original prophecy in Isaiah referring to a 'young girl' conceiving and bearing a son was later misunderstood to mean a virgin. The Immaculate Conception, the perpetual virginity, and the Assumption of Mary are inventions of the later Roman church. As the Roman Empire came under increasing pressure in the fourth century and its administration increasingly chaotic, bishops came to be seen more and more as the only effective 'managers' of civic society. From this fact developed the symbiotic relationship between Church and State, which increasingly corrupted the idealistic vision of Jesus and his early followers of a faith community which was without hierarchy and banded together for mutual support under an increasingly oppressive Roman regime.

All this made it possible for me to see the institutional Church as a flawed, human organisation rather than a body divinely appointed by some authoritarian divinity. It followed that its doctrines and culture were not set in stone; that it must renew and refresh itself continually; that it must revise and reinterpret its inherited mythology (and I do not use that word with any pejorative intention); that it must work to earn the support of its adherents, by its example of godly living, the compelling attractiveness of its teaching, and by adopting forms of worship meaningful to its followers and doctrines relevant to contemporary conditions. But all human institutions have a tendency to develop certainties about their monopoly of truth, and from that to seek to impose with increasing brutality their own vision of that truth. The Christian Churches are no exception, and their record of intolerance and brutality in defence of not only truth (as they saw it) but power and status also, is an enduring blot upon their history.

Their treatment of women is but one illustration. I have never had any problems with the issue of women priests. There was little or no scriptural argument against their ordination, as even Michael Ramsey, the recent and deeply scholarly archbishop of Canterbury acknowledged, and therefore none against their appointment as bishops either. In fact I am not entirely clear whether in the very early church the status of prophet (or apostle), where women seem to have been accepted, was not of greater importance than that of bishop, which was initially a largely administrative office. No doubt scholars will hasten to put me right on this. Objections to such developments were largely due to the ingrained conservatism of the religious institutions, vested interests, male chauvinism, cultural tradition, and perhaps an element of pure superstition. Jesus had no such inhibitions. In fact women priests have proved the salvation of the Anglican churches and in time even Rome is almost bound to move in the same direction.

Opponents of women priests insist that the alleged and unproven 'failure' of Jesus to choose female apostles requires that only men can be priests. The logic of this surely demands that only Jewish males (presumably circumcised) should be eligible for priesthoods or bishoprics. This is patently absurd. The idea that God chose a man to be his son, and therefore only a male priest can represent him on earth falls before the same argument, as well as before the myth that Jesus was literally God's son. Michael Ramsey's profoundly honest comment on the matter was that he 'rather wished that the theological arguments against women's ordination were stronger.' He very much wanted to preserve the possibility of church unity, to which he had devoted much of his time in office, and which at that time was enjoying a considerable thaw in relationships. The admission of women priests would have made his task more difficult than it was. Once retired from office as Archbishop he conceded that there was no evidence in the New Testament against women as priests, and that he expected it to happen at some time, even in the Roman Catholic Church.

As a result I now remain silent during the Creed, but I still participate hesitantly in the Eucharist, whose liturgy seems increasingly archaic and simply one form of worship out of several. It continues to appeal to me less than Matins and Evensong for routine church attendance. Its magical overtones offend some; they simply lack meaning, and I have no requirement that the elements should have to be consecrated by an ordained priest. Nor did the early Christians, according to Vermes. For some a priest's incantations may add solemnity to an occasion; but they add nothing to the elements, which remain for me entirely symbolic. On a desert island after (say) a shipwreck, I would happily accept them from anyone who tried to do the job decently and reverently.

For me the Eucharist is simply a ritual of ceremonial remembrance, which evolved naturally in the early Jewish-Christian communities, before churches were even formed. As a memorial service I find it much less compelling than Remembrance Day, and perhaps if it became similarly rare each year, its force would increase. I am sure I remember being taught at confirmation class that Queen Victoria regarded three communions per annum as perfectly sufficient, while I read somewhere that the Council of Trent (1545-63) settled for one such attendance. The significance of the bread and wine in the Eucharist seems to me to lie not so much in its creedal or doctrinal pronouncements as in its symbolic meaning as a shared meal, a social construct, looking back to its origins among early Christians, who met together for mutual support in hard times, and looking forward in an act of binding solidarity among those whose faith committed them to share everything and to work for the common good.

My reading over many years has come to mean that though I miss the childlike simplicity of my early faith, I am much more comfortable than I was in remaining a member of my Church, because I no longer feel the need to regard faith as 'the power to believe what you know isn't true', to use the famous schoolboy definition, or to defend to sceptical friends beliefs which I cheerfully admit are indefensible. There is, for me, no longer 'a divinity which shapes our ends.' But there may well be a divinity, which grows as we grow, expanding ever to elude, sustaining existence, and offering us meaning and purpose in our lives. On the existence and nature of that Divinity I remain cheerfully open-minded. The true enemy of faith is not doubt; it is certainty. Certainty is a denial of faith.

Just as I happily watch my grandchildren in their Nativity plays, and collude with their parents in the myth of Santa Claus, I tolerate the limitations of worship and try to maintain the regularity of my attendance. I wish it were different – and better. But it is all there is. If I were still a cricketer, I would accept the discipline of regular practice in the nets, knowing full well that it bears little resemblance to playing out there in the middle; so too I endure (that is nearly always the most accurate word) the worship which the Church offers, in the expectation (or at least the hope) that it will in some way prepare me for my next outing in the middle, and improve my performance. But it does not surprise me that the majority of my contemporaries cannot see the point; nor do I blame them for it. The Church is failing them, not they the Church.

Attempts to avoid the appearance of gender prejudice often necessitate tiresome repetition of the word God. To use 'she' seems to me simply an affectation; 'it' would be offensive. Convention has always used 'he' for most indeterminate beings or things, except for ships. It is probably easier to treat the masculine pronoun as the pronoun for any being or body of unspecific gender definition and hereafter that is the procedure to be followed. I would never attempt to offer any suggestions about the surely non-existent gender of the Almighty. The God I seek is indefinable. I still search for a better account of how he operates. I incline to think that the insights of poetry, such as the works of R.S. Thomas, offer the best verbal access to the idea of God; the example of good and holy men and women the best model; the incontrovertible virtues of common humanity (what St Paul calls the Fruits of the Spirit) the best guidelines for living.

I cannot pray to God in the conventional manner, asking for blessings or outcomes, which he manifestly cannot and does not provide. A God cannot be all-powerful in any conventional sense who, despite the endless prayers of the faithful, 'allows' a world to exist, where evil and cruelty, famine and deprivation, sickness and suffering, greed and ambition, and regimes of manifest unfairness and injustice prevail, not least because prayers are often contradictory and therefore inevitably unanswerable. To assert, as Dame Julian of Norwich did in her 13th Revelation that 'God recognises the existence of evil in the universe, but all shall be well....' is no real answer to this dilemma.

In fact, we need a different paradigm, a new vision, a totally different understanding of the nature of deity. And as always, once we try to reduce God to language, we are reduced to inarticulateness, and ultimately silence – what the mediaeval mystics would have called the 'apophatic' way.

I do not think of myself as radical in my views; but I do want to be rational, even though I readily concede that rationality has its limitations. My bishop friend called me latitudinarian; I prefer to see myself as possibly progressive, but more simply as liberal. I recently came across as good a definition of a liberal as I have seen in a tribute to Donald Hilton, one of the founder members of Free to Believe. Of liberalism he said this: 'Liberalism is a call to pilgrimage. Such a pilgrimage is not easy. It can be difficult to survive. Certainty is so much less costly; the path is clear and well-trodden. But we can survive the pilgrimage that moves between joyous adoration and critical analysis because, when we do so, we stand with the Gethsemane Jesus, who longed for the joyous burden of God and hated the consequences of it, but survived through faith; we stand with the searching Jesus who wrestled in the Lenten wilderness to know God's will; and with the crucified Jesus, who knew God could never disown him, but feared that he had. That is the developing tension of the Christian faith. That's what it means to 'live with questions'; and if it was true for Jesus, what right do you think we have to evade the tensions or the questions?'

It is, of course, perfectly possible that there are dimensions, literal or metaphorical, which are simply beyond the capacity of our species to grasp in our current phase of evolution. 'If horses had gods, they would look like horses,' as one of the early Greek philosophers acutely observed. My dog may not yet be fully up to speed on the Darwinian theory of evolution; humanity may similarly not yet be fully up to speed on the nature of the deity, still unable to 'give an account' (Socrates' phrase) of that deity's qualities, capacities, and functions. But that does not mean we should not try. Here is one attempt; it is not the answer; it suggests an approach. I quote Bishop John Shelby Spong in a recent message on the Internet.

> Suppose we try to envision God as the Source of Life, then we worship God by living fully, and we experience God as power flowing through us when we become the source of life to another.
> Suppose we conceive of God as the Source of Love, then we worship God by loving wastefully, and we experience God flowing through us when we become the source of love to another.
> Suppose we conceive of God as the Ground of Being, then we experience God by having the courage to be all that we can be....
> If we can entertain that understanding of God, then....

prayer becomes not a petitioner imploring an external authority, but an activity in which each of us is deeply involved;

God becomes not an external force invading time and space, but the power of life, love, and the sharing of being.

Maturity replaces childishness in worship and we recognise that God is part of who we are and we are a part of who God is.

CHAPTER TWO

On Lost Certainties

(Edited comment from a friend)

Where do I start in response to your interesting paper concerning religious belief? I suspect that I have said it all before, but matters of faith I find deeply interesting, if not at the depths to which you go to ponder and worry over these questions. In the margin of your first paragraph I wrote 'Santa Claus.' I beat you to it; he came up in the next paragraph. You will have read Dennett; he compellingly rehearses the argument that religion is a human construct. My own lack of belief, not by the way a bleak prospect, is strengthened when I read that there are billions of galaxies with billions of stars in each. It is thus surprising that God incarnate in the form of Jesus cropped up just two thousand years ago on this small planet. It reinforces the notion that the Christian religion is highly improbable. As to life after death, everything that one knows about nature, all creatures great and small, make me consider that eternal life is not improbable but preposterous.

And another telling argument concerning the truth of Christianity is the multiplicity of religions. Yes, all civilisations have created their religions. Most of them put forward the idea of some sort of afterlife. Why? Because humankind is the only form of life, we presume, that can contemplate its demise. And so we construct ideas of a life after death or reincarnations and that sort of thing.

I attend church because I love big services that go well and I have been fortunate in living within reach of Canterbury Cathedral and York Minster in my time. If I lived in London I would often attend All Saints, Margaret Street, with its fine music and catholic ceremonial. I note that you do not say the Creed. And yet, if you cannot accept it, then what are you doing by being there? If most of it is denied, then why attempt to construct a set of beliefs that you can accept?

God the Father, maker of heaven and earth. How can this mean anything? If there is a creator, what came before that? What caused the Big Bang? Perhaps, one day, mankind will know. Perhaps we are like our pet dog, which is unable as yet to understand the euro debt crisis and how to get out of it (not that we chaps seem to have the answer). Jesus, Son of God, conceived by the Holy Ghost - highly unlikely to say the least, and yet some of my rectors (interviewed in my latest book) consider this an essential fact that must be accepted. Descended into Hell. It is hard to believe in either hell or heaven. Rose again from the dead – impossible to swallow. Ascended into heaven, sitting on the right hand of the father, from thence he shall come to judge the quick and the dead. How often in church do we ever hear of the second coming these days? Never. Who believes it? The resurrection of the body and the life everlasting – surely preposterous? That's why churches are empty on a Sunday; it is not only because modern living offers Sunday alternatives; it is because most people regard Christian doctrine as incredible and ridiculous.

I suppose one can take the same line as Holloway, Spong, and Don Cupitt and interpret it all as a lovely myth, with the wise instruction to love one another, but is this not playing mental gymnastics and doing what I reckon you are doing – knowing that Santa Claus does not exist but unable completely to shake off the comfort and thrill of expecting him to visit on Christmas Eve?

And prayer! There is absolutely no evidence that a prayer has ever been answered. Good and bad people die of cancer, unaffected by prayer. And are you puzzled, as I am, how church services have to be set up and held whenever there is a terrible tragedy (when we thank God for the nurses, doctors, and rescue services)? Yes we know all the conventional answers: God does not answer all prayers, or at least give us the answer we seek; and horrible things happen in this world, because we have free will; otherwise life would be indeed be very strange.

Yes, says the modern believer, there is the problem of suffering and we cannot see the answer. It is much simpler for the non-believer: suffering is a consequence of life. It is not so much the selfish gene as the a-moral gene. Think of all forms of life existing by living off what is below them in the food chain. We are as guilty of that as a bacterium, as we tuck into our Sunday chicken. Consider the animals that David Attenborough shows us chasing and devouring other animals.

Actually you and I are not far apart; I reckon that I am a tad more honest in facing up to Christianity's illogicalities; then, there is the fact that you and I cannot comprehend what goes on in the minds of nice people we know who can swallow much more of this that can we. I do not completely go along with Christopher Hitchens, quoted in his *Times* obituary today: 'Religion is violent, irrational, allied to racism and tribalism and bigotry, invested in ignorance and hostile to free enquiry, contemptuous of women and coercive toward children.' Not quite the dear old C of E, but there is a grain of truth there.

To which (also slightly edited) I replied:

You could be the next Hitchens – there is a job going there. I could have cited his *God is not Great* as one of the books on my 'influential' list. You write with something of the same vigour, and though I agree that our views are not far apart, perhaps my greater willingness to contemplate the possibility that I am wrong leaves me inclined to be a little more gentle in my expression of what I think. My objection to the likes of Hitchens and Dawkins is that they too often seem to be so angry about it all. At least you are not guilty of that. Aggressive unbelief is as unattractive as belief.

I still concede to the purists that, just as your pet dog is still not entirely up to speed on the euro debt crisis, so perhaps we are not, as a species, fully up to speed on the creation of the cosmos and the possibility of divinity. I too still want to know what happened before the Big Bang, and at last I think some scientists are beginning to catch up with me on that. (Muttering about the arrow of time and there being nothing before the Bang seems to me about as weak as most religious arguments for the existence of God.) Messrs. Polkinghorne and Peacocke try very hard to reconcile the two belief systems – science and religion. Neither, for my money, succeeds. But both seem to be nice men – and sincere in their attempts to reconcile what may be irreconcilable.

My real complaint, which I fully share with you, is the amount of absurd nonsense we are still officially expected to believe, if we wish to be considered 'real' Christians, though I would not state it quite as baldly as you. You say that, 'there is no evidence that prayer is ever answered.' It is, in fact, answered quite often – but not, I agree, by God – or not necessarily. Rather, by the cumulative effect of united wills and desires and, probably, a degree of good luck or blind chance. The will of the community, whether expressed by prayer or by ballot box, can achieve desired results – sometimes. But if we attribute such successes to God, then we must also convict him of gross unfairness, inconsistency, and injustice – the whole amounting to incompetence.

But I would always remember that scientists, who are currently deemed incapable of error, have misled us throughout history with their own legends of creation and the universe – even the Higgs boson is unlikely to be seen, as opposed to merely deduced and measured by its effects upon a photographic plate (like a ouija board?). Their merit, however, is that unlike theologians they have been relatively willing (if not delighted) to prove themselves wrong. And wrong they have been, and will continue to be; as a result, no-one complains that they have seduced us through the centuries with their mythologies of creation. In the end, however, many of their theoretical assertions sound little different from theological ones. Both depend on metaphorical analogy to some degree. After all it is only about twenty years since Fred Hoyle was asserting the truth of Steady State....

I like Matthew Parris' comment in *The Times* recently, quoting Disraeli's *Endymion*: 'Sensible men are all of the same religion.' 'And what, pray, is that?' enquired the Prince. 'Sensible men never tell.' Auden suggested that 'Truth, like orthodoxy, is a reticence.' But best of all is Dickens' Dick Swiveller, in *The Old Curiosity Shop*, who observed, 'What is the odds so long as the fire of the soul is kindled at the taper of conviviality, and the wing of friendship never moults a feather?'

Not a million miles, I think, from good Queen Bess, who observed that 'There is only one faith; the rest is dispute about trifles.'

CHAPTER THREE

A God for the Gaps?

In our parish we recently had a discussion between some parishioners and the clergy on the decline in church attendance and the ever-growing 'Gap' between churchgoers and non-churchgoers, between the faithful and those who are lost, strayed, or disillusioned. Regrettably, it seemed to be largely a discussion about where to place the deck chairs on the already sinking *Titanic*, with some of the clergy and most of the laity acting out the part of the band, playing heroically the same old tunes as the ship went down. We never really addressed the Gap, its causes, and its remedies.

Has the church any sense of what this Gap is, who are part of it, and what are their problems? And do they really care? That the Gap exists is too obvious to need stating. But I would argue that though it is a regrettable phenomenon, it is also an extremely healthy sign of a general rejection of outdated modes of theology, thought and worship which the church continues to purvey. It is an essential precursor to renewal one day. But I suspect neither I, nor my children, will live to see it.

Despite my age, I see myself as very much one of the Gap people, though I have remained a regular churchgoer and communicant all my life. I find that the conventional church (in its worship and its teaching) has ceased to speak to me and certainly offers no ministry for me and my kind. Though my own vicar is immensely patient and understanding, in my worship I now find no solace in the somewhat dreary banalities and over-busyness of modern Family Communion, whose language and imagery (sacrifice, drinking blood, eating flesh etc.), are rather appalling and largely meaningless to the modern mind.

My children are similarly Gap people, benevolent to the church, confirmed, irregular churchgoers, perhaps because they feel no great need of the church. They don't really know what to teach their children in this modern age about the Bible and Jesus (cf. Ch. 39), and I doubt if Sunday School has much to offer beyond a fast track to fundamentalism.

In our parish discussion, we dodged instantly away from any suggestion that the theology we offer is seriously flawed and that the fundamental 'narrative' of the faith now lacks credibility for thinking people. But where thinking people are today, the generality will be the day after tomorrow. The clergy are well aware of this, but dare not educate their people in the new insights born of modern science and biblical scholarship.

Someone at our meeting asked a deceptively simple but critical question: what are the needs of the people whom the church seeks to win back or attract? We ducked that too! We kept drifting back to the needs of church people, not of Gap people. The moment such an uncomfortable question was asked, an understandable defensiveness crept in and we were regaled with lists of all the different things the church was doing, the different services, the groups and circles, the church schools, and so on. In our parish all schools are primary schools, with the result that no one even mentioned teenagers. Yet this, I suspect, is where the church loses its following for ever. I have taught the secondary age group all my life, many of them from church-supporting homes, and one could see the irrelevance of the church and its lack of credibility all through the 1960s–2000, which my career spans.

I entirely agree that the church needs to be seen to be with people where they are, not where they ought to be. But in the end, a plethora of small initiatives resembles nothing so much as the activity of a headless chicken, which rushes in every direction but (alas!) has no idea where it is going. That I am sure is the weakness of the current church. ('Got all the gear; but no idea'). In seeking to be all things to all men, it is in danger of being nothing to anyone. It must decide..... What is the core mission? What is the core narrative? Get that right and the rest will follow.

One problem is that Jesus got it wrong too. He thought that the Kingdom of God was at hand. It turned out that it wasn't (at least in the form that a first century Jew would have conceived it) and that has posed a problem to the church ever after. Jesus never formed a church – he sent his disciples out to preach the good news. And then the good news did not happen. The second coming, the End of the Age, and the Last Judgement failed to materialise. As for The Church (in capitals), it was really only formed, or at least firmly crystallised, round an agreed faith, in the 4th century by Constantine (the Great Pragmatist, who cared less about what people believed than that they should all publicly agree on what they believed).

But at least turning the signs of the coming Kingdom into a reality gave the church a sense of purpose, and to some degree that will remain a task for the foreseeable future: helping the blind to see, the lame to walk, seeking liberty for the captives etc. But here too it has a problem. That battle is won. Its values have, broadly, triumphed and every civilised society, in the Christianised West at least, seeks (however inadequately) to care for the weak, the oppressed and the underprivileged. With the deplorable exception of its attitude to women, Christianity can claim credit for that, whatever its other failings. The church certainly has a residual task in this area: to fill the gaps in the welfare state and to keep the state and society up to the mark. But, like Britain, it has 'lost an empire and not yet found a role.'

The second part of the mission (relationship with God) might be expressed in the words of the disciples: 'Lord, teach us to pray.' Here Jesus came up with a pretty good answer and example. Retreat to silence and inwardness; seek purity of heart (they are the ones that shall see God); obey the two great commandments; the Lord's prayer – a model of simplicity and lack of verbosity by contrast with what some writer called 'sad, talkative Christianity'; and lead as best you can the model of life set out in his teaching and example. I don't think he ever suggested that 'blessed are the churchgoers,' though I concede that he was probably a regular at synagogue.

Two millennia of theology and church obscurantism have made such relative simplicity of life and worship almost impossible. Modern civilisation has, in addition, so complicated the situation that Jesus' model is probably only possible in a monastery. But let's at least get rid of the theological clutter, the mumbo jumbo, the pre-Darwinian ideas. Let's really re-design (not just re-brand) the product - the theology - and perhaps the customers will return to the stores.

The issue of forms of worship is – or should be - peripheral, not central, since decline in church attendance is only a symptom of wider failure, not a cause. But the basic, routine Sunday service needs re-examination. We need familiarity, stability, regularity, order, and at least some instruction in a modern faith. The current emphasis on the Eucharist is no help to the Gap people, the uninitiated, uncommitted, and unimpressed, and is most unlikely to bring them back into the fold. It should be perfectly possible to design a form of regular worship, which meets the requirements of the ordinary worshipper (who may be a newcomer) and of the initiated, who may well seek a more devotional or Eucharistic style of worship.

- It should be regular and familiar, which means we should abandon excessive variety (as exemplified by the eight varieties of Eucharistic prayer).
- It must not be difficult for the uninitiated or embarrassing for newcomers (which the Eucharist undoubtedly is).
- It should recognise the importance of dramatic climax, and build towards it. Liturgical worship is in many ways akin to drama, but modern services seem to have lost sight of this.
- It should reduce verbiage and encourage stillness and contemplation.
- It should be reasonably short – TV programmes tend to last thirty to forty minutes: that is the sort of time length required by the modern attention span.
- It should happen at a time convenient to the modern worshipper and modern lifestyles.
- Children should be welcome (even at the Eucharist, and whether confirmed or not). But it should be clear that the main service is a service for adults. Concessions to children make for gimmickry and, however well intentioned, disturb the flow of a service and often seem patronising, almost to the point of insult.
- Other services should of course be available to suit other more precisely defined needs, such as those of children.

We need two elements: a common worship element, along the lines of Matins/ Evensong and a more devotional (Mystic) element. The Mattins/Evensong type element (Ministry of the Word) should restore the Old Testament and the Psalms to their historical place in our worship. This would make it possible to help worshippers to understand that the Bible is not literally the 'Word of God', but the record of a faith-journey towards God by a faith-filled people, whose successors we are. They, like us, lapsed repeatedly but kept coming back for more. The service could, probably should, include a sermon, which would be part of a structured and integrated teaching programme (a sort of adult Sunday School, if you like) at some other regular time, and should follow a programme drawn up by the incumbent to suit the needs of his congregation. Keep the Bishop and central authority out of it.

The second element of worship, the Eucharist (or some other form of devotional and spiritual meditation) would be intended for those who seek a deeper refreshment for the spirit. For some it may well have a profound significance – but that is no reason to exclude others. So it should be open to all, with no attempt to exclude those unconfirmed from participating. It will certainly need some re-writing.

A speaker at a recent conference pointed out to us that at least two generations are lost to the church: the 20-35s and the 35-50s. I think he underestimated. To judge by what I see and hear and the comments of my own friends, the 50-70s have been pretty well lost as well. Yet among all of them there is, I suspect,

- a yearning for spirituality, a residual belief in (or at least open-mindedness towards) the Divinity.
- a sense that Christianity's record is pretty poor and its resistance to all forms of modern ideas little short of deplorable.
- a certainty that Christianity is not the only answer and that all faiths are expressions of humanity's search for God and meaning.

For this reason, all faiths should be honoured for what they are: part of man's common exploration in the search for God. All talk of missionary activity (which in inter-faith dialogue can be as a red rag to a bull) should be abandoned

- a distrust of mumbo jumbo (I am afraid I would put the language and imagery of the Eucharist on that list), outdated theology (amongst which I would put the idea of Bible as the literal Word of God - we should stop using the phrase at the end of readings), and superstition
- a general scepticism (which I share) about the literal truth of Christianity's foundation myth – and the word 'myth' is not intended to be offensive.

The virgin birth, physical resurrection, miracles, Jesus' divinity, and so on are now obstacles to belief. Though an inspired teacher and prophet, Jesus as 'Son of God' is metaphorical, true only in the sense that we all are God's children. The title is either a deliberate challenge to the Roman emperor, or the product of Midrash, which required the Messiah to be born of the Davidic line, and therefore entitled to one of David's titles. Even the Roman centurion said only that 'truly this was a son of God,' or even, 'a god's son,' as the Greek makes clear.

- A broad indifference to the church's obsession with sinfulness and sexual mores (wait for the Lambeth Conference to see it in action)

Our problems derive primarily from two outdated ideas: the Bible as the literal and inerrant Word of God, and the divinity of Jesus. If we could accept that both ideas are no longer helpful, many of the theological problems of our faith would be resolved. An improvement in our relations with other faiths would also become possible. Even the most sceptical of critics will generally concede that Jesus was an inspired moral and ethical teacher and prophet, the source of profound insights into the nature of God and man's relationship with Him. In the ancient world, which accorded divine status to many of mankind's real or legendary heroes and benefactors, it was entirely natural that Jesus too should have received the same accolade. But in this modern era, it is outmoded and inappropriate.

None of this is new to any cleric, who will be fully aware of modern developments over the last century in biblical scholarship. But they have kept it all as a deadly secret from their congregations and as a result the church is now reaping the harvest of their dishonesty and lack of faith in the good sense of their flocks. We may have lost our inheritance of true religion, but we still live in a strangely superstitious age, much of it born of ignorance. Fundamentalism thrives on such ignorance and superstition. However uncomfortable, it is time for the clergy to modernise worship and educate their congregations. If they do, in time fundamentalism will wither on the vine.

(Since that article was written, we have had the depressing vote of the Synod against the proposal to allow the appointment of women bishops, due to the obstructive tactics of a minority in the House of Laity. For me this illustrates all too clearly the price we have paid for the failure of our Church leadership over perhaps the last hundred years. The Bishops and Clergy were clearly in favour of the proposal. But a century's cowardice, disguised as a perfectly understandable reluctance to disturb and distress the faithful, has meant that the laity have never really been taught by their clergy the realities of what modern scholarship has shown us of the origins of the Bible, including the New Testament record. The distorting effects of a belief in its inerrancy and divine inspiration lies at the heart of what I can only regard as a tragically lost opportunity. Perhaps this setback may be interpreted as God calling us to greater honesty, improved instruction, and better leadership in the future)

CHAPTER FOUR

On the State of the Church

(Letter to a Friend)

I share all your views of our Archbishop – a bit of a disappointment after the hype and the hope. He comes across as somewhat obscure in his writings and pronouncements. I have always believed that the really good minds write and speak with a clarity and coherence, which is deceptively simple, leaving one convinced that one could have written or said it oneself – until one tries. Bertrand Russell and Michael Ramsey are two of my models in this respect. As for the current issues under dispute, which seem to generate more heat than light, they are total trivialities compared with the issue of outdated theology. I am certain it would be best to kiss the Nigerians and other fundamentalists goodbye, together with all those who are hastening off to Rome, and certainly make no provision for the latter to take their church buildings and property with them.

When I saw *The Times* headlines recently about the decline in numbers of C of E congregations, I penned a letter to the Editor which, as usual, got nowhere. Here it is.

I read with interest your report in Saturday's Times of the problems of the declining Anglican Church and its clergy in this country. I have myself been an Anglican and a regular worshipper for almost all of my 72 years, and might therefore be expected to join in the chorus of lamentation, which will inevitably accompany the news you bring. My grandfather was an Archbishop for forty years, and nicknamed The Marble Arch for his rock-like defence of the certainties of his faith. Yet even he is said to have remarked, once, to a friend that, 'it may be that the true mission of the church is to disappear.' In that spirit I would actually rejoice at the news, which you report.

I look round at my own and similar congregations, and suspect that the average age of 67, which you promise us for 2050, seems already to be upon us. More interestingly, I so despair of the dead hand of the church's traditional teaching and theology and the largely traditional teaching of its clergy from the pulpit, that I have felt compelled to find my way into an encouragingly radical movement called The Progressive Christianity Network. Here, predictably enough, I find fresh thinking, open discussion, and thoughtful ideas about the nature and truth of our Christian faith. But to my great surprise I have also found that the average age of the small groups with whom I have met is similar to that of my own congregation, and that the membership includes a significant number of retired clergy, freed at last (I assume) from the shackles of the church to think and speak with an honesty, which they were denied by their oath of office, their bishops, and other authorities (including their usually conservative congregations) while they were still serving as priests within their parishes.

From this record of decline I would, in my earlier days, have concluded that God was trying to tell his churches something – and that they (or at least their leaders) were not listening. Now, however, I am very clear that whatever God may be, he does not interfere with our tiny world in all the vastness of the universe. We must, out of our own resources, find a wholly new theology, a different way of thinking and talking about God, a demythologised account of Jesus and his ministry, a radical rejection of the whole concept of sinful man redeemed by a benevolent deity, derived from the primitive view of Man's fall from grace in the mythical Garden of Eden. We are not fallen angels; we are risen apes, who have discovered self-awareness, mortality, and rightly or wrongly a sense of the divine, as part of this the latest stage of our evolutionary journey.

The young have largely, and sensibly, abandoned the traditional churches, which have little to say to them, leaving the field to the simple-minded fundamentalists so rightly berated by thoughtful critics like Richard Dawkins. But I find it very significant that so many elderly people and retired clergy seem similarly disenchanted by conventional religion and the worship of the church.

It seems to me that our best hope must lie in a new kind of faith for a new kind of religious believer, and that the present churches (not just the Anglican) indeed may well be fulfilling their true mission, which is to disappear.

Having failed, predictably, to get this letter published, it was to my great surprise that a further letter, which I sent to the Editor of *The Times* in September 2011, did get published. It was sufficiently provocative to prompt one of my friends to express great surprise that I had 'got it past the censors.' It followed a similar train of thought to that given above, but its brevity perhaps made it more acceptable. Here it is.

A New Theology

The news that the Archbishop of Canterbury may be going to retire next year (report, Sept 12) is regrettably welcome to those who like me had high hopes of him but now cling precariously to the wreckage of the traditional faith, which he has failed to reform. But the list of the possible candidates, < whom you describe as jockeying to replace him – *deleted by the editor* > offers little encouragement, given the skills which you suggest they offer. The ability to twitter and blog, to generate somewhat gimmicky appeals to the media, or even to appeal to the young, who are far too sensible to be attracted for long to such devices – these are hardly serious qualifications for high office.

What we all need is a new theology for a new age, a theology which will win the assent of thinking people, who have abandoned the traditional churches and their outdated mythologies, while sensitively weaning traditionalists to a more mature understanding of the way in which modern scholarship and science have transformed our interpretation of the gospels.

It was not long after that the Archbishop announced his retirement, leading me to feel some remorse that my criticisms had come at what was already a painful time for him. He was lauded as a great scholar, a man of saintly patience and endurance, and a priest of deep spirituality – but I share what seemed to me the general opinion that he was not cut out for the role of leadership of such a divided institution as the

Anglican Communion, which he strove to hold together at some cost to his own Church of England.

A splendid article in the *Spectator* of 31 March 2012 by Keith Ward said much of what needed to be said far better than I could ever hope to do. In it he argued that we seem to have forgotten or become afraid to state that the Church of England is a Protestant Church, and its priests and bishops (according to Roman Catholic teaching) just lay people and not priests at all; that it is a national church embracing a wide range of beliefs with no place in it for people who insist that only their sort of Christians are 'real' Christians; that the Protestant heritage can best be expressed as the encouragement of freedom of thought and rational criticism of all authority; that the church should raise and encourage the exploration of the big questions about human meaning, purpose, and value; and that to do so requires a liberal and humane approach to the Christian faith.

As a consequence the Church of England would have to stop pretending to be part of one unified worldwide Christian church, its ministers should stop pretending that they alone are true Christians, but rather part of one inclusive church with many diverse interpretations of scripture, based not on the acceptance of some formal creed but an objective morality and loyalty to a God believed to be revealed through Jesus, with many interpretations of that revelation being possible.

My third letter, penned in irritated haste after the fiasco of the Synod discussions on women bishops, on which the claim was made that church members had been 'widely consulted,' also failed to achieve publication. A friend of mine commented that he was not surprised. Had he published it, the editor might have faced excommunication. Here it is.

Seeking the views of church-goers (on women bishops)

My own experience mirrors that of Charles Nixon-Eckersall. It is not only the young who are never consulted. A church-goer all my relatively long life and for a time secretary of two different parochial church councils, never do I recollect being canvassed for my views on any issue outside that of my immediate parish.

My own perception of this is that those who claim to be the leaders of the Church of England are terrified of the ordinary man or woman in the pew, whose views (if given full weight) might well undermine an untenable status quo within the Anglican communion, and no less terrified for them, lest the discoveries of biblical scholarship and modern research, if preached from the pulpit, might undermine a similarly untenable status quo of theological assumptions – of which the inadmissibility of women bishops is but one.

All in all, it is difficult for the ordinary thinking man or woman in the pew to feel there is much hope for the church while its leadership remains so lacking in the steadfastness of a good courage.

CHAPTER FIVE

A New Inquisition?

(Letter to the Bishop)

I read with some dismay the report in today's *Times* that the Church of England is likely to introduce measures to try as heretics clergy who preach liberal doctrines on such matters as the virgin birth and the bodily resurrection of Jesus, not to mention 'mere' ethical issues such as homosexuality. I wonder how many of the church's would-be faithful adherents, currently holding onto our membership with some difficulty, will be finally alienated by such a decision.

I am not a theologian, though I have always tried to be a thinking Christian, with a life-long layman's interest in theology, albeit at a pretty humble level. The result has been that in liturgical practice I am conservative, preferring traditional Matins to the dreary banalities of our modernised liturgies, and I long to return to the glories of the King James Bible and the language of the BCP. But in my thinking about the faith I am wholly unable to accept in any literal sense the traditional formulations of church doctrine.

As one who had read Classics at Cambridge, it struck me almost before I became interested in things theological that the 'unique' divinity of Jesus was a difficult claim and the uniqueness of the resurrection challenging, precisely because they were relatively normal features of traditional, classical mythology and in a sense there was nothing particularly special about them. My mother, an absolutely faithful church member all her life, once assured me that even she and her contemporaries had rejected the idea of the virgin birth in the 1920s and that my 'modern' views were not modern at all.

When one observes the thought processes of the ancient world, it is perfectly clear that human benefactors (e.g. Hercules, Pompey, Augustus) were often accorded divine status; that the idea of resurrection was not uncommon, since descent into the underworld and return was part and parcel of legendary material (Orpheus, Theseus etc.), and the conquest of death was a common religious claim (cf. the ancient mystery religions such as Orphism). Indeed, even Lazarus' revival is presented as a form of resurrection; and the combination of divine and human parents was so common as to be the very stuff of most of the legends of Greece and Rome. As a result, within the thought processes of the time, it is hard to see how the Christian story could have been presented in any other way.

As for the idea of salvation, 'saving' the world from the wrath of a vindictive deity, that has long seemed to me a deeply negative idea, typical of early superstition and apotropaic religion; I am sure the Almighty can do better. 'Saving the world' I take poetically, as implying that in showing us the principles under which the best human life could be lived, Jesus showed us our highest potential as humans; and in challenging or even inspiring us to live up to that potential instead of reverting to the animal instincts which are our inheritance, he did indeed 'redeem' us. I have not believed for a long time that we are fallen angels - rather (as I am sure Darwin would have agreed) we are risen animals, reaching for the stars of heaven. *Superata tellus sidera donat* - as Boethius so splendidly put it. 'Earth conquered gives the stars.'

The trouble is that much of this imagery is no longer appropriate for modern man, with his very different understanding of the process of oral transmission of 'history,' as well as of the biological processes in the world and the origins and operation of the cosmos. By clinging to outmoded imagery without conceding that only poetically speaking can it still be claimed to be true, the Christian churches have rendered their faith unbelievable to many ordinary thinking people. Many of my own contemporaries, entirely supportive of the Christian faith and reared in its traditions, find themselves unable to say the creed with conviction or to accept the Church's teaching in its traditional formulations. The problem – indeed the tragedy – is that the Church's doctrines are still wrapped in the packaging of the 1st Century AD, and in the end implausible wrappings tend to destroy real substance – as perhaps one day in the political field even prime ministers may discover.

The message of Jesus, his all-forgiving death on the cross, his re-formulation of the law of sacrificial love - all these remain as true and powerful as they ever were. For thinking worshippers like myself a literal resurrection is a major impediment to belief, more like a gimmick than a proof of Christ's divinity, though quite what the concept of divinity now implies, I am not certain. By contrast the crucifixion seems the nearest a human death can get to being divine - calling down blessings on those that would destroy you. Socrates' death in ancient Athens at the hands of his political enemies had something of a similar quality.

The problem for religion in the twentieth century - and I fear science is much to blame for it - is that we have lost the capacity for poetic or symbolic thinking. The nature of scientific language is to be literal and exact, limiting and limited; the nature of poetic language is to be suggestive and imprecise, full of implication. The language of religion is far closer to poetry than prose, to symbol, image and implication, than literal and defined exactness. That surely is why until the coming of the Enlightenment (which brought new forms of darkness as well as light to Man) people would have had little trouble with the language of the Bible; now, restricted to a misconceived idea that scientific truth is the only kind of truth, they have forgotten how to think poetically.

In asserting the divinity of Jesus, it seems to me we are probably using the language and thought patterns of the 1st century AD. If we could accept him as a great prophet - even the greatest of the prophets - we could, I suspect, render him more credible and incidentally (though not specifically for that purpose) make a small step towards accommodation with our Muslim brethren. To the ancient world, especially in the Middle East, the application of divinity was really not much more than a courtesy title or a lofty compliment which, in the case of the later Roman emperors, became the expression of nothing more than the perquisite of office born of courtiers' need to flatter.

I like this reply to worshippers consulting the oracle of Apollo at Claros in about the 6th century BC. It really makes the ancient pagans sound somewhat more advanced than our 'modern' churchmen. To the question 'Who is God and what is his nature?' the God replied:

> Self born, untaught, motherless, unshakeable,
> Giving place to no name, many named, dwelling in fire,
> Such is God. We are a portion of God, his angels.

An old friend and a much better scholar than myself once told me that my grandfather (an Anglican Archbishop for forty years) had said to him that 'it may be that the true mission of the church is to disappear.' It sounds to me increasingly prophetic in these modern times, when superstitious traditionalism and primitive fundamentalism are uniting to suppress fresh thinking about our faith. Thinkers will soon not dare to open their mouths for fear of pillory or something worse.

Thomas More in Robert Bolt's wonderful play said that 'man was born to serve God in the tangle of his mind' and that if he could have found a form of words with which to placate the king, he would gladly have offered it. I still remain a communicant member of my parish church, though the weekly worship with our modernised (sic) prayer book and its utterly banal language is something to be endured, not enjoyed. But it sounds to me as if I shall not be wanted much longer.

When, all too rarely, clergy and senior members of the church show that even within the system there is a degree of willingness to re-think the more fundamental tenets of the faith, it is an enormous encouragement. If such courageous leaders are now to be hounded out, the fragile adherence of people like myself will become impossible.

But there may be hope amid the gloom. It is just possible that, as in politics, New Labour brought fresh life to a moribund political party clinging to outmoded doctrines, so too a New Christianity under a benign and intelligent leadership will open up a fresh Resurrection for our faith.

> To this letter I received a charming and (it seemed to me) somewhat complacent response, which suggested to me that the recipient saw no reason to agree with me, and therefore no cause for anxiety.

CHAPTER SIX

Changing Lives – A Diocesan Initiative

(Letter to my Vicar)

Thank you so much for letting me see this document. My instant reaction is such that you will despair of my negativity. My immediate response is that the proposals are indeed necessary, but they do not address the heart of the problem. Not quite shifting the deck chairs on the *Titanic*, but only one degree better – tying them together perhaps to make a few rafts on which a few additional passengers can float until the rescuers arrive.

Here is Petronius Arbiter, ca AD 50, on reorganisation:

> We trained hard but every time we were beginning to form up into teams we would be reorganised. I was to learn later in life that we tend to meet any new situation by reorganising – and a wonderful method it can be for creating the illusion of progress, while producing confusion, inefficiency, and demoralisation.

The Draft document has nothing to do with changing lives or even changing the church – it is all about reorganising structures, and as Petronius pointed out long ago this is the first refuge of poor leadership, which is reluctant to confront fundamental problems but wishes to appear dynamic. 'Proclaiming the faith afresh in each generation' – that is indeed what the church should be trying to do. But having made this ringing pronouncement in paragraph 1.1, it has avoided asking the really profound question about how the faith should be proclaimed in a modern age, and retreats into a discussion of structures.

Now as it happens, I do agree that structures need to be addressed; the church is extravagantly and inefficiently staffed, is much too busy about non-essentials, and shows no sign of wishing to make serious use of the benevolent laity or indeed worker-priests. The priestly closed shop is to continue, as of course I would expect, since every closed shop defends its territory to the bitter end. There is some useful tinkering round the edges, which should reduce the financial pressure on parishes.

I personally, of course, do not believe in mission, whether at home or abroad. If the church has something to offer, people will find it. Mission is wasteful and pointless. The only mission that makes any sense is faithful witness to the faithful and by the faithful to others. But that is a private hobby-horse. I also remain deeply sceptical of many of the peripheral activities, which are still deemed an essential part of the church's activity. I have doubts about most of the things for which the state now accepts responsibility and on the whole does much better (including schools). At the heart of the Church should be a faithful and worshipping community bearing witness to their faith by the quality of their lives in their daily living, not rushing about like second hand car salesmen trying to drum up custom. I was appalled by the Bishop's presentation to the deanery synod: amateur slickness; empty clichés; not an original idea; nor anything profound in the way of thinking about fundamentals. A Blairite PR style exercise not very well done. I am so glad no-one ever asked me what I thought of it.

I am very interested to find that my first thoughts on this document are very similar to my thoughts on the Church of Ireland Commission on Communication, which invited comments from the laity over twenty years ago on a similar initiative. I enclose a copy of what I wrote then in response. They faced similar problems earlier and showed the same failures of leadership. They too started with a ringing declaration about the heart of the church's activity being spiritual and then in my words 'dropped spirituality like a hot brick and busied themselves with safe questions like structures. Everybody,' I said, 'likes structures because we all think we know about them and can contribute.' Nothing changes.

Thank you for letting me see it. I am sure they mean well. But then, so do I.

CHAPTER SEVEN

Fresh Expressions – Another Initiative

(Letter to a Diocesan Speaker)

I was a member of the audience at your talk on Monday evening when you gave us an excellent Beginner's Guide to Fresh Expressions, for which I thank you.

I hope you will forgive me when I say that my respect for the quality of the presentation (which was very good) was not matched by my reaction to the contents thereof. I recognise completely that it takes all sorts to make a world – and a church congregation – so I offer my thoughts, not because I believe I am right, but in order to offer you a somewhat different perspective on the very serious problem, which we all acknowledge, of the church's declining appeal and dwindling congregations. I am still a regular if somewhat restive member of our parish church. Cathy probably sighs every time I write her a note with my thoughts!

I signed up for the whole FX course under the clearly mistaken impression that this would be an exploration of fresh expressions of the underlying theology of the Christian Faith – that is, an attempt to find better and more meaningful ways of expressing our belief in God and our understanding of the meaning of Jesus' mission. Instead, as I fear almost always happens, I found myself in the usual discussion of how best to shift the deck chairs tidily round the deck of the already sinking *Titanic*.

My usual analogy is derived from commerce: if the goods are shoddy or past their sell-by date, no amount of salesmanship is going to sell them. The churches have always retreated into salesmanship rather than examine with an honestly critical eye the quality of the goods on offer. Their depressingly outdated theology – very much reflected in the language you yourself used, I am afraid – remains at the core of Fresh Expressions, as you described them. You yourself, for example, spoke of Jesus being 'sent down from heaven by God, our Father, to redeem us from our sins.' The very idea of humanity as fallen beings needing redemption by the sacrifice of God's Son, is meaningless to ordinary modern secular people; it is to use language as anthropomorphic as the language used of Zeus and the other gods of the Olympian religion. To defend its use as metaphor, as some do, is to dodge the issue of what it says to the non-believer.

Instead, under FX, we are to busy ourselves with activities, doing things that will drag or entice people back to church, without any thought for the underlying belief which might persuade them to come of their own accord; we are to show people how to develop communities, as if those who are not church members had no idea how to go about it without the help of the churches. But when I look around our own village and all the community activities that go on without any church connection, I realise that this idea that the church has a unique or superior idea of community is pure fantasy. It would be much more impressive if the church was to say to the unchurched, 'show us how you develop the idea of community so that we can learn from you.'

For me the whole idea of Mission is misguided, and your own notes (MYTHS) quite misleading it seems to me in their assertions of what FX is NOT. It is all about evangelism, a bridge into the inherited church etc. To say that Jesus commanded us to go out and 'make disciples of all nations' is to take literally what was almost certainly something that Jesus never said, but was written more than half a century later by the individual evangelists to express as best they could what each of their particular communities of followers of The Way had come to believe was the world mission of the as yet infant and not yet institutional church. To quote the Jesus Seminar's view, 'Jesus probably had no idea of launching a world mission and was certainly not an institution builder.' I am put off by all forms of active – even aggressive - evangelism; my own preference would be for quiet good living, as an example that might interest others, without any overt attempt to do so; and if they are not interested they should be left in peace.

FX, as I now understand it, is exploring ways of winning back the unchurched (what I would call the lapsed or marginalised, those who for whatever reason have left the church), and of winning over the never-churched – those who have never had anything to do with religion. My 'simple' thesis is that the unchurched (and the marginalised, like me) have lost faith in the conventional religion offered by the churches, while the never-churched are not going to be won over until the church expresses its teaching in new and more meaningful ways.

That is why I personally think that the Eucharist, as the routine core feature of regular church worship, is a mistake. Its language is highly specialised. It can only appeal to those already committed to or comfortable with the traditional teaching of the meaning of Jesus' mission. It has a place – even a central place for the committed – but its language as expressed in the liturgy must be almost offensive to the uncommitted or unconvinced.

I shall, of course, continue to attend the course, and I have no doubt that I will gain new perspectives from the experience. But I would be less than honest if I did not say that I was disappointed by my first encounter with FX, (of which I had not even heard until I joined the course), and that I do feel that while every initiative is a worthy sign of endeavour, my own suspicion is that this one is pointing in the wrong direction.

It would be a good idea, I think, if at the end of it a short questionnaire could be issued asking people what they had wanted from the course, what they had expected, and how far their wishes and expectations were fulfilled – and then perhaps what single thing they would make their absolute priority for the church in the next five years.

One of my companions (not my wife) at the meeting has even suggested in an email that we should 'set up a three-way discussion (with guests) to open up the subject of Outdated Theology.' So, to my surprise, I find that I am not entirely alone.

I attach two articles, which will, I hope, illustrate more fully the nature of the problem as I see it. One I wrote myself a couple of years ago, for the Newsletter of the PCN (Progressive Christianity Network) and the other written this week in the Emailed weekly newsletter of TCPC (The Center for Progressive Christianity), its sister and founder organisation in the USA, where not all are fundamentalists, and some actually far more go-ahead in their thinking than we are – witness the work of the Jesus Seminar.

But thank you for your talk. In the end those that are not against us are for us. So we are both on the same side, though I accept that it may not always seem so.

Hardly surprisingly, I never received an acknowledgement or an answer.

CHAPTER EIGHT

The Sort of Church I'd Like

(Talk to North Somerset PCN Group)

No two people will want the same sort of church. No church can be all things to all men. The best I can do is set out a series of propositions. Call them sound bites for a policy, if you like. Socrates would have started by asking 'what is the church **for**?' He might well have gone on to ask 'What are priests for?' I prefer to start with an assertion - that.... The idea of God is the only necessary pre-supposition for any religion. The rest, as our First Queen Elizabeth might have observed, is 'dispute about trifles.'

John Polkinghorne has recently pointed out that even for scientists Creation is sufficiently full of surprises to make it irrational to discount the possibility of God – and therefore it is perfectly rational to search for him. The purpose of any church must be to help its followers in that search and then to guide them in their effort to serve Her or Him. How it does so is a proper subject for debate.

The Negatives

The easy side of the discussion is to describe the sort of church one does not want – and my answer is, 'broadly, the church we have got.' The churches, their doctrines, and their priestly castes are no longer fit for purpose. They have resisted every intellectual advance that mankind has produced. The church as an institution/organisation should be simplified and built upon the priesthood of the laity. Hierarchies should be abandoned. Priests should remain only as specialist advisors on theology and perhaps worship. Doctrine should be redefined and rewritten.

Jesus saw himself as a reforming prophet of Judaism. He had little time for priests and the Temple authorities. His followers elevated him into a Messiah and the Son of God. This is at best the Christ of Faith, not the Jesus of History.

The Positives

The sort of Church I'd like, to which I would add, 'to belong to, worship with, and to live among (as best I can and however inadequately) as an expression of my faith, such as it is.' All Negatives need to be countered by the positives implied by that phrase.

Who was/is Jesus? The disturbing thing is that after the crucifixion, even his followers found it very difficult to recognise Jesus. Mary thought he was the gardener; the two disciples on the road to Emmaus thought he was a fellow traveller; in the upper room, he was suddenly amongst them. The key thing is that followers suddenly came upon him or saw him in ordinary people and casual acquaintances. The old pre-Christian myth of entertaining gods or angels unawares carries the same disturbing implications. Christ is, or is to be found in, other people. The novel by Patrick White, *Riders in the Chariot*, explores the same idea.

Is this also the implication of St Mark's story in the second last verse (excluding the late additions) of his final chapter, when the angel in the sepulchre told the women that 'he is going before you into Galilee; there you shall see him, as he told you.' Was the message simply this? – 'Go back to your ordinary lives among ordinary people, and there you will find the Lord.' Not in churches or vast organisations, perhaps, but in chance encounters or where two or three are gathered? For me that idea has a bearing on the church I want to belong to.

Jesus' reported sayings, whether actual, mythical, or legendary, are also relevant. They include the following:

- *God is spirit, and they that worship him must worship him in spirit and in truth.* Give me a church whose worship offers refreshment to the spirit, teaching for the mind. Too much of its current worship is noisy, verbose, superstitious; its preaching rarely speaks to the spirit and never to the mind.
- *Where two or three are gathered together in my name, there am I in the midst.* Not two or three million. Zechariah once asked: 'who hath despised the day of small things?' Like any secular company, the church is obsessed by numbers, finances, and extensions to its range of activity; it cares less for the quality of the experience.
- *The Sabbath was made for man, not man for the Sabbath.* The emphasis upon Sunday worship and the one size fits all Eucharist has, perhaps, forgotten this principle.
- *Know the truth and the truth shall make you free.* The church is terrified of the truth; it has fought against every scientific discovery, and has conspired to conceal from its congregations all the insights of biblical scholarship for the last two hundred years. I want a church that explores the truth fearlessly and tells it courageously.
- *In my father's house are many mansions.* St Augustine says that God welcomes his children by whatever road they come. Let's abandon the idea once and for all that Christianity is the only way to God, or church worship the only worship. I like the phrase in the prayer 'bearing about with us the infection of a good courage...' The church should be in the business of infection, not evangelization and mission. Indeed, missionary activity (other than by the example of good living and sacrificial service of humanity) should be abandoned.
- *Inasmuch as ye have done it to one of the least of these, you have done it unto me.* Effectively the Golden Rule – terrifyingly difficult to follow. Sufficient moral guidance to be going on with. The church is as materialistic as any

other human organisation; it should be grateful that it shares humanity's wider prosperity. Until it has sold all that it has and given it to the poor, it should observe a decent reticence on the subject of materialism in society, cultivating economy and poverty in all its ways.

- Then, two other suggestive sound-bites, the first from the Psalms (46.10); the second from I Kings 19.12:

Be still and know that I am God

Be still and know; be still.

And after the fire, a still small voice

After the fires of life, stillness is a balm for troubled souls; a quiet, sequestered pathway up to God.

- Finally, here is a near contemporary comment from Pliny, the Roman Governor of Bithynia, a civilised man forced by imperial policy to be an unsympathetic observer, dated ca. AD 110.

They met regularly before dawn on a fixed day to chant verses alternately among themselves in honour of Christ, as if to a God, and also to bind themselves by oath, not for any criminal purpose, but to abstain from theft, robbery, and adultery, to commit no breach of trust and not to deny a deposit when called upon to restore it. After this ceremony it had been their custom to disperse and reassemble later to take food of an ordinary, harmless kind.

(Pliny Letters:10.96)

In summary: I would like a church with the courage to be and to become, rather than to defend tradition with its last breath. I would like a church which respects intellect as well as encouraging faith; which welcomes fresh ideas; a servant church, determined to abandon its roots in the domination cultures of a masculine and hierarchical past.

I would like to worship there in a way that celebrates past, present and future. Our faith is rooted in its Jewish past. It grew through the insights Jesus brought to his own inherited faith. It has been refined through the millstones of history. I lament the near abandonment of many parts of the Old Testament in regular worship; I miss deeply the singing or reading of the psalms; I accept the importance of the Gospels and such of St Paul's Epistles as are genuine, as guides to the central mysteries of our faith, even though I would personally describe those mysteries as mythological more than historical. I would like a church whose structures and worship reflect something of the simplicity of the early Christian communities.

CHAPTER NINE

The Curate's Three Questions

In a sermon on the Parable of the Talents, our curate challenged the congregation to answer three questions:

1. What talents do you think you have?
2. In five years' time where would you like to see the church? (It was not clear if he meant Yatton Moor or the C of E)
3. What talents will be needed to achieve this?

Sara and I decided to treat this as a serious enquiry, rather than the usual clerical rhetorical question. Typically, I fear, my answer is rather longer than Sara's.

My answer

My talents are (I think):

- I have an interested and reasonably good mind, an ability to write and speak with clarity, a determination to think for myself, coupled with a degree of scepticism about received wisdom in many matters, not just religion. None of this, I have come to believe, is welcome in the church as it now is.
- I have read quite widely at an amateur level in modern approaches to theology. I studied Classics and Ancient History and have taught it all my life. It has shaped my understanding of the Christian faith and nurtured my increasing scepticism of its mythology.
- I hope I am also well organised and efficient; I find administration easy.
- I am old – which is a 'natural' talent. On the plus side it brings experience and sometimes a greater patience with and sympathy for others; it can allow me more time than those who still have to earn their living. On the minus side, declining mental and physical energy, and (probably) a degree of conservatism in outlook.

In five years' time I hope that the C of E

- will have been disestablished;
- will have developed the ministry of the laity into something worthwhile and

ended the clerical closed shop;

- will have decided to reduce drastically the financial burden it places on the laity by such measures as :- the reduction of bureaucracy, the elimination of services already offered by the state (e.g. schools), a vigorous rationalisation of clergy numbers, a much more active use of part-time clergy (most of whom should become worker priests), and a greater willingness to use lay people in the conduct of worship;
- will have committed itself to annual reductions in the Parish Share, as an outward and visible sign of an inward and spiritual focus and realisation of the previous point;
- will have closed many more churches with small congregations;
- will have reduced the overall number of bishops. Like admirals in the navy, they seem to increase in number as membership declines;
- will have appointed several women to bishoprics;
- in its teaching and preaching will have adopted a vigorous policy of educating its congregations in the insights and understandings of modern theology and biblical criticism, thus putting an end to biblical literalism;
- will have abandoned active evangelism and proselytising.

In five years time in Yatton Moor I hope that we shall have:

- Just one church, staffed by a maximum of two full time clergy;
- a richer variety of forms of worship, many led by lay people, and some at least designed by their brevity, form, and content to appeal to the un-convinced;
- a rich variety of preaching and teaching, some at least designed to stimulate and challenge the comfortable, as well as answer the needs of those whose faith is more 'progressive' or 'radical' than the norm;
- a church so welcoming, so outward-looking, so open-minded that it will offer itself for inclusion on the PCN-B map of progressive churches.

The talents required to realise the above 'vision' are:

- A new vision, probably inspired by a new prophet;
- A new maturity of belief in the wider church;
- A willingness to let go of privilege, prerogative and pre-supposition;
- Courage;
- Leadership at the top;
- A 'post-adolescent' mindset (as per Von Hügel).

Sara's answer (She is characteristically far too modest)

My talents are – I hope:

- an ability to empathise and to listen.

In five years' time we should have:

- only one church operating in Yatton Moor. In addition to services, it will offer a weekly 'Sunday School for Adults' (not necessarily on Sunday), a study group for anyone interested in religion, faith, and post-modern Christianity.

The talents required will be:

- a willingness to relinquish one's local church and instead worship weekly as part of the team ministry, looking out for one's neighbours, offering and sharing lifts;
- To see the church as being its members out in the community, living out their understanding of Christianity without evangelizing;
- Valuing people of all faiths and none.
- To be willing to be open-minded.

Probably predictably, to this exercise there was no feedback, no action in response, no indication that the findings had been studied and ideas passed on to higher authority. Perhaps this is what the church authorities call 'consulting widely.' It is rather like the approach of modern politicians – lots of noise and talk about consultation, loudly publicised 'initiatives,' futile photo-opportunities, and little evidence of follow-up or effective action.

Section B: Groundwork

*A wise man… built his house upon a rock; a foolish man
…built his house upon the sand.*

Chapters 10 and 11 try to set out what I might call ground rules for debate and discussion. Chapters 12 to 15 are derived, in whole or in part, from my answers to friends' letters, in which I tried to set out my best approach to questions they had raised. Chapters 16-17 were my contribution to a Parish Colloquy (less pretentious than a Conference), which was an admirable attempt to invite ordinary parish members to think out where they stood on a fundamental element of our faith: the Nature of Jesus for a modern Christian.

Axiom - Greek axioma: a self-evident proposition - is defined by the OED as a 'self-evident truth'.

Hypothesis – Greek *hupothesis*: defined by the OED as 'a supposition made as a basis for reasoning', or 'as a starting point for investigation' (without reference to its truth).

Euclid used axioms as the starting point for his geometrical proofs. One might say that an axiom is an hypothesis that is 'self-evidently true.' But the testing of hypotheses to destruction is inherent in all good scientific reasoning. Hypotheses that have been accepted as axiomatic (such as the idea that the world is flat or, until more recently, the idea of the three-tiered universe in which heaven is above the earth and hell below) have sometimes turned out to be wrong. But the acceptance of a working hypothesis as a basis for a theory until it is overturned, is entirely normal and the only practical way in which to pursue truth.

Wherever I have lived I have watched with fascination the progress of new building – whether of roads, houses, or public facilities. It is always the same – the groundwork, which really means the below-ground work, seems to take far longer than the final superstructures. Nothing much seems to happen at first; and then, suddenly, with remarkable speed the final edifice appears. The groundwork matters more than the final edifice, as Jesus is said to have remarked of the 'foolish man who built his house upon sand,' but neglected his groundwork.

For me the Christian churches have failed to recognise that their faith, which once upon a time seemed to be based on foundations of solid rock, has become sadly vulnerable to the shifting sands of its all too unstable foundations.

One cannot argue productively about religion (or anything else) without getting the groundwork right; that means starting the discussion from common ground. This is why so much religious argument can seem so pointless. If one cannot establish an agreed working hypothesis with one's opponent as a starting point for discussion, or better still, agree upon something that is self-evidently true (axiomatic), there is little point in carrying the conversation any further.

Ideally one should try to establish similar common ground with one's readers, if at all possible, by agreeing the premises from which we argue. In any religious discussion, however, I suspect that what seems to one person to be self-evidently true, or at least a sensible working hypothesis, may seem less so to others. Nevertheless, the list below represents propositions, which are for me either axiomatic or at least working hypotheses. They are where I start from. It is an attempt to clear the ground in a way that should make discussion possible with those who are of like mind. A question that will occur to any reader is whether any of these propositions are axiomatic (i.e. self-evidently true), merely working hypotheses, or sheer folly.

CHAPTER TEN

Towards Belief

(Some Axioms or Working Hypotheses)

Science without Religion is lame; Religion without Science is blind - Einstein

God

1. The only necessary hypothesis for any religion, which fundamentalists will, of course, take as axiomatic, is the existence of God. I take the possibility – not the certainty - of his existence as my working hypothesis, if not axiomatic; his non-existence remains as unprovable as his existence.
2. If there is a God we are one kind of creature; if there is not, we are another. That is why it is important to try and find out.
3. The idea of God is common to all cultures. This is not a proof of his existence; it may be an indication.

Man

4. Man is a risen ape, not a fallen angel;
5. In the search for God, reason alone is not sufficient; but without reason, any faith is as a house built upon sand.
6. Man was 'born to serve God in the tangle of his mind.'
7. 'All knowledge is human; it is mixed with our errors, our prejudices, our dreams, and our hopes; all we can do is grope for truth even though it is beyond our reach. Truth is beyond human authority.'

(Karl Popper, abbreviated)

The Bible

8. The Bible is not the Word of God in any literal sense. It is the record of the spiritual journey of a whole people, written by men and women for men and women in words that could, of course, be said to be inspired, but only in a metaphorical sense, just as poets are said to be inspired.
9. There are many kinds of writing. Language operates on a variety of levels. Religious writing aims for illumination by accumulating illustration. Scientific

writing aims for proof by a logical sequence of demonstrable facts. It is important to be clear about the poetic, metaphorical nature of religious writing and to try to agree about it with potential opponents, before any religious discussion can take place.

Jesus

10. Jesus was a normal human being, not born of a virgin, which is a mistranslation of the Greek (and, I think, of the original Hebrew by the translators of the Septuagint). It is also a biological impossibility.
11. Jesus, therefore, was not the Son of God in any literal sense. A God who is Spirit, as Jesus himself said, would be unlikely to have an 'only son,' whether in this world or eternity. It is all poetic and religious imagery, attributing divinity to an inspired prophetic figure. In Jesus' day there were lots of Gods and their offspring were the very stuff of religious belief.
12. Jesus was exalted/deified in much the same way as the emperor Augustus. Augustus became a God, and was honoured as Son of a God (*divi filius*). Augustus was the adopted son of the deified Julius Caesar. King David was also called Son of God. The Messiah, as the second King David, was bound to be given the title Son of God by those who believed that he was the promised Messiah.

Resurrection

13. Resurrection myths are common in the ancient religions. A literal, physical Resurrection (though by definition within the powers of an omnipotent God) is highly improbable. It is an impediment to belief and Jesus seems to have rejected such 'supernatural' methods in the Temptation story. It was, rather, a spiritual event, experienced by his followers, who later described it in physical terms, as would be entirely normal practice then.
14. By contrast the manner of Jesus' life and above all his death was sublime, inspirational, a model of what at its noblest and best humanity can be; in that sense only can he be said to have 'redeemed' humankind.

The Church

15. The Church is a human organisation, not a divine creation. It exists to further the worship of God; but regrettably it serves also to sustain priestly power – and has always done so. But, organisations are necessary (sadly!) for most human activities.
16. The Creeds of the Church (like the Ten Commandments before them) are the product of human rulers or leaders, imposed in the case of the Creeds by the emperors Constantine and Theodosius in the 4th Century AD to put an end to factional squabbles in the various sections of the church. They are not the result of divine dictation or imposition.
17. Priests and theologians have a vested interest in preserving their specialist

patch through mystification. Their technical language is called theology; their mystification is called ritual; their closed shop is protected by their 'divine calling' and sanctified by tradition. Their claim to know the mind of God, or his wishes, is spurious. What they call God's will almost always seems to coincide with their own inclinations or prejudices.

18. Though I find the idea attractive, it seems to me unlikely that the apostolic succession has remained unbroken since Jesus' day or uncontaminated during the Middle Ages, when the Church was fundamentally corrupt. It simply exploits human superstition, is a pretty tradition, and is a matter of minimal importance.

Scholarship and History

19. Modern scholars have transformed our understanding of the New Testament as well as of the Old. However distressing to the faithful, it is important to acknowledge the validity of their researches, where their consensus is substantial. Since even the synoptic Gospels were first recorded (in Greek) at least forty and as much as seventy years after the death of Jesus Christ, and were written for an infant church which was spreading widely through much of the Greek speaking Middle East, it is inevitable that their content reflects the mindset and assumptions of their authors, and the outcome of various controversies and differences of belief with which the church leaders had to grapple.

20. What purports to be Jesus' teaching as well as his actions contains a considerable proportion of editorial matter. Events may well be included to lend authenticity to the claims of Jesus' divinity made by the expanding church.

21. Mankind is a maker of stories. Legends are good stories about the past. Myths are legends which have endured, because they carry true insights beyond their literal meaning. To call something a myth is a compliment, not an insult; its truth may not be literal or scientific, but could well be illustrative of something more profound.

22. History does not stand still. Historical truth purports to record facts, but in the end it is all too obvious that history is written by the winners, and then re-written by historians in the light of their own prejudices and under the influence of contemporary perceptions.

CHAPTER ELEVEN

The Basis of Religious Certainty

(From a Seminar Discussion Paper)

Extract A

The basis of religious certainty is the individual consciousness....

A certainty that rests on authority only, whether the authority of a book, such as the Bible, or the authority of a body such as the Church, or the authority of a fact or of a person may have a certain temporary value, but it is only temporary. It may constrain the man, but it does not enlarge him – at any rate only indirectly. Spiritual teaching, taken on authority only – professed from sense of obedience and not from sense of its intrinsic worth, - is a spiritual thing outside me. Faith is the individual's apprehension of truth: and where you accept a thing because you are told to do it, there is no apprehension – no personal consent, and therefore no faith, only servitude. And that is not enough: for <it is> not submission, but self-direction <that> is the ultimate end of life....

But the real faith – or the real spiritual vision – is that which sees into truth and sees through truth; which needs not to be told, 'Thus saith the Lord'; which needs not to count heads or know the utterer's name before it accepts a thing; which leaps at a truth by sheer intuition, seems in league with the truth by some natural and eternal compact....

Abraham, for example, was inspired we say, because he was so made that he alone in a dark age was able to see that God was a spiritual being. His distinction, his inspiration lay in that he staked his all on a truth that was never for a moment in doubt with him. This, of course, is no explanation of how Abraham was what he was. It is simply a reminder that his composition differed from that of his contemporaries, because it was ahead of them. He had it in him to be what they had not – in his generation, he was a spiritual freak, a sudden variation to a higher type of visionary, despite his apparent willingness to sacrifice his own son without challenging the orders of his God. It was the same with the Isaiah's, and Hoseas, and John Baptists: the same with Buddha and Confucius and Zoroaster, the same with Savonarola and Luther: it was not that their truth rested on an authority outside them: but, what verified to them the message they felt impelled to proclaim was the witness of their inner consciousness....

The great aim in life is to know truth for what it is – at first hand; to have it in you for your own. Any one who rests on authority and lets it steer him surrenders the right of growth, which is the only justification for living. We are put here to be educated and enhanced – and second hand truth will only do that in a very small degree. We must all begin, of course, by accepting truth at second hand, just as the child has to receive its daily bread for years before it has the strength to earn it. But once men and women receive second hand truth and rest in it, and think that it is enough to accept it and that there is no necessity to interrogate it – they have cut themselves off from real progress, and therefore from the true end of religion....

Authority is anything but discredited. It has played a stupendous part in the past.... because it helps the intuition-obeying minds by rendering them dissatisfied, while it rules the authority-obeying minds by taking all initiative out of their hands. Authority has a most beneficent part to play, provided always that it be remembered that it is only a temporary, provisional, and makeshift.

For the postulate at the bottom of my argument is that human nature may know itself to be a partaker of the Divine – 'that Heaven kindly gave our blood a moral flow' – that truth is not alien to us but natural, so much so that Plato suggested that all our learning of it was merely a recalling to memory of things learned before our incarnation here ...

Truth does not need such support as the *ipse dixit* of the Bible. It is not the final court of appeal for us – our consciousness is gradually and rightly usurping that place for itself. The Bible is a storehouse of spiritual truth: we can never germinate and originate truth; but our duty is to take no truth offered us without sifting and weighing and questioning it, as judges....

Authority has gradually trained up the human consciousness through truth received at second hand, and pondered till it is possessed at first hand, till now the human soul is 'finding itself' in increasing numbers of people, and individuality of consciousness is asserting itself as never before. A new era is dawning. An ever-expanding largeness of nature is open to men and women, according as they employ the capacity that is in them. They will feel an added sense of responsibility, as they enter on a closer personal wrestling with truth ...

By no means all of us will feel the difficulty of accepting an external authority. But those of us who *do*, have one point that they can start from in their reconstruction of the spiritual fabric – a rock that is unshakeable by any criticism – a single vantage-point from which they can reach out into the world of spirit and the world of matter – their own individual self-consciousness.

Extract B

Whatever verbal definitions we have of the Person of Christ are human and not divine. The Synoptic Gospels present Christ, as He presented Himself, a life and not a formulated dogma. It is possible to regard the Life there presented as not necessarily more than human... The distinction must be enforced between Christ, what He said about himself, and Christ, what His interpreters say about Him. Now where do Paul and the Fourth Gospel draw the materials of their Christology from? There is a Divine and a human source. The Divine is their personal conviction that Christ was God, wrought in them by the indwelling God; but the human source is pre-existing speculation, which suddenly found itself confronted with a reality that needed clothing in words. The Wisdom-Doctrine was waiting to be used, and Paul and John drank copiously of it. ...

If Christ is to be the living Christ for us, and not merely a Christ of the Apostolic Age and of past history, we must learn to distinguish carefully between Himself, the Divine Figure eternal in the heavens – and the doctrines about Him, even Bible doctrines, which are just as likely to fetter Him as to present Him. The more completely we acknowledge the humanness and the occasional-ness of the NT doctrines concerning His Person, the more completely will our soul be thrown back upon Himself.

In summary: Any statement about the Person of Christ is really symbolic, relative, approximate, an economical formula, accommodation, shifting, liable to be displaced.

Some Possible Questions for Discussion

1. Do you think this was written

   a) ca.1750 at the start of the Enlightenment
   b) ca.1900 at the end of the Victorian era?
   c) In the 1920s, after the Great War to end all Wars and before the Depression of the 1930s.
   d) in the 1960s after the discovery of DNA and the publication of *Honest to God*?
   e) Recently?

2. Do you think passage B was written by a different author? If so, why? Is it less intellectual – more based upon intuition, inspiration?
3. How old do you think the writer of A was when s/he wrote it?
4. Do you think it was written by an agnostic philosopher, or a believer?
5. To what sort of audience would you think it was addressed?
6. Is the individual consciousness really a sound basis for religious certainty?
7. Is real faith 'that which leaps at truth by sheer intuition?'
8. Is s/he right to downplay the importance of Authority and Tradition?
9. Could the description of Abraham in para five be applied equally well to Jesus?
10. Do you agree with the writer that 'a new era' of human consciousness is dawning? Or is it over?
11. Would you accept the writer's strong linkage between human self-consciousness and a sense of God?
12. Spong (*A New Christianity for a New World*) suggests that the idea of God became essential once Mankind acquired self-consciousness. Has he anything in common with the author of the passage?
13. Do you agree that 'letting your faith rest on authority is to surrender your right to growth'? If so, what is the Bible for? If not, are you abandoning your integrity as an individual?

14. If it is our duty to take no truth offered to us without 'sifting and weighing it as judges', is there a danger of creating such a destructive level of doubt as will destroy all faith? Does this matter?

15. Does the author of passage A set too great a store upon intellect and too little on revelation?

16. How would you help an over-intellectual, rational 21st century person find 'a living Christ.'?

17. The writer(s) set great store by rationality. If you are to have a rational discussion about religion, you and your interlocutor need to agree the premises from which your discussion will begin. What do you regard as the axioms, the self-evident truths, about religion on which you and your opponent should base your discussion?

CHAPTER TWELVE

God - Some Thoughts

(Letter to a Friend)

Thank you for your latest, with its interesting enclosure by Peter Jones, whom we got to know when I was lecturing on one of the Swan Hellenic cruises – he was a fellow lecturer, great fun, and very committed to the popularisation of the Classics.

I like his thesis that to the early Greek philosopher/physicists divinity was not a necessary part of the explanation of the material world. I suspect he is oversimplifying in order to make a debating point: after all Zeus threw thunderbolts, Poseidon controlled the sea and earthquakes, Apollo the sun etc., and within their mindset I would incline to think that perhaps Sophocles' comment (in the *Trachiniae*, I think) that 'here is nothing that is not God' would have been closer to the ideas of the ordinary man on the top of the Piraeus ox-bus. But that said, it is a telling point to make, if for no other reason to restore a degree of balance in our ideas of what we might arrogantly call early society's primitive superstition. Certainly Epicurus, following on the teaching of Democritus (born ca.460 BC), the great 'inventor' of the atomic theory, argued that there were no gods, and that if there were any they were indifferent to human circumstance.

My own embryonic thoughts on the subject are moving in the direction of trying to reconcile the possibility of God (which I do not find difficult) with what little I understand of the physical universe. I was listening to Stephen Hawking the other night talking about the future of the solar system and, by implication of the cosmos. His entirely factual discussion of what physics tells us is likely to happen to our solar system in about eight billion years time was completely devoid of any anti-religious polemic or bias. This makes him far more compelling than some of the more aggressive atheists.

But it raises the dilemma of where God might be in all this. If he is not the Creator, nor the Prime Mover of the Cosmos of Aristotle, what is his job description? And what sort of creation is it that explodes into existence and then implodes into non-existence, with or without his assistance? And if he is Spirit, what is he doing around the cosmos in the meantime, since he is clearly helpless to prevent both our total annihilation and that of the whole of Creation, when it reverts as it may to a singularity once again? We end up with an Epicurean divinity, possibly real, but clearly pointless.

All this leaves me trying to reconcile the irrelevance (so to speak) of God to creation with the undeniable fact that mankind has always had a sense of divinity, and constantly invented metaphors for its divinities, whether singular or plural, and has no less constantly deified a few of its fellow men (and women, in other religions), whose merits or significance seemed hugely significant (even if the context within which they displayed those merits were insignificant, like the ruler of North Korea).

Man has always invented his gods, and still does: but does this matter? In Jesus' time Pompey was worshipped in the Middle East; and before him Alexander the Great; and after him Julius Caesar followed, and more deservedly, by Augustus; the legendary Heracles was deified as the supreme benefactor of mankind; Mithraism remained popular well into the 4th century AD; the Egyptians worshipped their kings; etc. etc. Even Jesus, in those terms, merely invented a new version of the old Jewish god, whom he nicknamed Abba. Our sense of belonging to something greater than ourselves, and indeed to the sum total of all there is, seems a very general (though not universal) perception. I still find a kind of comfort in the idea that we are made of star-dust and to the stars we will return.

One could in fact end up with the proposition that the only way to deal with the question is to state, as an axiom, a self-evident proposition that is beyond argument, that GOD IS; and then argue that he is so utterly beyond our understanding and comprehension that it is pointless to worship or relate to him, except by metaphor, and that great mortals are the best if not the only models, metaphors, or paradigms by which we can seek to describe Him. We should, therefore, admire - even idealise - such mortals as our best inspiration and guide to the problems and meaning of existence. Which means we should be quite happy to have as many gods as we like – which of course in a sense we do!

All that sounds dangerously Roman Catholic. You cannot get to God except through the Saints, etc. But the problem with the Roman Catholic saints is that they are two-a-penny, and their very status seems to depend on the whims of individual popes, and so they fail by miles to fit my criterion for divinity – the fact of being outstanding human beings and benefactors of mankind. I discount their alleged miracles as being largely, if not entirely, fictitious. By contrast I would willingly enough accept the deification (in the sense I have described) of Jesus, the Buddha, Mohammed, the Mahatma etc. Some of the modern fringe cults have already done that sort of thing, without perhaps selecting for their veneration human beings of indubitable merit and general benefaction.

Because my thoughts are as yet tentative, not even convincing to myself, I'll leave it at that.

CHAPTER THIRTEEN

Eternal Life?

I love the idea that the English, being an unimaginative people, invented the game of cricket to give themselves some understanding of the nature of eternity. A friend of mine, a church organist, but to his own regret, I think, an admitted atheist, asked me once what I thought about Eternal Life. That put me on the spot, not least because I suspect that it is the underlying angst of many people, and one which perhaps keeps them hanging by their fingernails to the church in hope of something comforting. The best I could immediately offer was as follows (slightly edited):

What do I think about Eternal Life and the hereafter? In the traditional Christian presentation of Paradise - which sounds rather like the Muslim version - the whole idea seems to me at best metaphorical, but more probably mere superstitious twaddle. I doubt, also, that we shall all be resurrected at the Last Trump into our physical bodies.

I think my grandfather in 1940 made an interesting stab at a rather different idea – you will find it on the final pages of *A Faith Unfaithful*. I am finding some people are wrestling with the same sort of concept nowadays. It is no great comfort to the anxious credulous, since the gist of his argument is that Eternal Life is here and now, and to the extent that you believe in God you also have eternal life already – which sounds to me in some ways like having your cake and eating it. But he was a profoundly spiritual man and immensely intelligent, and thought deeply through a lifetime about his faith. So he cannot be dismissed in the same breath as all the simpletons who adhere to more fundamentalist beliefs. Nevertheless, to any rational and seasoned critic his line will seem a bit of a cop out. So in any literal and physical sense, I'd subscribe to your proposition that it is the final curtain.

What I find myself unable to do, yet, is to dispense with the possibility of God – I put it no stronger. Dawkins would of course put this down to wishful thinking, and Freud to something Oedipodean. They may well be right. But like Wordsworth, I too have felt at times 'A Presence that disturbs', etc. – read all the middle bits of Tintern Abbey - and if that seems to you nothing more than pantheism, I would probably agree, while suggesting that pantheism (and its modern half-brother panentheism) has a long and in some ways respectable history, born of that same strange sense so many mortals share, that there seems to be something 'beyond', or numinous, with which we often most easily get in touch when we get close to Nature.

And if there is a God, then the possibility remains that, in some sense which we cannot possibly define, something of our essence may yet survive, not just in the memory of those we leave behind, but also in some absolute existence which we cannot begin to understand, but which for convenience we call metaphorically Heaven.

Recent DNA technology, too, has recently become able to reveal that some modern people still carry in their genetic makeup traces of our original human forebears from some two hundred thousand years ago. Though the male (nicknamed Adam) is middle eastern and the female (Eve) is African, these two originators of our species are apparently specifically identifiable. Though separated geographically and chronologically and therefore never aware of each other's existence, they are, I understand, the prime ancestors of us all. If we can get thus far with a technology still in its infancy, who knows what may not be added in time to our understanding of the concept of eternal life.

I continue to accept, even hope for, occasionally pray to, the God-hypothesis, while becoming increasingly dismissive of the literalist and fundamentalist nonsense promulgated by the churches. I strive to think about the idea of God, not, of course, as an old man with a beard sitting up on a cloud in the seventh heaven judging the quick and the dead. I focus more on a kind of God-shaped possibility – because, as Hamlet observed, 'there are more things in heaven and earth than are dreamed of in your philosophy, Horatio.' I fully accept that man evolved his ideas of God in order to account for what he did not understand or very much feared (of which extinction was probably the worst). But if he had to begin somewhere, that seems a perfectly logical place to start.

The expression coined by St Paul, I think, that we 'feel after him and find him' is perhaps nearer the mark, and I find much to ponder in the poems of R.S. Thomas, for whom God is often a Great Absence. I am not really sold on Tillich's idea of The Depth and Ground of Our Being, which is becoming somewhat fashionable once again, having had a considerable following in the 70s. My trouble is I don't know what it means. Finding God within is a perfectly sensible thing to do – the mystics have tried it since the beginning of human thought. But if God is the Depth & Ground etc., then he can be nothing more than the essence of our own humanity – and that is not enough. I prefer Teilhard de Chardin's noosphere, as pointing forwards one day, perhaps, to a Theosphere, in which we will all participate having achieved the divinity of our full humanity.

Analogy is always dodgy and should never be taken as an argument. But it can illustrate the possibility of a possibility. Just as the insects of the world pursue their own lives in almost total ignorance, and indeed awareness, of mankind's existence, unless we happen by mischance to feed them or exterminate them by accident or design, so too I find it possible, in ways I cannot begin to conceive, that we too pursue our funny little lives in blissful ignorance of another world (dimension/superstring?), of which we only become aware by chance or mischance, and probably with little or no awareness of what it is we have encountered.

As for Jesus. I am totally comfortable with the idea that he was simply a great religious teacher, nothing more perhaps than another Socrates, and like Socrates put to death for his beliefs, his allegedly pernicious influence, but above all because he (like Jesus) was seen as a threat to the established power blocs within his own society. Because power tends to corrupt, it is consequently ruthless in its own defence. I am content to see Jesus as Son of God only in the same sense that Jewish Kings were accorded the description as a sort of courtesy title. He was not born of a virgin; his father may have been called Joseph, but that is a name with significant overtones in Jewish history also. Physically he was not resurrected, since it was Roman practice to leave crucified bodies for the dogs and birds.

But his spirit 'lived on' by the power of his teaching and the memory of his life, just as the spirits of many other great human beings seem to endure. (Many modernists call this resurrection, but I suspect that this is simply a misuse or even abuse of language). Socrates lived on in the memory of his disciples, and in the writings of Plato, who richly developed his master's initial teaching. So too with Jesus – his followers and then the institutional churches developed his insights into dogma and Jesus himself into an unrecognisably mythic or superhuman figure. But beyond that he died, as we all must die, unless, of course, the possibility of an after life proves correct; in which case we shall all meet again and 'bliss will it be in that morn to be alive.'

I do very much like Socrates' comment on all this in Plato's account of his *Apology*, but even more in the *Phaedo*. He says to his disciples:

> Do you think I have less divination than the swans? For they, when they know that they must die, having sung all their lives sing louder than ever, for joy at going home to the god they serve. Men, who themselves fear death, have taken it for lamentation, forgetting that no bird sings in hunger, or cold, or pain. But, being Apollo's own birds, they share his gift of prophecy, and forsee the joys of another world.

Most of the biographical details of Jesus' life were put together by the gospel writers at least forty and as much as seventy years after his death. They are very often theological additions to explain or justify religious practice or belief that had gradually developed after his lifetime. In a Jewish ambience it was perfectly natural. The Jews mythologised their history constantly – it was called midrash. So too the early Christians (who continued to attend synagogue and until about AD 100 saw their faith as a sub-set of Judaism) followed Jewish practice and re-mythologised their Jewish history to force Jesus into the Jewish mould - or Judaism into the Jesus mould.

There may possibly be a God; and I am pretty sure that the only way to explore that possibility is to act as if there is, or on the assumption that there might be. If there is one, we are unlikely to discover him by denying the possibility, and ceasing to practice our religious batting skills in our religious nets. Hence my own practice of still going, often very reluctantly, to church. Meanwhile, the one practical thing that must be done is to try and live a good life, follow the Golden Rule; and in this respect the Jesus Way (another currently fashionable concept) seems as good as any and better than many. Only in that very limited sense can I 'take Jesus into my life' or, in that phrase that used to make me curl up inside when used by my CICCU friends, 'know the Lord Jesus.'

CHAPTER FOURTEEN

Salvation

(Letter to a Friend)

You asked me on the phone, 'What do you understand by the term 'Salvation'?' My instant response was 'Very little. It is one of those Christian clichés inherited from our traditions, which once meant something to believers, but no longer does. But I'll think about it and send you a short essay.' So here goes. It is not so much an essay as an attempt to think aloud. It makes no claim to authority, profundity, or originality.

I am not a theologian. So I approach theological questions partly, I hope, through the application of common sense, partly as an ancient historian, since this often gives me an appreciation of and a context for ancient ideas, and partly as one who has tried for fifty years to read his way round the problems of traditional Christian belief, in which I was reared and which I find increasingly incoherent or unbelievable.

My vicar generously offered me a thought. 'People not of a Christian background,' she suggested, 'might interpret it these days in psychological terms (self-fulfilment, actualisation, wholeness etc). Maybe there is a very Anglican middle way – self-transcendence as attained by growth in Christ/Self which leads to the desire to work for the 'shalom' of others/community/planet.'

I intend to confess to her that I am not sure I know what that means (its obscurity is a bit Rowan Williams-ish), but she is a very good expositor and I have no doubt that clarity will ensue.

To be saved, I assume one must be saved **from** something. So our salvation, even in psychological terms, must imply that we are saved - but from what? Our worse nature? Human delinquency? Moral decay? Or just plain death? Every religion and every philosophy will, I am sure, offer no less. Christianity can make no claim to any special merit in this regard, let alone any claim to be unique.

We must do better.

A quick flip through Cruden's Concordance suggests to me that in the OT there was little problem. 'Salvation' really meant no more than 'preservation from trouble or danger' (to quote Cruden), God promising to fight on Israel's side to ensure that they won.

Such beliefs are part of the wider general proposition (pagan as well as Christian) that God answers prayer. It really is extremely hard to see how he can, without believing Him guilty of outrageous favouritism and incredible inconsistency. But that is another story.

If I was being naughty, I would call this the Bush/ Blair approach – twentieth century naivety allied to media-based spin. Trying to ensure that innocent people think that they are on the side of the angels and that God is naturally the 'real' captain of their team. All protagonists in battle have believed (or at least asserted) that God is on their side since time immemorial, and Constantine adopted the Christian god specifically because he thought – or pretended to – that he was a god who delivered the goods. The Israelites thought the same.

The idea is deeply primitive. The psalms are full of it; God is the god of Israel's salvation. Jonah prays to the God of his salvation and is vomited out of the fish; Isaiah often seems similarly uncomplicated, but we do find in him the beginnings of an idea of righteousness associated with salvation. But I suspect that this is tied into the idea that afflictions such as the Exile are a punishment for unrighteousness (i.e. turning away from God) and therefore salvation is still little more than rescue by God from misfortune or disaster – you could call it God extorting money or obedience 'with menaces'. And one might wonder whether it is moral qualities, or merely detailed adherence to ritual requirements, that constituted righteousness in the eyes of the Jahweh of those days. I would be tempted, without the knowledge to demonstrate it, to think it was the latter, given the importance of ritualistic behaviour in all the societies of the Axial Era, as is strongly brought out in Robert Bellah's recent book, *Religion in Human Evolution*.

Cruden's second definition is 'deliverance from sin and its consequences'. This again is initially relatively uncomplicated. Israel's repeated backslidings from faithfulness to their god was seen as the reason for the disasters that befell them. A return to righteousness was the source of salvation or rescue from disaster.

I may be wrong, since my reading is inadequate, but I get little impression in the OT that for the Jews the idea of 'going to heaven' as a reward for being 'good' figured in their calculations. In that sense they were a very secular people – working out their 'salvation' on earth from entirely terrestrial enemies with the help of a somewhat ferocious and occasionally capricious divinity. Mount Sion, a citadel of safety, God's holy hill on which they placed his tabernacle (Ps 15), may have been – or become in time – a symbol of something more complex, but I have no clear idea of what it was. But effectively 'death closes all', though the concept of Sheol and the lovely verse from Eccleiastes 12.7, which you quoted, does suggest that perhaps I overstate the case a little. 'Then shall the dust return to the earth as it was: and the spirit shall return unto God who gave it.'

But lest one imagine that this 'spirit' is an embryonic suggestion of the soul, the New English Bible very honestly states in a footnote that it could/should be translated 'breath' – which is consistent with the picture in Genesis 2.7, where God 'formed man of the dust of the ground and breathed into his nostrils' so that 'he became a 'living soul' (says the AV), 'living creature' (says the NEB). All this, of course, aligns the word closely with the Latin *anima* and the Greek *psyche*, which both primarily convey the idea of 'breath of life' but carry some sort of idea of a (departed) spirit or ghost as well, but very much only as secondary meanings. As you suggest, this verse is 'all ye know on earth and all ye need to know'. As an *envoi* for the departed it says all that needs to be said or can be said with confidence, and offers comfort where it is needed. It has the power of true poetry.

As long as this naïve approach to Salvation persisted there can have been few problems. Be good and God will be on your side and keep you safe. Be bad, and punishments will follow. Turn again to your God and he will forgive you. If you are naughty, God can be appeased by sacrifices (though Amos 5.21 ff might not agree), and while you are about it you had better do some sacrificing in advance just to keep Him sweet.

Sacrifices continue down through the NT period and in all ancient religions. But in Israel the process clearly had become sufficiently corrupt for Jesus to be affronted by it. But like the Church through the ages, the Temple priests will have realised that a substantial source of revenue to the Temple (and less directly of power to themselves) was not something to be lightly cast away.

As long as sin and retribution were handled as little more than the settlement of a kind of debt, as long as punishment for misdemeanour could be more or less successfully anticipated by sacrifice or cancelled out by expiatory action, the fierce OT patriarchal God remained plausible, comprehensible, manageable, and usually able to deliver the goods. He was remarkably patient with the shortcomings of his people too; indeed his patience, though sorely tried, seemed infinite.

Monotheism (and they were not, perhaps, quite as monotheistic as common perceptions suggest) and specific rituals apart, there seems little to distinguish OT Judaism from the religious practices of the ancient world in general. All gods were the same – capricious, ferocious, jealous of their prerogatives, benevolent to their favourites. State religion in the ancient world demanded a degree of outward respect for ritual; but as long as you made a show of respect for the official deities, what you did the rest of the time was up to you. Paganism was a model of tolerance compared with later Christianity.

Greek religion from the time of Homer onward saw Hades as a dim, monochrome world where the shadowy ghosts of the departed lived out an entirely futile existence to all eternity – such that Achilles in Homer said he would rather be the meanest serf on earth than Lord of the kingdoms of the dead. In time the idea of punishment of the great sinners entered the equation – but their sins were offences against the gods, not against their fellow men. The fear of death was simply part of man's natural aversion to extinction; fear of eternal damnation linked to deficiencies in earthly virtue I think comes later. Socrates/Plato probably started it; Christianity made a meal of it.

Fear of (instead of acceptance of) death gradually develops. Where there is a need, in time there will always be an attempt to satisfy that need. Hence the mystery religions emerged (based on such things as corn rituals, music, mathematics) with their promise of blessed and eternal life for their adherents, and they acquired significant followings. Life beyond the grave became 'negotiable.' This must in time have influenced religious outlooks.

The expansion of the Roman empire must also have complicated the issue somewhat. For a people who knew not the God of Jacob they did extraordinarily well and by the time of the Jewish revolt and the fall of the Temple (AD 70), it must have seemed that their gods (plural) were a rather more successful proposition than poor old Jahweh, though after Constantine one might say that Jahweh had the last laugh.

Jesus greatly complicated things. As a conventional Messiah he would have been fine. If he had led the movement to drive out the Romans by a national revolt in the name of Jahweh, it would have been entirely consistent with the old idea of Salvation – God defending his people from their enemies. But his teaching, his refusal to lead an insurrection, and above all his death (leaving aside the issue of resurrection), must also have greatly undermined the age-old simplicities and left a real problem for his followers and interpreters. St Paul and later theologians through the ages have simply made matters worse. The result has been two thousand years of theologians dancing on increasingly tiny pin heads as they try to find forms of words that make sense of the idea of Salvation.

Instead of the simple proposition of disobedience and retribution (= defeat by enemies); obedience and reward (= triumph over enemies), we now have a god who sacrifices his own, blameless, son to himself; a god who suddenly settles for one 'full, perfect and sufficient sacrifice', though note that he still wants a sacrifice; a god who forgives sins free of charge, but only because Jesus has paid the charge on our behalf; a loving father who forgives and forgets; a god who keeps a warmer welcome for the dregs of society than for the toffs. Whatever you make of the theological propositions that ensue, it must be clear that for believers at least with the coming of Jesus things changed utterly.

I went back to an old text book: Alister McGrath, *Christian Theology – An Introduction*, Chapter eleven. This quick survey does not do it justice.

He summarises in some thirty pages the doctrine of Salvation in Christ, as it developed through the years. I find that when I originally read and annotated the book I wrote at the end of this chapter, 'Not at all clear what salvation is. The best I can gather is an equivalent of the old mystery religions – immortality for those who are so privileged. He tries desperately to avoid Gnosticism, but fails.'

At the end of the chapter he sets questions for readers to wrestle with, including:

1. From what are we saved?
2. Is a human response to salvation necessary?
3. How are the cross and resurrection related in Christian understandings of salvation?
4. Assess the importance of the following approaches to the meaning of the cross: a victory over sin and death; forgiveness of sin; a demonstration of the love of God towards humanity.

Which, I think, leaves you and me back where we started. But it is a useful chapter as a summary of the problem as it developed over the centuries and some of the answers offered. Instead of throwing out the bath water – at the risk of throwing out the baby as well – theologians have steadily increased the amount of water in the bath, with the result that the baby is probably drowned by now.

The focus of the discussion is all the time on Jesus and the links between salvation and his life, death, and resurrection: what did he do; what difference did he make; did he 'reveal' (illustrative) or did he 'achieve' (constitutive) something? If so what? Is salvation past, present, or future – i.e. is there an eschatological dimension to it? (The magic words are: justification; sanctification; salvation).

This whole topic is called soteriology – the theory of salvation, also called theory of atonement. It covers two main areas: what is salvation and how does it work? And, how does it relate to the history of Jesus? I am glad to say that the focus seems to be more on the meaning of the Cross, which is not factually in doubt, than on the resurrection, which can at least be said to be debatable. We get four images, says McGrath: the cross as Sacrifice, as Victory, as the source of Forgiveness, as Moral Example.

Sacrifice, is understandable, though much debased by its increasingly secular overtones – we are all in favour of sacrifices for the common good, provided someone else makes them. But what is the common good for which the Jesus sacrifice is made, if not the OT idea of the wrath of God, punishment of our sins etc? We are no further forward.

Victory: over sin, death, and Satan. Again, we are all in favour, but how is it done? Is there anything that cannot be done by a good man, such as Socrates/Plato envisaged? There is nothing specifically Christian about it beyond the assertion that the victory is won by Jesus. And again one must ask, to what purpose?

Forgiveness: Jesus' death 'allows' God to forgive sin. A very feudal idea, derived from Anselm. Sinful man cannot make satisfaction to God for his sins; but a god-man can do so - and thus impose an obligation in law on God to forgive and save one representative man – and having done so he must save all, because all (believers) are 'in' Christ.

I may have got this wrong. This idea appealed it seems to the 16th century, which was very alive to the importance of human law and saw it also as a model for God's forgiveness. To me it smacks of lawyers' language – obfuscation designed to deceive the jury.

Moral Example: there is a difference of degree but not nature between Man and Jesus; the cross has no objective value beyond its impact on mankind; it serves to inspire and encourage, and Jesus is therefore to be seen more as a martyr than a 'saviour'.

This is a rather more modern concept, I think. But it still leaves open the question of what is the nature of Salvation and what we are being saved from.

So what is Salvation?

Deification – eternal life? Derives from the old slogan 'God became human in order that humans might become God.' Good sound bite – not sure it means anything outside the ancient world where, by deification, humans quite often became gods. Grandfather's sermon at the end of *A Faith Unfaithful* perhaps offers some illumination on this.

Righteousness in God's sight: how without it could any man stand before God? Jesus brings deliverance from condemnation. Not easy for modern man to accept and the mechanics of such deliverance are not clear.

'Authentic' human existence - a truly question-begging answer. An existentialist concept – life characterised by faith in God is deemed 'authentic'; life fettered to the material order 'inauthentic'. Who will define authenticity?

The trouble is that it can only be self-authenticating and subjective; this is Humpty Dumpty language – words mean whatever I choose them to mean. If I do not like your definition of authentic, then your idea of human existence is not authentic.

Political liberation; God and Jesus express a preference for the poor to whom He brings liberation through his teaching and life style. This makes Jesus a South American model. But it is back to an OT idea of salvation from defeat and deprivation at the hand of mortal enemies and tyrants.

Spiritual freedom: victory over subjective forces which enslave humanity and trap it in inauthentic (sic) modes of existence. But what the Early Fathers treated as objective forces have now, under the influence of the Tillich school, become subjective.

All of these attempts to define salvation require a forced or entirely subjective interpretation of the word, without really making clear what form that salvation takes and what it is that we are saved from.

Objectivity is the problem.

In the good old OT days, it was entirely clear what you were being saved from: enemy forces (the tribes of the Holy Land, Egypt, Assyria, Babylon, Rome or whatever). Jahweh, your tribal god, seemed a reliable ally, and in the best traditions of ancient peoples generally, if things went wrong, you accepted that it was never the god's fault. You had done something wrong; your sacrifice was blemished; you had not followed ritual exactly; your god's attention was distracted; or whatever.

Death was a fact of life. You could not do much about it. At best there was a shadowy post-death existence, to be endured. Your moral conduct did not really have a bearing.

Morality crept in: Socrates and Plato preached the care of the soul; Greek philosophers developed their ideas; Hebrew prophets developed the concept of righteousness, which came to include moral conduct and not just backsliding from the commandments of Jahweh.

Mystery religions flourished, with their promises of eternal (and by implication blessed and happy) life beyond the grave to those who were ritually purged and acquired 'The Knowledge.' Such initiates were *makarioi* – blessed. The Gnostic heresies (so called) developed much the same approach, but with specifically Christian slants.

Christianity transformed the model by eliminating objectivity and changing all the rules. Salvation was a return of the prodigal to his father's house of unlimited mansions; unconditional love; forgiveness of enemies; acceptance of the rule of a conqueror; quality of living, not quality of life; sacrifice of self; death as victory.

The only constant was the promise of eternal life, which was never defined. The only objective threat from which salvation can still be offered is death.

If salvation means anything, it can only mean some form of survival of the soul beyond the grave; some form of return to the arms of a loving god. If it is to be earned, then it must involve for Christians at least a sincere attempt to conform our lives to the Jesus Model. For non-Christians I would have to believe that any moral equivalent code of life will suffice. In that sense alone we are 'saved' by Jesus, because he shows us a 'more excellent way.' But such salvation can never truly be earned, since we can never achieve the perfection of our model. But I cannot believe that for that reason God regarded Jesus' death as a necessary or 'sufficient' sacrifice for our inadequacies.

However, the mechanics of this have been argued about for two thousand years and no doubt will continue so to be.

No doubt to traditionally minded fundamentalists it still means that in some way Jesus has bought us off the flames of hell-fire, exactly in the same way as ancient apotropaic sacrifices bought-off the anger of local divinities. This has the great merit of clarity and comprehensibility. But they do not make clear what is to happen to the rest of us who can't quite swallow the idea of such a scenario. I merely hope that God is a little more advanced than that.

In fact, for simple folk like us the only thing is to take refuge in the words of Socrates: either death is a sleep and a forgetting – and we have nothing to fear from that. Or else it is the journey of the soul to another place and of this we can be sure – no evil can happen to a good man. Seek the Good. Care for the soul.

That is the best I think I can do. I have no satisfactory answers beyond my original suspicion that Salvation, in all but some poetic sense, is a concept that has passed its sell-by date.

CHAPTER FIFTEEN

Ye Must Be Born Again

Today our Rector preached on Nicodemus (St John 3.1), the famous passage which is the source of the command to all believers that 'Ye must be born again.'

I have long shared Nicodemus' incomprehension as to what Jesus may have meant by this particular phrase, which has always seemed to me meaningless, especially when employed by the well intentioned if somewhat naïve missionaries of various religious groups who from time to time come knocking at my door. It also offends me when smug fundamentalists seem to imply that those of us who cannot, or will not, make such a claim are doomed or even damned.

The passage was also the gospel reading for the day, and the Rector read it from some modern version (possibly the International RSV) and startled me into attention when he announced that, 'Ye must be born from above.' 'Another of those sloppy translations,' I said to myself, reaching for the Bible in the pew to check it, and slightly smugly looking forward to consulting my Greek Bible and in subsequent conversation pointing out to him with a mildly superior air the error of his reading.

To my great surprise I found that he was absolutely right and that Jesus may well have never said that we must be 'born again.' Born from above, born spiritually, seems to make rather more sense and is acknowledged in the AV as an alternative translation to the conventional 'again.' Slightly disappointingly, the NEB offered no such variant, instead translating the Greek *anothen,* as 'over again.'

I thought I would pursue the matter a little further. It would be such a blessing to be able to tell all those people who claim to be Born-again Christians, that they have wasted their time and that Jesus never said it.

First, to Cruden's Concordance: how often is the phrase 'born again' actually used? Apart from this one passage, never. So everything hangs on this one passage from St John, where a variant translation is acknowledged.

I heard a lecture two weeks ago in Oxford by Profession Keith Ward, a leading and very distinguished biblical scholar, who asserted that very few NT Scholars think that anything St John's gospel tells us that Jesus said was actually said by Jesus. (The Jesus Seminar concurs). Certainly the lengthy discourse, of which this passage is a part, is uncharacteristic of Jesus' more normal form of discourse, as described in the Synoptics.

So far so good. Jesus probably never said any of this to Nicodemus, and Prof Ward's comment does no harm to my particular attempt to invalidate the command that we must be 'born again.' Even if he did say it, he didn't say it in Greek.

Then to my Liddell & Scott Greek dictionary to check on the Greek. The key word is *anothen* – whose common meaning is 'from above', 'from heaven', or variations of that idea. So on the face of it, if Jesus said this at all, he probably said that, 'except a man be born **from above**, he cannot enter into the kingdom of God.'

The Oxford Bible Commentary confirms this, pointing out that it is the earthly Nicodemus who misunderstands Jesus and takes him to mean 'again.' This reinforces my suspicion that those who tell us that we must be born again are perhaps quoting Nicodemus rather than Jesus. I am less convinced by their assertion that *anothen*, meaning 'again', is 'quite possible in Greek'. As far as I can see, it is rare.

I like this translation, because it is a simple metaphor, much clearer than 'born again', suggesting simply that as well as a conventional birth, a man needs a spiritual birth, a birth born of or inspired by heaven, a birth '**from above**.' Jesus seems to reinforce this idea by saying in explanation (verse five) that, 'Except a man be born of water **and** of the spirit, he cannot see the kingdom of God.' He goes on, 'that which is born of the flesh is flesh; and that which is born of the spirit is spirit.' Spirit he says is like the wind (in Greek *pneuma* means both 'wind' and 'spirit'); you cannot tell where it comes from or where it is going. Those who are born of the spirit are like that.

So if the Greek word *anothen* probably does not mean 'again', and Jesus (or rather, John interpreting Jesus for us) said simply that you must be born 'from above', then being born 'again' is an unnecessary qualification for any Christian.

I thought I should pursue *anothen* a little further. There are only four examples of its use cited in the dictionary when it may mean 'again.' The first comes from Galatians 4.9. Here it has nothing to do with being born again; Paul asks the Galatians how, once they have known the true God, they can possibly return to their feeble and beggarly old gods, 'to whom you desire to be **back** in slavery **again**.'

Here in his emphatic manner he uses two words, *palin* and *anothen* – both apparently meaning 'again'. *Palin* is the usual Greek word for again. And it is certainly difficult to give *anothen* its usual meaning of 'from above'. But *anothen* can carry a secondary meaning of 'from an earlier point or time', whether in a book or a philosophical argument, and this is conveyed by the word 'back,' which again the AV offers as a variant translation. We often find in dictionaries or reference books such expressions as vide supra (= 'see above') used in exactly that sense. So I have translated it 'back.... again', because a) the Galatians have gone **back** to their earlier gods, and b) 'back again' is an emphatic English way of saying 'again'.

There are only two other uses in Liddell & Scott of *anothen* possibly meaning 'again', neither of which I could check. The first is in Josephus' *Jewish Antiquities* and the other in Artemidorus' *Interpretation of Dreams*. Four uses, two of them from the Bible and acknowledged as uncertain by the AV, is not a large number to set against the conventional use of the word as meaning 'from above.'

Richard Ferguson in his *Listen to the Gospels* offers an interesting additional insight, when he suggests that the story may owe something to contemporary controversy, perhaps even in the author's own community, between Jewish and non-Jewish Christians. Jesus' words, he suggests, would for the Christian community have pointed unmistakably towards Baptism, as being of the spirit, as opposed to circumcision, as being of the flesh. The Nicodemus story then becomes a validation of the Pauline view that there is neither Greek nor Jew, and that circumcision was not necessary for initiation into the Christian community.

Stephen Verney in his *Water into Wine* has contrived, ingeniously or perceptively (depending on your point of view) to have it both ways. He suggests that the two Greek words, *ano* (above/up) and *kato* (below/down) are key ideas of St John, who is writing on two levels: at the human (*kato*) level he is describing mundane events which happened on earth, physically (e.g. a wedding); but at the spiritual (*ano*) level he is describing a transforming experience, a new birth into the spiritual realm of Agape, Love, and you must indeed be born-again-from-above (all one word). It certainly reinforced my view of St John's Gospel as a great literary creation, where the author, like all great writers, is working on several levels of meaning at once. But a simple and accurate historical record it most certainly is not.

Now of course being born again, for those so fortunate as to experience it, may suggest a spiritual encounter, a new birth 'from above' through the spirit, in which case I have no quarrel with them and my argument is little more than a quibble. But over the years I have met very few people who have ever claimed to have been blessed with a profound spiritual encounter, such as is implied by this passage, yet there seem to be large numbers of people claiming to be Born-again Christians. This suggests to me that their view of being born again is somewhat different and considerably less awe-inspiring than such a spiritual experience is likely to be.

So I shall save up my arguments for those who come to my door and ask me with a confidence born of naivety whether I have been born again. And instead of saying simply, as hitherto, that I fear that I have not, I shall assert that it is not in the Bible and that the Greek makes it quite clear that Jesus never said it. It is overstating my case somewhat, but they have overstated theirs for far too long and now I feel it is my turn to do so.

CHAPTER SIXTEEN

Towards a Christology for the 21ˢᵗ Century

(A Parish Colloquy Jointly with Rev. Francis Miles)

Francis Miles is a wonderful speaker and a spiritual counsellor. I will gladly travel miles to listen to her. She also has the enviable gift, which I lack, of being able to speak without depending on a text, a knack of thinking aloud as she goes along in a way that brings her audience with her. Our talks alternated. After my first section, Setting out the Problem, she dealt with Biblical Sources. I then returned to the fray with a survey of the Greek and Roman background; and then Francis led the discussions.

Part 1: Setting out the Problem: Who is, or was, Jesus?
Jesus, Son of God: Foolishness? Stumbling Block? Myth? Revelation?

OT: Son of God; Messiah; Servant of the Lord.
NT: Christ; Lord.

For the Jews require a sign, and the Greeks seek after wisdom; but we preach Christ crucified, unto the Jews a stumbling block, and unto the Greeks foolishness; but unto them that are called, both Jews and Greeks, Christ the power of God, and the wisdom of God. Because the foolishness of God is wiser than men; and the weakness of God is stronger than men.

(1 Cor.1.22-7)

Our highest truths are but half-truths. Think not to settle down forever in any truth. Make use of it as a tent in which to pass a summer's night, but build not a house of it or it will be your tomb. When you first have an inkling of its insufficiency and begin to descry a dim counter-truth looming up behind, then weep not but give thanks. It is the Lord whispering: 'Take up thy bed – and walk.'

Arthur Balfour *(PM 1902-1905)*.

I hope those words of perhaps the most scholarly of all our 20ᵗʰ Century Prime Ministers will help to set for us an appropriate mood of thoughtful exploration in our discussions today. I spent a long time wondering what to take as my text; when these words came to me at about midnight last night, I fell asleep at once. I only hope they will not have the same effect on all of you.

Let me start with two apologies: first, for reading a paper rather than giving a talk. I am not a natural speaker and when developing an argument I prefer the security of a prepared text. The great 17th century essayist Francis Bacon tells us that, 'reading maketh a full man, conference a ready man, and writing an exact man.' Like him I should wish to be exact. But he goes on, 'if a man read little, he had need of much cunning to seem to know that <which> he doth not know.' Given the deficiencies of my theological reading, no conference can make of me a ready man, and I fear that my cunning will not measure up to the task of seeming to know that which I know not.' My second apology is for my presumption in speaking to you at all. I have no training in theology, though all my life I have read theological books, as I sought the intellectual underpinning for my faith, which the church never seemed to offer. As a classicist with no knowledge of Hebrew the only credentials I have are those of a benevolent layman, with many generations of clerical families behind me. My upbringing in the Church of Ireland was liberal in attitudes but evangelical in content; I was well grounded in my bible and catechism and it never occurred to me to doubt any of it till my university years. My goodwill for the church is sincere; my sorrow at its apparent decline no less so, though many no doubt will argue that the Almighty has the matter well in hand. I suspect that I have no business here at all; but for that you must blame my vicar, Cathy Horder, who is a most persuasive lady, with a nice line in two-edged compliments: 'even you,' she said, 'must have something to offer.' It was the 'even' that got to me!

I do speak as one who has a real sense of desolation at the church's inability to offer me a faith that is intellectually coherent in the modern world. Like many other thoughtful laymen and women I am alienated by the spurious modernisation of the church's worship and demoralised by its failure to modernise its thought. Why modernise the presentation without modernising the content? Why offer the dreary banality of modernised liturgy and hymns, when mystery and wonder should be at the heart of worship? I hope I speak also as a thoughtful pilgrim; though as Julius Caesar once remarked of Cassius, 'he thinks too much - such men are dangerous.' But men who think are, I believe, less dangerous than men who are certain. Certainty breeds intolerance; uncertainty, I hope breeds humility. Men of certainty tend to be unwilling to face the challenge of new ideas, taking refuge instead in a flight back to the womb of their intellectual infancy. My own views are always provisional; I have more questions than answers. If what I say offends you, I am sorry; but I speak the truth as I see it and we have it on good biblical authority that the truth will set us free.

How, then, do I as a classicist, view the Jesus phenomenon and why has my training as a classicist and an ancient historian forced me to change my view of my religion and the faith of my fathers? In the years of my early maturity I became increasingly aware of two great contradictions: the first, obviously, between our modern understanding of the world and the cosmos in which we briefly sojourn and the Church's response, which has been to resist all new insights since the days of Gallileo and Darwin. But, unlike the Church, I have few problems with science, because in my view science and religion live, so to speak, in parallel universes, the one a material universe, subject to inevitable change and decay; the other a non-material universe of spirit, whose very nature we cannot begin to understand. So they speak different languages; neither can disprove the other. They may, of course, and do offer insights to each other; and indeed I incline to think that today scientists rather than the church should be seen as the true stewards of God's mysteries. As Einstein once said: 'Science without religion is lame; but religion without science is blind.'

But second, and more significantly, through my interest in Greek and Latin language, literature, and history I became increasingly aware of the contradiction between what I learned about religion and mythology in the ancient world and Christianity's claim to uniqueness. Where my faith claimed to be unique, I felt that I could see many similarities with other and older religions, reinforcing my perception that religion in general evolves. There seemed little to choose between the Christian narrative and traditional mythologies - where gods incarnate were two a penny, resurrections barely unusual, marriages of gods and mortals entirely normal in the birth of any legendary hero, and gods coming down to earth from heaven a regular occurrence. Even Zeus was born as a squalling infant and hidden by Corybants from an infanticidal ruler, his Father Saturn, in a cave in Crete. In other words, whatever the essence of the 'new' Christian religion, the language and imagery by which it was purveyed to its adherents was pretty conventional, not least in its concept of a three-tiered universe, with heaven up above, earth below, and the land of the dead beneath.

In ancient society miraculous foundation stories were the norm. Aristocratic families, cities, institutions, and religious cults all had them, and in this respect the foundation 'myths' of Christianity seem to me to run true to form. Historically, the birth of Jesus simply could not have happened as St Matthew puts it 'on this wise' (1.18) and to insist on the literal truth of the story is to lose credibility.

There are four Gospel stories, two of which make no reference to Jesus' birth at all. In the other two, Jesus was born, allegedly, under Herod the Great - who died in 4 BC; but also when Quirinius was governor of Syria - in AD6. Take your pick. You can't have both. Augustus never issued a decree that all the world should be taxed. Local censuses were directed towards raising money; so they were based on property, not genealogy. Nazareth in Galilee was ruled by a client king and therefore not subject to Roman census or taxation at all. So Joseph would not have been required to travel to Bethlehem to register. But the story had to send him there, because of the connection with David and the new Messiah. Virgin birth is a biological impossibility and would require God to break the rules of the universe he created. But in those days some kings and every hero or demigod had a divine ancestry and it would have seemed essential to give Jesus one, even though such a miraculous birth denies him the full humanity which is supposed to be part of the package. The Greek word *parthenos* can mean young girl as well as virgin, and that I believe would be the correct translation of Isaiah's original Hebrew, *almah*; where *betulah* is the word for virgin.

But of course none of this matters in the slightest, nor need it have the slightest effect upon one's faith, once we accept that this is not history but a foundation myth, typical of its times. It is of the same type as the myths of the birth of Dionysus, god of wine, the origins of Zeus, or the descent of Orpheus into the Underworld and his defeat of death, which was the basis of the origins of the Orphic mystery religion. Perhaps the most delightful of these resurrection myths is that of Kore, or Persephone, the daughter of Demeter, the earth mother and Corn Goddess. She was carried off to the underworld by Pluto, god of Death. All the crops on earth died in sorrow. So Pluto relented and allowed her back to earth for six months of the year, which is broadly the time from sowing of the corn until its harvest. It is a much more poetic resurrection myth than the Christian one. But Jesus does not require such miraculous fairy tales to be the founder of a great religion, though in the context of his times a resurrection might well have seemed essential.

The Bible is also literature: and from a literary perspective similar perceptions and problems grew. Everyone has heard of Homer, the great epic poet of the Greeks, whose two works, the *Iliad* and the *Odyssey*, were as near as the Greeks came to having a Bible of their own. Indeed the poems were regarded with such reverence that their texts were even used centuries later as a basis for settling legal and territorial disputes; they were regarded as historical fact, as infallible as our scripture. Homer, the author, was naturally seen as inspired by the Gods, and the mouthpiece of Apollo, god of the arts and enlightenment. But then Milman Parry came along in the 1930s and demonstrated beyond dispute that these poems were the products of centuries of folklore and recitation by bards. So far from being historical records of a cataclysmic 'world war' around 1200 BC, they were the product of generations of story-telling in which tales and conditions of an iron age culture were superimposed upon those of an earlier bronze age. Though there is some residual fact behind it, the whole story was built up by the imagination of bards and poets, working with a massive repertoire of verbal formulas, which were constantly refined to literary perfection by centuries of public performance. Only later, much later, were they finally written down and became fixed and 'scriptural.'

The similar development of the biblical stories from inherited folklore became for me a hypothesis too obvious to be easily dismissed. Now, for example, with two distinct creation myths in Genesis, and with four different sources acknowledged for the Pentateuch, none of them Moses, the argument seems to me settled. I cannot say this too often: such discoveries are immensely comforting, not distressing. No longer do we have to resort to what is really intellectual dishonesty to reconcile biblical contradictions and inconsistencies. They are simply inevitable, because of the nature of oral literary transmission. The truth sets us free.

Story telling is the only way in which primitive peoples can record their history, and the development of such stories follows familiar patterns, whether in history or religion. Divine epiphanies, for example, were common and correspond quite closely to the pattern of Jesus' post-resurrection appearances to the disciples on the road to Emmaus, or to Mary in the Garden of Gethsemane. This is not to cast doubt, necessarily, on the truth of the stories; simply to point out that the way the story is told is exactly what you would expect in those times. Gods constantly appear to their mortal offspring and are often unrecognised until they withdraw. Think of the Emmaus story as a parallel. In pagan cults, a divine epiphany often led to a wish to publicise the event or set up a permanent shrine or priesthood – just as Peter wanted to do at the Transfiguration. In Lydian villages centuries before Christ they used to set up stones to record gods' manifestations. It was a standard response, still echoed in Christian practice to this day.

Such visions remain common. In the past thirty-five years, I have read, the Virgin Mary has made 352 appearances accepted by the Roman Catholic Church as authentic; in Spain there have not been as many appearances as in the 20th century since the 1400s; there are claims of over two thousand appearances in Yugoslavia since 1981. (Robin Lane Fox, *Pagans and Christians,* makes fascinating reading on divine epiphanies). I am not commenting, except by implication, on the authenticity of these appearances – simply remarking that epiphanies are still, as they always have been, part of the religious scene. Of course any sacred narrative had to and still has to include such mysterious events. They are part and parcel of the divine package.

Then again, in ancient writing authority was important. To attach a story or line of thought to some great figure of the past was normal – almost an act of homage. Prophecies could be thrown back, anachronistically to explain current events; laws attributed to some ancient prophet or lawgiver; ideas attributed to great teachers. For example, Plato's philosophical ideas are put into the mouth of Socrates, who may have been their inspiration but was certainly not their author. Dare one suggest something of the same with St Paul? To the ancients this was entirely normal and not seen as dishonest but a mark of respect.

On the plus side, such considerations all helped me to become comfortable with historical inaccuracies, inconsistencies, and false attributions, which increasingly modern scholarship seemed to be throwing up about biblical accounts. On the down side, the idea of infallible scripture, the literal Word of God, became for me impossible, as it became increasingly clear to me that religion and its sacred texts are the products of an evolutionary process, adapting to and reflecting the changing times and the intellectual development of any given cultural group. And of course, from the very start of Christianity, there were different sects and power groups in the infant church, each pushing its own viewpoint and contriving to find authoritative support for it too, by adjusting the texts to suit their arguments. It is still going on. The more I read, the more unhelpful I find the idea of an infallible Bible and a supernatural founder of my faith. Other religions managed perfectly well without.

But in defending its own mythology, the Church has always failed to distinguish the essence from the peripheral. It wastes its resources defending an inessential perimeter, which inevitably will go on shrinking; it fails to defend its central fortress, let alone build up new and more tenable defences. Jesus may have inspired, but it was mortal men who founded and constituted the Church, and in typically human – or at least masculine - fashion were soon squabbling about who was in charge and what the mission statement was to be. There is no one unequivocal source of truth that represents the sum total of Christian knowledge and insight. Even the Nicene Creed had to be imposed as a compromise to still the squabbling of the various factions.

Jesus' divinity itself was an issue for several centuries. According to Luke (Acts 2.22) Peter himself described him in his Pentecost address as 'a man approved of God among you by miracles and wonders and signs.' St John's Gospel in about AD 100 was the first to introduce the idea of Jesus as the Logos of God, co-existent with him before time began. It was not until AD 325 that his full divinity was made official at the council of Nicaea. Indeed, earlier in the 4th century, Pope Liberius signed his name to the Arian creed, which challenged the divinity of Jesus, and Arianism only became an official heresy at the Council of Constantinople in AD 381. Karen Armstrong has pointed out that whatever Western Christendom may have thought, for those in the East and the Greek orthodox churches, Maximus the

Confessor finally produced a definitive formula only in the 7th century. This asserted that Jesus had been 'wholly deified, because he was entirely permeated by the divine.' It was the insistence on Jesus' divinity, at least as much as any desire to honour Mary, that encouraged the development of doctrines such as the immaculate conception (violently disputed in the 13th century between Dominicans and Franciscans), her perpetual virginity, her Assumption, and the various dubious developments of her cult. Such doctrines may serve the psychological needs of the religious; they are no help to the uncommitted.

The effort to show that Jesus was at once wholly man and wholly God naturally led to impossible intellectual contortions. Yet, as someone once wisely remarked, 'If there is one thing Jesus did not think he was, it is the Second Person of the Trinity.' Was he *homoiousios* (of like substance) or *homoousios*, (of the same substance) with the Father? It would not have worried him one iota, but it took nearly four hundred years for the Christian churches to settle the point, probably wrongly and certainly pointlessly.

All this is why for me even the Bible came into my category of peripherals, not essentials - a guide to the essence of our religion, but not the essence itself. Religious motivation is always the same: a search for meaning and purpose, anchor points in an otherwise pointless universe. But the answers inevitably change through the centuries and I have no doubt they always will. I continue to have few problems with the possibility (indeed probability) of a divinity; I have increasing problems with a religion which claims to be other than a human construct, designed for the time being to bring its followers closer to that divinity. And I can no longer accept any religion's claim to be uniquely true or man's sole source of salvation, whatever we may mean by 'salvation.'

I also came to see a real distinction, in any religion (I suspect) and in my own (certainly), between the life and thought of the Founder and the subsequent efforts of his disciples to interpret to others the essence of their Founder's thought. Witness the relation between Socrates and his great interpreter Plato, or, (though I know little about them) the bifurcating streams of Islam represented by the Sunni and Shia traditions, or between Jesus (whose emphasis seemed to be Jewish) and his great interpreter Paul, whose view of Christianity as a universal religion led my namesake but no relation, A.N. Wilson, to suggest rather naughtily that he is the real founder of Christianity. Christian theologians and interpreters have much to answer for, because over the years in their efforts to define the indefinable they have made complicated and obscure what was originally relatively simple.

Indeed, for me, the essence of Christianity is very simple: God as revealed to man by Jesus Christ. All else is external and of relatively less importance, including the Church and the body of writings and experiences, which make up the Bible. The Church, for me, is a man-made institution; the Bible a man-made record of humanity's endless search for God. It is a record passed from mouth to mouth, people to people, generation to generation, over centuries, changing and renewing itself through new visions and interpretations in the minds and hearts of ordinary men.

Finally, there is the problem of language, the vehicle for human ideas. We live in a very literal-minded era. But if you take all language too literally, you face problems, as I did when reciting a poem the other day to my three year old grand-daughter. I puzzled her greatly when I told her that 'the sea is a hungry dog, giant and grey...' Thinking metaphorically is difficult for the mind of a child, which deals only in what the psychologists call 'concrete operations.' Our approach to religion is too often similar. When confronted by the more metaphorical or poetic conceptual patterns of earlier centuries, our own concrete, literal-minded age can turn sceptical. In the 16th century, part of the power of Shakespeare's language lay in the fact that in his day there was little distinction between objective and metaphorical modes of thought and expression. But today, words can be problematic, when used to convey to people of a different era and culture the meaning and essence of the life of Jesus.

What, for example, do we actually mean by the idea of a 'sacrifice for the sin of the world'? Historically it is a relatively modern concept (Robin Lane Fox: *The Unauthorised Version*), not commented on in Jewish writers until about 200 BC in the writing of Ben Sira, the author of Ecclesiasticus. Does God seriously want human sacrifice? I doubt it. The prophets such as Micah, Hosea or Amos had doubts about even animal sacrifices. Did Jesus really, literally, mean 'this is my body...' at the last supper? Even if the Greek text (1 Cor 11.23) was entirely reliable, which it isn't, I myself doubt it. But in primitive religion it was thought that if you ate part of a particular animal, its desired characteristics (its *mana*) would become part of you. So it would have been a less difficult idea in a largely pagan world, though even then early Christians were at times suspected of cannibalism.

The whole issue caused problems for the Popes until at least Pius IV in 1564. And What about Jesus as 'Son of God'? Or doctrinally as 'God the Son'? What does it actually mean? 'Son of God' was originally simply an honorific title for King David, and then - if only by implication - for his descendants, who included the expected Messiah; so of course, it was used of Jesus himself by his followers, possibly even as an implicit challenge to that other Son of God, the Roman Emperor. But what does such an assertion as Son of God actually mean? Such imagery and symbolic language was perfectly adequate for over one thousand years – but in this our literal-minded and scientific era I suspect it is no longer. In the ancient world, which was full of gods, the idea of elevating a man to divinity was relatively common. Great benefactors were often deified by their communities. Sophocles, the Athenian playwright, became a god; Pompey, the Roman general, who brought peace and stability to the permanently troubled Middle East, was widely worshipped there; Augustus himself was *divi filius*, Son of God, because he was the adopted son of the deified Julius Caesar – talk about deification by proxy!

Thereafter the cult of the emperor was the most powerful single unifying factor in the Roman empire, and after conquest, the first thing to be built in any new centre of government was the temple of the Imperial Cult. Augustus permitted his own worship in the Eastern empire, though not in the West. And look what happened to Paul and Barnabas in Lystra, in response to a single, relatively modest miracle. (Acts 14.8) The crowds shouted that 'The gods have come down to us in human form and they called Barnabas Jupiter and Paul Mercury, because he was the spokesman. And the priest of Jupiter, whose temple was just outside the city, brought oxen and garlands to the gates and he and all the people were about to offer sacrifice.' In those days gods and mortals regularly overlapped.

There is more than one kind of truth, and we all speak several languages every day. Too often the Church claims for its doctrines a truth inappropriate to the kind of truths it is proclaiming - it is simply speaking in the wrong language. Its exposition and defence of its doctrines have become too often intellectually disreputable. And that for me is a brief summary of the problem of Jesus, Son of God, who in metaphorical language that we still use, and which the ancient world (with its three-tiered universe) would have fully understood, 'came down to earth from heaven.'

Part 2: The Greek and Roman Cultural Background
(The Era between the Testaments)

In the first part of my talk I explained in general terms why I find the Bible stories and traditional Christian teaching about them unsatisfactory and what a relief it can be to feel able to discard them as unwanted religious baggage on one's pilgrimage. Now in the very limited time available, I want to do three things to reinforce my argument: first, to say something about the pattern of religious development in the ancient classical world where Christianity was born, and in so doing to give you a context within which, as I see it, the Christian 'myth' or 'narrative' evolved; second, to suggest that our present religious turmoil is of a similar kind to that which confronted the pagan religions at the time of Christ, and is a natural part of religious development; third, to suggest that we should not be depressed by this, but feel encouraged to be released from the burden of defending the indefensible. It is a sign of religious maturity, of health not failure.

So let me first say a little about the development of ancient religion and suggest similarities with today. The stage sets are different, of course; but stage sets are only paint and canvas. The actors who prance before those sets, whether in Classical Athens or 21st Century Britain, seem strangely similar, and it is worth remembering that we are only about seventy-five generations away from the Greeks who heard St Paul on the Hill of the Areopagus in Athens. In evolutionary terms that's nothing.

Gilbert Murray, an atheist but probably the greatest classical scholar of his generation, suggests that we can discern five distinct stages in Greek religion – and I suspect that the pattern applies more generally.

The first of his five stages is the primitive world of superstition. It doesn't need much explanation. It was closely tied to sympathetic magic and the manipulation of natural forces, and all bound up with early man's chief concerns: crops, survival, and reproduction. Its divinities are strongly female. Like the Athenians on the Areopagus, we probably think we have left that stage behind long ago – I tend to doubt it, given the modern obsession with sex, obesity, astrology, black magic, and alternative therapies. Residual superstition is still all about us.

Stage two comes in with the tribal migrations that brought new peoples and gods to the region, from around 1500 BC onwards, and represents a most significant change. This is the great anthropomorphic stage of religion. The gods became recognisably human, masculine of course, supplanting the female mother- and nature-goddesses of more primitive times. By then warfare was becoming a significant activity, superseding the relatively peaceful and feminine culture of the preceding agricultural communities, whose increasing prosperity made them attractive to the increasing acquisitiveness of the emerging masculine societies. Greed and domination are typically masculine characteristics – and to a degree their gods reflect this as the familiar Gods of classical mythology take over.

Zeus the King, Father of Gods and Men, Lord of the thunderbolt rules over all from his throne above, on Mount Olympus instead of Sinai, whence gods regularly commuted between earth and heaven, often for lascivious purposes. It was the world of Apollo, god of the sun, enlightenment, reason, healing, and the Arts; the world of Athene, a primitive war-goddess, who sprang fully armed from the head of Zeus, but in stage two became transformed into the embodiment of pure thought and of intellect (feminists take heart!). Instead of Satan, Hades reigned in the underworld, where the wicked were punished and the rest lived out a shadowy semi-existence. The familiar three-tiered universe of heaven, earth, and Hell is thus established and persists to this day in our own religious imagery.

It is sometimes easy to forget what an enormous advance such divinities represent from their predecessors. They bring Greek religion into the sunlight after the darkness of magic and primitive superstition. Their motivations and behaviour are human; so they are comprehensible, easy to placate or bribe, and fiercely territorial. In fact, apart from their great numbers, they were very like the jealous God of the Old Testament, though their outlook was rather more international than Jehovah's narrow Jewish favouritism. This is what most of us still regard as the Pagan World, in the midst of which Christianity was formed and from which, somewhat naively perhaps, we like to think it rescued us, though in fact at the popular level we have barely developed beyond it. Paganism was a far more tolerant and inclusive religion that Christianity ever managed to be. Remarkably, these Olympian gods lasted for the better part of 2000 years, about the same as Christianity so far. Yet I suspect that we would not find their characteristics or powers very different from those of our own God. They were, for example, all powerful and consequently expected to answer prayers – usually at a price – just as today.

Only in the fact that they were many and ubiquitous were they significantly different. Their temples dominated the scene, whether urban or rural; their shrines littered the landscape; their statues filled the streets. Every hill or woodland or spring, every river or mountain had its attendant deity. The streets of every town were chock full of religious clutter. Think of Paul on the Areopagus, commenting on the Athenians' excessive scrupulousness about religion: they were, he said, *deisidaimonesteroi*, – 'over fearful of the gods' – or 'too superstitious', as the Authorised Version puts it. There were shrines to every known deity, and for insurance purposes, in case they had left one out, they had even put one up To the Unknown God. With something better to offer, Paul must have seen this as a marketing opportunity. By AD 50 Olympianism had long been in decline. As early as 400 BC, long before St Paul, the seeds of the gods' destruction were being sown and their effects were visible - at least to anyone who thought about it. This is the period I now want to focus on in rather more detail, since I find many parallels with our situation today.

As the Greeks grew up intellectually, morally, and politically, thinking men became increasingly troubled by the inadequacy of gods, whose conduct and motivations were a-moral, irrational and arbitrary. By 400 BC the democratic city-state was fully developed and with it secular man's sense of community. The citizen's awareness of his duty to his neighbours, as well as to his gods, his sense of the mutual dependency between man and man, was increasing. New ideas were all the rage – in theology, for example, four world-class dramatists were at the height of their powers – drama was theology then; in philosophy and science, great thinkers were speculating about the material universe and the nature of knowledge; in politics, the habit of public debate and free speech were fully established. Trade and travel were helping to increase prosperity and broaden horizons, and a growing empire gave to all a sense of national pride and personal self-sufficiency, a confidence that man was master of his fate and captain of his soul; some now denied the existence of the gods altogether. It was, in fact, the climax of what is often called the 'Axial Age.'

In an extraordinary leap of imagination, Greek scientific thinkers had long suggested that all matter was derived from a single substance – a hypothesis that marks the birth of the physical sciences in the western world. Around 600 BC Thales (fl.585) proposed that this substance was water, and that the world originates from and returns to it, so that water is eternal and divine. Heraclitus suggested (like St John, some five hundred years later) that Logos (Rational Principle) or transcendent wisdom and elemental fire was the origin of all things, that it spans the universe, but depends for its own existence on the cosmic processes. Parmenides (ca.450) wrestled with the concept of being, thus anticipating the linguistic basis of much modern philosophy. Finally, around 420 BC Democritus proposed that the basis of all matter was a single, uncuttable, fundamental particle which he called the atom, and that the origin of the universe was a chance collision of such atoms, fusing together in the vacuum by a kind of chain reaction. The only thing he left out was the Big Bang.

These physical explanations of creation naturally led to increased speculation about the reality of existence and the very nature of knowledge, asking whether one can really know anything at all. As a result, thinkers inevitably began to challenge the validity of moral values, with some suggesting that objective knowledge was impossible, and that morality was entirely subjective, simply a matter of choice. For the educated and the young, the traditional tales, what we would call the 'mythology' of conventional religion, came to seem 'little more than poets' wretched lies,' to quote a contemporary. Certainty gave way to uncertainty; there were no absolutes; all was relative. The more you knew, the more you doubted. In fact, established values seemed to be crumbling away amid the increasing materialism and secularism of the age. The more conservative complained bitterly that the young lacked all respect for their elders, for traditional religion, and accepted codes of morality.

It all sounds uncomfortably familiar. We too are in the midst of an intellectual revolution, with horizons vastly expanded by travel, trade, and exploration; with our minds expanded by increased knowledge; with all our certainties challenged by free thinking intellectuals; and with prosperity massively increasing, which always tends to undermine religion. Only a few weeks ago I read a newspaper report that the Astronomer Royal was arguing a similar point: that the universe may not actually exist at all and that we might all be part of a virtual reality inside a gigantic cosmic computer experiment. How do you know we are not? Can you prove it? For the Greeks, as for us, traditional value systems were seen increasingly as a matter of individual choice; opinion replaced knowledge; authority and objectivity were dead. One famous sound-bite summarised this position: 'Nothing is; if it were, we could not know it; if we knew it, we could not communicate it.' Another said simply, 'Man is the measure of all things.' Gods were becoming superfluous, like today.

In all this, the Olympian Gods (rather like modern church leaders) offered neither challenge to their opponents nor comfort and help to their adherents. Traditionalists and populist politicians blamed the liberal, intellectual elite, the so-called Sophists. This group of itinerant polymaths and lecturers were the media celebrities of their day, roughly a cross between TV pundits and left wing university dons. The Athenians even put one of them to death for 'atheism, impiety and corrupting the young.' His name was Socrates. As usually happens in a popular witch-hunt, they got the wrong man. Socrates' views were the absolute opposite of those of the Sophists. He was the most devout of all the Athenian intelligentsia, inclined to monotheism perhaps, but not atheism. As with Jesus, his death was as much a matter of politics as religion. Socrates challenged the prevailing intellectual fashions on every front.

The Sophists denied the possibility of objective knowledge, arguing that all knowledge was relative and that one man's opinion was as good as another's. Socrates insisted that true knowledge was objective, and values objectively real and eternally valid. The Sophists were fashionable, popular, trendy, and offered expensive courses in rhetoric. They cultivated an exclusive clientele among the aristocracy, for whom success in public life required rhetorical training in the art of winning arguments. Socrates charged nothing; talked to everyone; and sought to discover the truth, not to win arguments. He pioneered the techniques of logic and what we now call inductive reasoning, which is the basis of all scientific thought. This debate between the relativism of the sophists and the objective values of Socrates and his followers was the intellectual battle of the age and in many ways parallels our own debates between traditional values and individual libertarianism. The effect of his judicial murder was to turn his young aristocratic disciple, Plato, away from the normal aristocrat's career in politics and into academic life - probably one of the best things that has happened in the history of human thought.

It is from here that we can date the beginning of the eternal tension between science and theology. If we ignore purpose and design, and offer material solutions to the question of the origin of matter, then inevitably God becomes irrelevant. If we move to more abstract concepts like purpose and design, as the Greeks soon did, with Logos (Rational principle) or The One, or The Good, as the source of all being, then you run into linguistic problems and problems of proof: what do you mean by such terms, and how do you know? For Socrates and Plato, Beauty, Goodness, and Truth are all manifestations of the divine, and what we experience on earth is a pale imitation of an ultimate and objective reality, which is God. Scientists who discount such abstractions are inevitably atheist.

In this context, I suspect that St John at the start of his gospel was doing exactly what Heraclitus and Plato had sought to do long before – to reconcile the material experience of our senses with our perception of the numinous and the divine, which derives from some inner essence that we call the soul. By St John's day Greek was the lingua franca of the Middle East; and Greek thought as well as language was widely understood. As a result, educated and thinking men naturally expressed their ideas through Greek concepts. Indeed, Alister McGrath in his *Introduction to Christian Theology*, sees Plato as the key to many of the intense debates of the Christian patristic period.

Time is short but as a brief illustration of this general point, I have attached to my summary of this talk a note on the idea of Logos in the first four verses of John's gospel. The debate still rages to this day, with modern scientists perhaps rather less inclined than they were to boast that science has all the answers to the riddles of existence. And now some interesting ideas are emerging about physical, chemical, and biological convergence throughout the Cosmos, which for some may increase the attractions of the idea of a supreme Designer.

The suggestion is that such convergence means that all life must inevitably develop along similar lines, because the laws of physical and biological science apply throughout creation. If you did not watch Martin Rees, the astronomer Royal, in a series called 'What we still do not know' you missed a fascinating programme, which seemed to me to be offering real potential for the development of a new theology. For me Plato's use of Myth as the final step in the revelation of profound thought about God remains definitive in my approach to all problems of belief. It was Ian Ramsey, I think, the late great Bishop of Durham, who suggested a similar approach in his book, *Religious Language*. You can go so far with language, piling up insight and illustration, until at some moment, and you never know when, 'the penny drops' and understanding or belief dawns. Plato's Socrates works in the same way. He takes you as far a he can by induction, logic, and reason – but in the end he has to tell a story, which elevates the relentless force of cold reason to the realms of high poetry. It is only by such a process, which engages emotion or intuition or whatever you care to call it into an alliance with the rational side of our natures that we can hope to approach the perception of truth, which is God.

This remarkable period which I have been describing is the era of Gilbert Murray's Third Stage. In it the great schools of philosophy emerge, and with them the great –isms, such as Stoicism, Cynicism, Epicureanism. By that time the Olympian religion, rather like Christianity today, had come to seem intellectually indefensible; and inevitably the more thoughtful had begun to seek different solutions to the puzzle of existence. It was in this post-religious era of intellectual speculation, when Plato founded his great school of philosophy from which all others derive, that ancient religion lost the argument and Western Civilisation came of age intellectually. And that is a very sobering thought for those of us who support traditional religion. If religion, any religion, loses intellectual credibility (as our new Archbishop has acknowledged that Christianity has) in time it will die, as surely as Olympianism began to die 2500 years ago. Certainly for the Greeks new philosophies, Stoicism and Epicureanism particularly, now became predominant, though I hesitate to offer suggestions for what our modern equivalent –isms might be – materialism, perhaps, environmentalism, nihilism, consumerism, individualism? You pays your money and you takes your choice.

Stoicism taught that human existence was controlled by Destiny or Fate, and that the key to human happiness was to do your duty in that state of life unto which it had pleased Fate to call you. It appealed strongly to the Roman governing classes, and has strong echoes in the attitudes of our own Victorians, who in answer to the call of Duty, 'Stern Daughter of the voice of God', went out to rule an empire in the service of their country and their God. Epicureanism was the exact opposite: it was based on Democritus' atomic theory of the origins of creation, denied the existence of the gods or the afterlife, and taught that the key to happiness was a civilised atheism, a contented retirement in the confines of one's garden. 'Eat, drink, and be merry for tomorrow we die' is an unfair but popular parody of their approach.

But we must always remember that ideas take centuries to percolate down through the general mass of humanity, and for the vast, conservative, majority in the ancient world, life – and religion – went on much as before. By the time of Jesus the Romans (who rarely had an original idea, but were jolly good at conquest and drainage) had moved little further forward than the Greeks of some three hundred years before. For their ruling and educated classes the great philosophies of Stoicism and Epicureanism were now the primary guides to a good life, and religion was seen as an opiate of the people, a useful means of controlling them and promoting national unity. As the poet Ovid cynically observed: 'it is expedient that there should be gods, and, since it is expedient, we believe in them.' (*Expedit esse deos et ut expedit, esse putamus*).

The Olympian religion was a bit like all popular religion – approved of by the authorities; underpinned by popular superstition; reinforced by state cults, and sometimes brutally enforced by the rulers. For example, Pliny, the Roman Governor of Bithynia, in Northern Turkey, around AD 100, had problems with the Christians and referred constantly to the emperor Trajan for advice on how to deal with them. He reported that they were good people, but they would not even pay lip service to the state's cults. So should they be executed? Yes, was the reply. Even the normally tolerant Romans could not allow any group to refuse to acknowledge the official cults, if only for the sake of good order and social stability.

Two of Murray's five stages of religion yet remain. The first he called The Failure of Nerve and he dates it from the beginning of the Christian era. It is marked, he says, by a rise of asceticism, of mysticism, and of pessimism; by a loss of self-confidence and hope; a loss of faith in human effort; a despair of patient enquiry; a cry for certainty, for infallible revelation; a turning inward of the soul to God. The aim of the good man was now not so much to live justly and serve society, as to show contempt for the world, and to find pardon for his sins through suffering, ecstasy, or martyrdom.

The period sees an enormous increase in the worship of Fortuna (Luck) or Tyche (Chance), of the planets and astrology, and the eastern religions. There is a growing belief in visions, revelations, ecstatic experiences, and the redeemer gods of the Gnostic sects. Emperor worship thrives. I read recently in *The Times* that today we are seeing (and I quote) 'a marked growth in mysticism in opposition to credal Christianity and traditional patterns of worship. The new movements are individualistic and inchoate, offering various kinds of meditation and focused on subjective experience and self-development.' The writer could have been describing the year 300 BC or AD 100. Such phenomena are characteristic of any era when traditional beliefs are eroding and intellectual nerve and moral fibre fail, but it now goes by the fashionable name of post-modernism.

But what of Christianity in Murray's analysis? Here again, uncomfortable though his comments are, I find them revealing and a source of much food for thought. But always remember he was an atheist and a humanist. This clearly colours his analysis. I quote:

Historically speaking it appears to me that the character of Christianity in these early centuries is to be sought not so much in the doctrines it professed, nearly all of which had their roots and parallels in older Hellenistic and Hebrew thought, but in the organisation on which it rested. When I try to understand Christianity as a mass of doctrines - Gnostic, Trinitarian, Monophysite, Arian, and the rest - I get no further. When I try to realise it as a sort of semi-secret society for mutual help with a mystical religious basis, resting first on the proletariats of Antioch and the great commercial and manufacturing towns of the Levant, and then spreading by instinctive sympathy to similar classes in Rome and the west, and rising in influence by the special appeal it made to women, then the various historical puzzles fall into place.

This explains the strange subterranean power which baffled Diocletian; it explains the humanity, the intense feeling of brotherhood; its incessant care of the poor; its indifference to the governing classes and their virtues of statesmanship, moderation, learning, culture and public spirit.... But after the time of Constantine the governing classes come into the fold, bringing with them their normal qualities.

I would be tempted to add that with the advent of those 'normal qualities of the governing classes' came the beginning of the decline of Christianity and it has been in decline ever since. Its link to the temporal powers of this world weakened and possibly severed its link to the Lord of the next. Dare one suggest that the church's record in its first millennium and more reveals all the qualities one normally associates with governing classes and is the source of what I would regard as the unedifying spectacle of the church as a temporal power?

Christian doctrine reflects its origins in Jewish and Hellenistic thought, but its Church structure reflects the fact that it developed under the Roman Empire; indeed, I think it is a moot point whether Christianity took Rome captive, or Rome Christianity. I incline to the latter view. Constantine was entirely tolerant of other religions but once he reckoned that in the God of the Christians he had found his most effective divine military ally, it was what we would now call a no-brainer to enlist him under his banner. But the soldiers who fought for Constantine remained devoutly pagan in their beliefs and religious practices, and the ancient world in general did likewise for several centuries afterwards at least. Julian the Apostate is only the most notorious example of the inherent conservatism of all religion, whether pagan or Christian. Paganism survived for centuries after the coming of Christ. The survival of the ancient oracles is simply one testimony to this fact. For example, after the great revival of oracles in the second century AD, as late as the fifth century AD, the famous oracle of Apollo at Claros in Western Turkey had a Christian martyr shrine placed near. If the oracle had not been active at that late date, Christians would not have troubled to neutralise it with a shrine of their own.

Finally we have stage five - the last flowering of paganism before the triumph of mediaeval Christianity, which brought intolerance and a sort of superstitious certainty to the church and reached its culmination a thousand years later in the horrors of the Inquisition. Julian the Apostate (fl.AD 350) stands as a convenient symbol of this final stage. He restored the practice of universal religious toleration and led a retreat into what Murray calls 'a synthesising mysticism,' - a sort of monotheistic pantheism. He maintained that all gods were one God, and that what mattered most was the one great truth that the gods exist, that they are ultimately one, and that traditional pagan myths are simply different expressions of god and the goodness of the gods. Queen Elizabeth the first made much the same point, I think, when she stated that there was only one Faith – and the rest was argument about trifles. (Try telling that to a modern synod discussing the role of women bishops!).

I think I could go along with that without much difficulty and I find it difficult to see Christianity in its modern form as anything much more than the last and perhaps the greatest of the anthropomorphic religions. Such liberal thinking was not destined to last long and was soon ruthlessly eliminated by the emperor Theodosius. But in all this I see no grounds for despair. It is simply part of the cycle of man's evolving mind and spirit and that never ending quest for truth, understanding, and richer experience which is our real inheritance from Adam, and far more original than any sin of which he may once have been guilty. To quote Tennyson,

> Though much is taken, much abides and....
> All experience is an arch where through
> Gleams the un-travelled world whose margin fades
> For ever and for ever when I move.

It is high time both church and people were on the move once more, lifting our eyes to where the untravelled world of a reformed faith gleams bright against a dark horizon.

Conclusion

And the lessons to be learnt from it all are, I suggest, as follows: First, as man's mind evolves, so the religions that sustain it must evolve also. To treat even Christianity as something somehow fixed irrevocably for all time is to condemn it to a lingering death by asphyxiation similar to that died by the Olympian religion of old. Man's habits of thought change and unless religion's habits change also it will cease to speak to him or answer his needs. That is what is happening now, I believe. And though we are well into the era of our own great -isms, the philosophies such as Communism, Marxism, Egalitarianism, Materialism, Feminism, and so on, our thought processes, the tools and concepts of our religion, are still too often as primitive as the anthropomorphism of the Olympians.

There was a time, some five hundred years ago, when the works of the poet Virgil enjoyed a status not dissimilar to that accorded to the Bible today in much of the church's apologetic and homily. Such was the standing of the poet as a man of inspiration and divine connections that what was called the *Sors Virgiliana*, Virgil's lucky dip, if you like, was a common recourse for those seeking guidance in the anxieties of their daily life. Whether you wanted next week's winner of the Derby or advice on whether to marry, you took a random passage from the works of Virgil and duly interpreted them to suit the occasion of your worry. We would readily enough nowadays dismiss such an approach as superstitious, but similar practices still exist.

Yet much of the intellectual basis of the church's proclamation seems to approach the Bible in much the same spirit. This may be reasonable enough for those whose conceptual framework is adapted to it. But it will not do for a new generation which knew not Pharaoh. Christian apologetics must return to the classroom and learn its trade all over again, if it does not want to find itself preaching to an ageing congregation and a smattering of insecure beings who will surrender their intelligence as the price of a spurious certainty.

In this context I cannot do better than quote the late Professor Hanson, former Bishop of Derry and Raphoe, controversial though his views may be. In discussing the relationship of St John's Gospel to the other three and the fact that only in St John is Jesus attributed with specific claims to divinity and pre-existence, he argued that the fourth gospel was less an historical account than a theological commentary on the significance of Jesus - a view which he argues has been established for over three hundred years. 'Yet,' he goes on, 'clergy of all denominations seem to be either unaware of modern scholarly opinion.... or are engaged in a conspiracy of silence to say nothing about it and are content to assist their people to continue in ignorance of what must be, on any estimate, a vitally important fact for contemporary Christianity.... How far is one justified,' he asks, 'in sacrificing intellectual integrity in order to avoid upsetting the faithful. In the matter of liturgy and ceremony there is no problem. But intellectual integrity is another matter and one that should bite on the consciences deeper than apparently it does. And a non-critical, blindly conservative attitude to scholarship in the long run does deep damage to the church.'

Here is one layman from the pew who can only shout 'Hear! Hear!' For every one of the faithful that is offended or distressed by the intellectual challenge of modern scholarship, I would guess there are five doubters for whom intellectual traditionalism has become a major obstacle to belief, because to them it seems akin to the superstitions of Greek anthropomorphic Olympianism.

It is time for the church at large and not just its leading and sometimes way-out intellectuals to initiate a great debate about just where the central core of its belief and message is to be found and how it is to be presented. It seems to me that it is too often trying to keep the water in the bath only to allow the baby to disappear. Our Lord, after all, when pressed was able to get to the heart of his message in a single sentence, which, he claimed, embodied the law and the prophets. It is the church that has erected a vast and unstable edifice upon it. My own suspicion is that a most profound redefinition of belief is needed if we are to speak coherently to the growing generations of the 21st century, whose outlook is so changed that I believe they have less in common with the man of 1850 than that man would have had with a man of Jesus' day. The process of such accelerated evolution is extremely uncomfortable but I believe unavoidable.

I take, however, great comfort from Jesus' sayings that 'a grain of corn must fall to the ground and die' and that 'the man that would save his life must lose it.'

CHAPTER SEVENTEEN

Footnotes to a Parish Colloquy

(1) A Note on Logos

As a boy I was given a copy of Moffatt's translation of the Bible and was struck by the fact that he avoided translating the word Logos in the opening verse of St John's gospel. 'The Logos existed in the very beginning...,' he wrote. It still seems a sort of abdication, but how does one find a form of words which combines the overtones of the Hebrew, on which I am not competent to comment, with the rather different force of the Greek. Suggestiveness is an innate quality of poetry and the effectiveness of poetry depends in part on the richness of associations suggested. The power of the concept of Logos/Word in an OT context similarly depends on the richness of its associated ideas, since all religious language is closer to poetry than any other language, such as that of science or logic. The problem for any translator is to capture something of the poetic effect of the Hebrew overtones and ally them with the more rational 'scientific' overtones of the Greek word. I suspect it can't be done and that Moffatt was right to abandon the struggle.

To me as an ordinary layman, some of the associations which the Hebrew suggests are these:

1. 'God spake and it was created': creation is the expression of the creator, God. God's Word is equated with his Works.
2. Breath is a manifestation of our life force and proceeds from our mouths; so too the Word of God is the expression of his life force or essence (cf. Latin *spiritus* can mean breath and also spirit).
3. The will of God is expressed through his words, spoken by his prophets in the form of commandments, laws of conduct, wisdom and poetry. Such words are earthly expressions of his Word.
4. The Bible, as the written record of God's works/Word, is part of his Logos.
5. Jesus, to Christians, is the incarnate expression of the Word of God, a model of his will.
6. In ancient magic to know the name of something was to gain power over it – so Adam and Eve gave names to things; Jacob wrestled with an unknown stranger who would not reveal his name. There is a connection between power and language. God's Word is part of his power; and possibly to know

God's word is to know God.
7. Story or narrative – one of the three categories of Jewish writing

The Greek word Logos carries various meanings. From the dictionary we can extract the following:

1. Computation or reckoning – as in sums, account books, etc.
2. By extension, *logon didonai* in Greek means to render your accounts.
3. By further extension, to give an account or explanation of something. In Socrates' thinking, this was the key test of true knowledge or understanding, the ability to 'give an account' of what you believe. Without it you merely had right (or wrong) opinions. There are clear implications of logic, precision, and calculation, but also objective reality.
4. Relation, correspondence, proportion
5. Explanation, theory, argument
6. Rule, principle, law
7. Reason, law (as exhibited in world process, such as the laws of Nature)
8. Heracleitus (ca.500 BC) – Rational First Principle (equated with divine Wisdom and Fire, by which the Cosmos was created).
9. Inward debate of the soul, internal dialogue
10. Narrative, report, speech

How then might one try to translate the opening verses of St John's Gospel?

'There is a rational principle behind all created matter. Its source is the will of God and its expression is the manifestation of God himself.
All creation is the expression of God and exists outside of time.
He is the source of all being and his creation is the expression of that being.
God (once) gave living form to the expression of his will; and its life gave light to the world. That light shines for ever in the darkness and can never be extinguished.'

(2) A Note on Romans 1.1-3. The Nature of Jesus

Date: AD 55, so the passage probably predates the gospels and presumably reflects early attempts to 'define' the faith. A manifesto. Difficult to translate, as all manifestos should be, so that they mean different things to different constituencies.

NEB offers two renderings, both of which seem to me to force the Greek into meanings, which as a teacher of Greek, I would query from a pupil. NEB translates:

'on the human level he was born of David's stock, but on the level of the spirit – the Holy Spirit – he was declared Son of God by a mighty act in that he rose from the dead' OR

'was declared Son of God with full powers **from the time when he** rose from the dead.'

I would have reservations about

1. 'Son of God' with capitals – the Greek would as easily bear the meaning 'a son of a god.'
2. 'Declared' sounds like a royal proclamation; the basic meaning is 'separated out' or 'marked out,' usually of territorial boundaries. The whole phrase could most readily be translated 'he was marked out as a son of god.'
3. 'The Holy Spirit' is similarly forced – Paul may well be working his way towards such a concept, and by the time of Matthew's gospel the phrase is indeed 'holy spirit', though capitals were not normal. What Paul actually writes is not terribly coherent - 'marked out as a son of god according to the spirit of holiness.' We have not yet reached a stage where the Holy Spirit is a fully developed concept, deemed capable of being involved in human conception, let alone as the third member of the Trinity.
4. If we can take *en dunamei kata pneuma hagiosunes* as a single phrase, one unit of thought, then it would be nice to translate it: 'in spiritual terms, by the power of holiness,' thus contrasting it with 'in human terms – *kata sarka*'. But I suspect I may be interpreting rather than translating, and so forcing the Greek into pre-conceived ideas, rather as the NEB translators are. The most literal version would be something like: 'in power according to the spirit of holiness.' But does that mean anything?
5. The biggest issue is the final phrase *ex anastaseos nekron*: lit: 'out of/from the resurrection of the dead.' The NEB preferred version 'in that he rose from the dead' is the more natural rendering. Its alternative, 'from the time when he rose from the dead' is perfectly acceptable from the Greek, as the NEB suggests in its footnote, and is compatible with the alternative rendering. (*ex hou* in Gk can mean 'from the time when....'). This has considerable theological implications.

My own neutral (I hope) version might go like this <.....> = not strictly in the Greek:

> 'Paul, a slave of Christ Jesus, called <to be> an apostle, set apart for the gospel of god <sends you greetings>. This gospel was first announced through his prophets in holy writings concerning his son, Jesus Christ our Lord, who in human terms was born of the seed of David, but in spiritual terms by (lit: in) the power of holiness was marked out as a son of God as a result of (or: from the time of) <his> resurrection from the dead.'

In the Gospels

Mark, the earliest, ca AD 70, with no miraculous birth story, sees Jesus as acknowledged by God at his baptism, ?? aged thirty ??. Acknowledgement by a father was a typical formality in the ancient world.
Matthew suggests divinity at conception: Mary has conceived 'by the Holy Spirit'.
Luke has two goes: prior to conception, since the angel foretells the conception; says it will happen. Then at baptism (like Mark).

John, the latest, sees Jesus as the incarnation of the Word, and therefore pre-existent with God from the beginning.

The Roman centurion said (Matt.27.54) 'Truly this was a son of God' OR 'a son of a god.' The NEB concedes 'the son of God' as a variant rendering in a footnote.

Comments:

Is it possible to argue that the early years of Christianity did not themselves quite know what they thought about Jesus?

Is that why there was so much debate and wrangling about creeds and heresies?

Could one argue that they were much more flexible about dogma and doctrine than the Middle Ages, when The Church had acquired a dominant role in the secular world and was determined to prevent free thought?

Are we at last breaking free? Is this not a good thing?

(3) Other Ideas for Discussion Sessions

Consider the assumptions that are no longer a part of our own conceptual framework compared with, say, even our grandparents.

The Bible is no longer self-evidently true down to the last comma. Palaeontology, archaeology, Darwinian science, form criticism and modern biblical scholarship have all seen to that.

Heaven is no longer the upper tier of a three-tiered creation, with earth in the middle and hell below. The world is a microscopic and finite entity in an infinite cosmos, doomed to destruction, within a measurable time span, like our sun and its galaxy, which will collapse in upon itself and disappear like bath water down its own celestial plug hole - only they call them black-holes nowadays. Even the universe may be similarly finite, though we are not as yet sure about it.

Authority is no longer seen as god-given. There is no divine right of kings; the world is no longer the microcosm of God's creation; the habit of deference to traditional authority is eroded; 'because I say so' has ceased to be a legitimate argument; it was of course never a very rational one.

Man is no longer seen to be descended from the angels; it is clear that he has, if anything, ascended from the beasts; and not long ago, as we know full well, even the beasts came crawling out of the primeval sludge.

Life can be created out of non-life in a test tube in a laboratory.

Communications are now so instant that we can see what is happening anywhere in the world as soon as it occurs, and we are (like the Greeks of Herodotus' day) bombarded all the time with knowledge and comparisons, strange beliefs, and cultures, all of which must serve to undermine our own certainties. The world is now our village and a small square box embracing a cathode ray tube is our market place, the source of our gossip, the stuff of all our common chatter, and at its well we draw most of our refreshment and relaxation.

Travel is now so fast that like Ariel you can put a girdle round the earth in minutes in your satellite; you can circumnavigate the globe in twenty-four hours or less exotically travel five hundred miles in a weekend to see Aunt Flo.

The supernatural is no longer a normal assumption for the educated man and except in the fantasy world of celluloid he does not expect close encounters of the third, fourth, fifth or any other kind in real life. Only astrology, exorcism, black magic and other perversions remain upon the fringes of our certainties to be exploited by the cynical at the expense of the escapist and the gullible.

Relativism reigns supreme. Nothing is certain; all is relative. You do your own thing and leave me to get on with mine. You can only be true to yourself. Knowledge is impossible because what you thought you knew today is all too likely to be disproved tomorrow. The sum of human knowledge is growing at such a rate that clever men can only know more and more about less and less, while ordinary men must be content with potted knowledge purveyed to them by the trivialising simplifications of the mass media. The grasshopper has become a burden. And yet amidst all this turmoil we see the churches seemingly unchanged. That the values they proclaim should not change seems right enough - but on the whole those values are now also the values of the unbelieving as well as of believers. What worries me is that the whole apparatus - conceptual, linguistic, intellectual, practical - which underlies and used to underpin the proclamation of the church's message seems almost unchanged since the 1st century AD. It is this that leads me to use the rather pejorative term of 'anthropomorphic' or 'Olympian' Christianity.

Section C: History

Thinking about History and Faith

To know only your own time is to remain forever a child - Cicero

The more I have wrestled with my doubts about the Christian faith to which I belong, the clearer it has become to me that my problems of belief derived from the fact that, like any good fundamentalist, I had always been taught to treat my religious inheritance as if, from its beginning, it had issued fully formed for ever from the hand of God, infallible and unalterable. But it steadily became no less clear to me that if the doctrines of that faith were an affront to my God-given powers of reason and my relatively modern intelligence, then the faith by which they were underpinned was a nonsense.

There were only two solutions: either to abandon that faith or try to work out a more acceptable interpretation of its teaching.

As a classicist with several very distinguished clerics in my close ancestry, including two archbishops, a couple of bishops, and a monsignor, I had always had a general interest in religion, ancient and modern, as well a sincere sympathy for the church, and had even toyed for a time with the idea of seeking Holy Orders, until Bob Runcie (later Archbishop of Canterbury) persuaded me that I would be too uncomfortable within the institution. Sadly he was probably right.

All my life I have explored religious ideas, and even taught non-specialist RE to VI Formers. I had no training in theology, though a Cambridge don who influenced me greatly had told me that any educated man should have a book of theology on the go all the time. I believed him, and for much of my life I have done so. Had he suggested that I should read the Bible every day, I might well have abandoned the practice. Bible reading does not readily encourage one to think about ideas. And it was only when I got to Cambridge that I learned to think for myself. Boarding school followed by the army was not conducive to the practice.

But I had also one great and more unusual blessing: I had never been to Sunday school, which tended in those days to be a nursery for a fundamentalist view of Biblical knowledge. Instead until the age of 13 I had been to a boarding school in Northern Ireland, which had its own chapel, a choir in which I sang, and daily services. We learned by heart the Collect for the week, and as a result the language and rhythms of their language has remained with me all my life. We were entered each year for the nationwide system of so-called Church of Ireland Synod Examinations, with a well-planned syllabus rendered all the more attractive by the fact that everyone who entered seemed to win prizes, graded First, Second or Third. The result was that I had a more systematic familiarity with the best Bible stories and other 'good bits' of the Bible than many of my contemporaries. We even studied the three missionary journeys of Paul.

I went on to boarding school in England until the age of 18, where of course there was a chapel, a choir, daily prayers in the school hall, and (too many!) Sunday services. So I also acquired a long habit of daily and Sunday worship, through which I could not help but gain familiarity with the psalms (which I still love), and a systematic exposure to the church lectionary, including the Old Testament which has now largely fallen out of fashion. It was, I think, the Jesuits who said that if they had hold of a child till the age of seven, they would have him for life. Well thanks to my boarding schools, indirectly my religion had a pretty firm hold of me till 18 and has retained my interest ever after.

So, as my doubts about the traditional faith grew, the option of abandoning my faith was not something that appealed to me. Instead I sought to read my way to a more acceptable basis for my belief. Since then I have to some extent followed the writings of many of the more popular and fashionable theologians, though to call them 'popular' is not intended to imply any criticism of the quality of their work. Rather it is intended to suggest my gratitude to those who seek to make theology accessible to the ordinary man in the street, by marked contrast with some of those leaders of the church whose writings and public statements border on the oracular and the sadly numerous clerics whose sermons range from the cliché-ridden to the harmlessly bland.

In the end, and relatively recently, I have come to realise that my best hope of recovering a degree of conviction lies in discovering more about the very early days of Christianity from the perspective of an historian, not a conventional Christian. If I could see what it was that shaped Jesus and his mission and how in his own time he reacted to contemporary problems and situations and related them to his understanding of his own beliefs, then I might be able to find a new relevance to my own time, which my church makes no real attempt to convey. If I could reach some kind of view about what actually happened and why the 'record' took the form it did, I might have a sounder basis for understanding the origins of my faith than the largely mythological accounts on which I had been reared.

I have called this section History, not because it makes any claims to being a comprehensive account of the history of early Christianity. Rather it contains, I hope, some sort of outline of where my reading has taken me. I have listed in the final Bibliography some of the books which have figured in my more general reading. But nothing has had a greater impact on my understanding of those early years of Christianity than the writings of Dominic Crossan, Marcus Borg, Charles Freeman, Tom Holland, Bishop John Shelby Spong, John Churcher, and the body which calls itself The Jesus Seminar. Between them they have set me free and saved me from abandoning the Church of my fathers.

I should add, too, that my admittedly limited reading about the Dead Sea Scrolls reinforces my understanding of the evolution of religion generally and of the early origins of Christianity in particular. In their Epilogue to *The Complete World of the Dead Sea Scrolls* the authors say this: 'No new Life of Jesus can be plausibly written without these manuscripts. Jesus has not been found in the Dead Sea Scrolls, despite the claims of at least one scholar. Nor has John the Baptist or Paul. But the Scrolls came from the time of these pioneering figures of early Christianity, and they destroy for ever any simplistic opposition of 'Jesus' and 'Judaism'. Do they demonstrate that Christianity is older than Jesus? Strictly, no: but they expose very strong continuities..... The Scrolls underline the ongoing imagination and the desire of Jews to become attuned to the words and the will of God in the final days of the Second Temple. They represent the religious matrix of both rabbinic Judaism and Christianity.'

No religion emerges fully formed for ever from the mind of God. All religions evolve. All are the products of their time and develop in the context of their time.

CHAPTER EIGHTEEN

Thinking About History and Faith

(From the Forum Website of permissiontospeak.org.uk)

This is a thought that came to me as I was reading Crossan's Birth of Christianity. I wondered if it would make a good Forum topic and offered it to the P2S Forum Website.

In a tightly argued chapter in which he discusses and compares the accounts of the divine origins of the emperor Augustus and Jesus of Nazareth, Crossan (with admirable honesty) states the following:

> 'We cannot live without group ideology (or, if you prefer, theology), but we must be able to keep it in dialectic with public evidence - if, that is, we make claims to such data. My own position as an historian trying to be ethical and a Christian trying to be faithful is this: I do not accept the divine conception of either Jesus or Augustus as factual history, but I **believe** (his italics) that God is incarnate in the Jewish peasant poverty of Jesus and not in the Roman imperial power of Augustus.'

The trouble is that, when one compares dispassionately the record of these two historically factual characters, might one not be tempted (perhaps only by the Devil!) to argue the opposite case? After all, Augustus' legacy to the Roman world was an almost universal peace after a hundred years of civil war, a peace which led the poet Virgil to comment, very early in his reign but with poetic and perhaps prophetic insight, '*deus ille deus nobis haec otia fecit*' ('A god it was, yes a god, that brought about for us this state of civil peace'). By contrast can one seriously argue that the legacy of Christianity for humankind has been other than a long record of hatreds, exploitation of power, disputes, schisms, and wars, tempered perhaps by outbreaks of individual insight, goodness, and virtue, which led sometimes to social or community advances? In general Christianity has been no less imperialist than Rome.

Augustus' legacy did not last - arguably that of Jesus did, and its failings are due to the fact that it is still 'work in progress.' But as a test of divine providence, I wonder if the peasant farmers of Augustus' Italy would have given a higher grade of divinity to their Emperor, not least for the speed with which he delivered peace, than the peasants of Judaea and Galilee would have given to their (self-proclaimed?) anointed Saviour, whose programme for humanity's moral improvement has been an unconscionable time a-coming. It is a rather disturbing thought.

Ethical Historian versus Faithful Christian

Some further thoughts:

I like Crossan – he brings a historian's perspective to the examination of the gospel evidence (if one can call it that). His working definition of History is: 'History is the past reconstructed interactively by the present through argued evidence in public discourse.'

But, as he also says, 'When Christians **as historians** bracket from discussion or quarantine from debate specific events,' such as the divine conception of Jesus, 'but not all other such claims, past and present,' such as the divine conception of Augustus, 'they do something I consider unethical.'

He goes on, 'The earliest Christians lived in a world not yet bedevilled by either direct or indirect rationalism, a world where divine conceptions were quite acceptable, where in fact divine and human, eternal and temporal, heaven, earth, and Hades were marvellously porous and open to one another. They could never have argued that Jesus was uniquely singular because divine conception had happened to him alone in all the world. They could not, and they did *not*.'

It is part of a more general proposition that the gospels, written between forty and seventy years after the events, are already examples of the present 'interactively reconstructing' the past, since each is written from a different perspective and for a different community, contemporary with the writer, not the events being described, and not about a purely historical Jesus – if there can be such a person. Each of the canonical gospels, he suggests, goes back to the historical Jesus of the late twenties in his Jewish homeland, but each of them has that Jesus speak directly to the author's own immediate situation and community. In every case, there is a dialectic of then-and-now, of then-as-now – that is of the historical Jesus then as the risen Jesus now.

By seeking to close down 'public discourse' for nearly two thousand years, he seems to imply, the church theologians have diminished credibility for the gospels not just as historical documents, though they were of course not intended to be purely historical, but also as faith documents or, in his phrase, Biography Gospels. As a result they have seriously undermined the faith itself – both as faith and as history.

I begin to wonder in this connection whether one of the impediments for contemporary and marginalised Christians lies in the phrase 'risen Jesus,' which Crossan uses of the post-Easter Jesus. The adjective is inevitably taken as an assertion of literal and physical resurrection, which may never have been intended in early days. If we were to speak now of the 'Remembered Jesus,' I wonder whether it would reduce the obstructive force of the mythical (for want of a better word) overtones of 'risen', while encouraging a more general admiration, respect, and possibly even adherence to the teachings of the founder of our faith. Belief in and even love of the Jesus Christ of Faith might follow.

CHAPTER NINETEEN

Power, Politics, and the Early Church

(Letter to a Friend)

This is just a short note to thank you so much for sending me Verney's *Water into Wine* and the article from the *Times* by Charles Freeman on the works of the Emperor Theodosius in AD 381. I bought the book at once and have interrupted all other reading to complete it, because I simply could not put it down.

It is a fascinating account of how the Creeds came to be imposed on the church by the secular imperial authority, in the shape of three emperors. Initially, but to a lesser extent, there was Constantine, reinforced by Athanasius, a bear of relatively little brain. Constantine was relatively relaxed about paganism, which had a tradition of tolerance and intellectual free-thinking which compares very well, when set against Christianity's intolerance and inflexibility (witness the reign of Julian, the so-called Apostate). Constantine was at best a political rather than a practising Christian, and was only baptised on his deathbed. Then came Theodosius in 381, who with absolute unbending brutality re-imposed the dogmas of the Nicene Creed by law. Thereafter intellectual life and the eastern (Greek) tradition of intellectual discussion and free debate were extinguished.

Then the emperor Justinian (imp. AD 527-565) in the 6th century enshrined Theodosius' imposition in his Codification of the Roman Law, making it something to be upheld in secular as well as church courts, and this shaped and constricted the European mind for one thousand years. He was reinforced later by the ingenious Augustine, whose intellectual powers were formidable; he bent his mind to justifying the final and absolute status of the Nicene Creed. He thereby stifled all future debate until the time of Abelard, whose ideas were rapidly suppressed, and Aquinas who tried to release religious thought from its shackles, but not very successfully. Even Augustine was never able to resolve the intellectual contradictions of the doctrine of the Trinity – which is an intellectual nonsense, and (as he acknowledged) can only be defended as 'an act of faith.'

Not until the collapse of the Roman Catholic Church's authority in the 16th century and the rise of the protestant churches was any sort of intellectual freedom restored. Indeed Prof. Keith Ward has argued that the only hope for Christianity in the long run lies in the protestant liberal tradition, not in fundamentalism or the high church tradition, because without freedom of thought and vigorous debate, faith fails to develop and in time loses all credibility.

For me this book shows, beyond peradventure, that the church of Constantine in Rome and then Constantinople, and after it the church of the Holy Roman Empire which ultimately became the Roman Catholic church, is the creature of politics not God. It shows, too, that power, prerogative, privilege and wealth were the primary motivating factors in the post-Constantine battles that shaped the medieval church, and that it was so deeply corrupt that (for example) a child of two was made a bishop, some were appointed bishops before they had been baptised, and that the whole story is of an unholy alliance between the secular authority and the developing church, which ultimately lived parasitically off the power of the state. In fact, power politics was the name of the game from Constantine onwards. Until then Christianity was a small minority in a broadly tolerant empire. My limited reading suggests that Islam in its own early centuries proved to be a rather more enlightened faith, but with not dissimilar problems of doctrinal definition.

I turn back to Verney's *Water into Wine*. It has been, I confess, a little disappointing. It has good moments of useful insight, but it reads more as a devotional exercise than an intellectual study. It is presumptuous of one who has no modern Greek to doubt his interpretations of some of the key words from the Greek testament that he discusses. But to me it reads very much like the works of some of the literary critics of the 20th century, who ceased to study texts to find the intentions of the author and instead began to use them as vehicles for their own creative interpretations. This was the period when subjectivism became all-pervading and has now, if I understand the term aright, evolved into post-modernism which is nothing more than individualism erected into a totem pole.

I have been sitting with my Greek testament and William Temple by my side as I read. And where I find Temple still impressive and persuasive (for his time), I find Verney rather less so. Above all, he seems to take St John as Gospel truth, without so much as a nod to modern biblical criticism. Keith Ward the other day said in his lecture that 'virtually no reputable biblical scholar now believes that anything St John says that Jesus said is likely to have been said by Jesus.'

CHAPTER TWENTY

The 'Real' Death of Jesus

(On Charles Freeman's New History of Christianity)

Then felt I like some watcher of the skies,
When a new planet swims into his ken -

John Keats

The Final 'Victory' – or was it Defeat?

Any dispassionate reader could be forgiven for wondering whether Jesus would have recognised the victory of the late fourth century Imperial Church as a victory at all. My own feeling is that it was no victory – rather it represents a triumph of Christian intolerance, brutality, materialist aggrandisement by the church, its hierarchy, and its adherents, political opportunism, and flagrant dishonesty in the exploitation of superstition for the distortion of truth. It is fashionable nowadays to apologise for the excesses of the Crusades; the excesses of the 4th century AD are no less deplorable, from the time of Constantine and his later successors, notably Theodosius and his sons, Honorius and Arcadius, manipulated by the fanatical Bishop Ambrose of Milan.

The first three centuries of the Christian era were notable for the intellectual distinction of those who argued and discussed the truth of the Christian faith and the nature of God, divinity, Jesus and the Holy Spirit, as well as the existence of the human soul and the possibilities of eternity. There were of course extreme disagreements, riots, and disturbances in many communities; and many fine intellects doubtless danced upon pinheads in their efforts to reconcile the irreconcilable elements of the Christian faith, so analytically and accurately exposed by Celsus and others. But the vigour and quality of the debate is undeniable.

The period was no less notable for the variety of ideas and interpretations of religious and philosophical belief, as would be entirely expected in a world still dominated by the intellectual legacy of Greece. Paganism, particularly the philosophy of Plato, influenced Christian theology to a significant degree; Stoicism, Epicureanism (despite its atheistic stance), Cynicism, and of course Gnostic creeds of many kinds all found their place in the debates. Fine minds were deployed on both sides of the argument. Alexandria (with its great Library and Mouseion, and dynamic mixture of cultures and population derived from its position as the trading capital of the eastern

Mediterranean) was in many ways the centre of the Hellenistic tradition of open-minded argument and debate in this search for truth, while Carthage was to become one centre of a more inflexible western, Latin tradition.

'This was a city,' comments Freeman, 'where a tradition of tolerant debate made it possible for Christians to use philosophy creatively,' and men like Clement and Origen (184-254), called by Jerome 'the greatest teacher of the church since the Apostles', derive from that city, which was also the home of formidable scholars such as the great astronomer and geographer, Ptolemy. Origen's advice to his pupil Gregory, the Wonder-worker, illustrates the broad-mindedness of the times: 'I beg of you to take from your studies of Hellenic philosophy those things such as can be made encyclic or preparatory studies of Christianity ... and apply the things that are useful from geometry and astronomy to the explanation of the Holy Scriptures.' Freeman comments: 'The idea that one should move through pagan philosophy into Christianity was to survive in Christian circles until the emperors of the late fourth century began to suppress paganism... Origen offers a model of Christian scholarship that is open to learning across the spectrum of disciplines. He could see how breadth of learning could help achieve a greater understanding of God and Christ.'

In a similar spirit my very scholarly grandfather used to point out that mankind was aware of and worshipped God long before the coming of Jesus, and commended the comment of Simone Weil, who said that she had come to faith in Jesus through God, rather than to belief in God through Jesus. I feel that my own comments on the 'God hypothesis' (see Ch.10) as the basis for belief reflect a similar mindset.

From AD 180 we get the first references to Latin speaking Christians and the tone of discussion becomes less civilised. Tertullian is 'typical of Roman Christians of this period in his obsession with discipline, heretics and rigid adherence to a rule of faith. His church is one where ritual has become important for its own sake and his austerity extended to welcoming martyrdom.' Cyprian of Carthage adapted familiar political structures to Christian purposes, arguing that a bishop was a representative of Christ just as a provincial governor represented the emperor, and insisting on the unity of the church and the proposition that there was no salvation outside of it. The third century was an age of social breakdown, weaker and short-lived emperors, and an empire subject to repeated attacks by barbarians. Bishops increasingly emerged as competent and effective leaders of communities, useful to the political authorities in getting things done. Yet by about AD 300, perhaps only 10% of the population of the empire were Christian. The social status and wealth of their bishops was growing, but the vast majority of people were still pagan. The bishops themselves had no means yet of achieving uniformity of doctrine, and theological problems remained intractable.

It was the 4th century emperors who delivered the solution. Their motives were often political, not theological, since they sought order and peaceful government within the empire and found in an alliance with the Christian church authorities a means to that end. Theological conviction came low on their list of motivations. The effect, says Freeman, was that 'a predominantly Christian state became established in both halves of a disintegrating empire, which went hand in hand with a transfer of interest from the Gospels, whose portrayal of a spiritual leader crucified by the

Roman authorities fitted uneasily with the new regime, to the Old Testament, which had far more texts supporting an empire whose survival depended on success in war and, in so far as authority needed to be reinforced over a sinful population, to the letters of Paul. Augustine's Paul became the cornerstone of western theology.' Geza Vermes (*Christian Beginnings*) describes it as 'a metamorphosis from the religious message of a 1st century Galilean rural holy man to the solemn proclamation of the Universal Lord.... as the eternal son of God, consubstantial with the Father.'

In fact by AD 400, the Jesus of history and the Gospels had vanished and the authoritarian Christ of Western Christendom and the Imperial Church, rich and powerful through its alliance with the political authorities, had supplanted him.

Constantine (Imp. 306-337) in his bid for empire knew the importance of having the gods on his side but showed no early interest in Christianity – indeed his coinage showed the image of *Sol Invictus*, the Unconquered Sun, until the 320s. His victory at the Milvian Bridge (312) made him ruler of the west. The idea that he told his soldiers to paint the sign of the cross on his shield is probably later 'spin.' It is likely that he had already decided to bring Christianity under the auspices of the state and realised that the best way to do it was to associate the faith with his great victory. In 313, by agreement with Licinius, emperor of the eastern empire, he passed the Edict of Toleration (Edict of Milan), which extended tolerance to all Christians in the empire. But he was himself not baptised and continued to use pagan symbols, which was sound policy in an empire with 90% of the population still pagan. But he developed a growing exploitation of Bishops in the administration of the empire. In 325 he defeated Licinius, and so became master of the whole empire, and decided to move his capital to the east on a new site in the ancient Byzantium, which now became Constantinople.

Within Christianity disputes over theology continued, regarded by Constantine as 'idle and trivial' speculations, best left to the bishops to sort out. But squabbles between bishops and the adherents of different theologies (not least the followers of Arius, who argued that Christ must have been a later but distinct creation of God the father – and therefore subordinate to him) were threatening to disrupt the order of the empire. So he summoned the bishops to the Council of Nicaea (325), determined to find a formula which would reinforce the authority of bishops and allow the different theologies to coalesce around it. Predictably there was no agreement until Constantine, by cajolery, implicit threats, and some 'persuasion' imposed a solution – the first version of the Nicene Creed, drawn up by an unknown adviser, possibly Eusebius of Caesarea. It included the phrase '*homoousios*' – 'of the same substance' – to define Christ's relationship with the Father but made no reference to the Trinity, and referred to the Holy Spirit in a single phrase 'And I believe in the Holy Spirit.'

In fact the Creed was 'a mine of potential confusion and consequently, most unlikely to be a means of ending the Arian controversy. But all this is understandable in the context of a Council that was more concerned with backing the authority of the bishops and the state than with theological precision' (Richard Hanson). It was a muddled formula, adopted for political purposes and intended to isolate Arius and his followers. In many of Constantine's pronouncements, says Freeman, 'Christ appears only as a symbol of order and unity, God's 'only-begotten, pre-existent Word, the great High Priest and the mighty God, elder than all time and every age' as Eusebius puts it. The human Jesus of the gospels is missing.' Constantine's reign sees the beginning of the Byzantine concept of the Christian ruler, appointed by God. 'The carpenter's son who had died a rebel on the cross now risked being forgotten in the transformation of Christians from outsiders to insiders, housed in rich buildings, and tied in with the successes of the empire in war.' Theological issues continued to be debated; and it is surely significant even for 21st century discussion that as late as the 4th century there was still no agreement about the nature and being of Jesus Christ. The final resolution was an imposed political, decision, not some moment of divine revelation.

Constantine had imposed and certainly encouraged, but did not enforce, uniformity. His successors (from 337-380) broadly upheld this freedom of debate, though Julian withdrew the right of Christians to teach outside their own churches. But the period was the swansong of creative theology. Issues included *homoousios* (of the same substance as the Father) versus *homoiousios* (of like substance with the F.); Subordination <of Christ to God> versus Equality.

The Dated Creed (359) replaced *homoousios* with a formula which described Jesus as 'the Son of God, distinct from him but begotten before all ages.' The Council of Seleucia (361) under Julian the Apostate (who, though born a Christian, was repelled by these squabbles over doctrine) replaced this with *homoiousios* (of like substance). Nothing proved generally acceptable. Into the fray stepped Athanasius (d.373), seeking in his earlier writings to enhance the status of the Holy Spirit and launching vigorous attacks upon the Arians for their 'diabolical' views of the subordination of Christ, which ultimately gave that issue the title of Arian Controversy. Against them stood men like the Cappadocian Fathers (Gregory of Nazianzus, Gregory of Nyssa, and Basil of Caesarea), champions of the pagan tradition of open debate and philosophical discussion and striving to define how each distinct hypostasis or personality of Father, Son, and Holy Spirit could exist within a single godhead, while Eunomius of Chalcedon, leader of the eponymous Eunomians, exposed ruthlessly the vagueness of the term *homoios* and insisted on the absurdity of any of the Father's substance being passed on to the Son.

With the coming of Theodosius (380) as emperor, all this came to an end. A Latin speaker, ignorant of the cultured tradition of intellectual debate in the Greek east, he issued an edict, an *epistula*, to the effect that only those who affirmed the faith of Nicaea could now be appointed bishops. It included a sweeping condemnation of the 'poison' of the Arian sacrilege. He summoned the Council of Constantinople (381), rigged the presidency like any good politician, and forced through a decision that Constantinople was the second bishopric of the empire after Rome, and issued a revised version of the Nicene Creed. There was still no mention of the Trinity and none of the consubstantiality of the Holy Spirit, but Jesus is once again described as *homoousios*, 'of the same substance' with the Father. Civil servants were instructed to impose the new faith.

In the face of widespread unrest, Theodosius called another smaller Council of Constantinople in 383; but after further acrimonious discussion, Theodosius lost patience and announced that he would accept only the Nicene creed and that all other views were heretical. 'He offered the wealth of the church only to the Nicene supporters and cemented his laws within a bedrock of privilege and patronage. The incentives for conformity were powerful' (Freeman). Theodosius' motivations were clear enough. He was a Spanish aristocrat and like most members of his class he would have been sympathetic to the idea that Jesus was part of the divine. If he were not, then it meant acknowledging the Jesus of the gospels as a rebel against empire and its rulers, and executed as such. There was consequently a considerable incentive to shift the emphasis of church doctrine away from one who preached that the poor would inherit the earth (bad news for aristocrats then, and thereafter at least for the branches of the hugely wealthy Catholic Church, whether Anglican or Roman), and to emphasise instead the rather more impenetrable concept of one who was the divine pre-existent incarnation of the deity.

Freeman's verdict:

> The imposition of the Nicene Creed was motivated as much by politics as theology. Imposed through imperial law, accepted by a council presided over by a hastily converted <pagan> senator, it was the theological formula which most fully met the needs of the empire for an ideology of good order under the auspices of God. Yet histories of Christian doctrine still talk of the Nicene solution as if it had floated down from heaven and been recognised by the Bishops as the only possible formula to describe the three members of the Trinity..... One result was that the Church was unable to provide a reasoned support for the Nicene Trinity and it is still referred to in the Roman Catholic catechism as 'a mystery of faith ... inaccessible to reason alone.

Only recently has Theodosius' considerable role in settling the great theological debates been recognised.... The result of the Council of Constantinople was to reduce the meaning of the word 'God' from a very large selection of alternatives to one only, with the result that when Western man today says 'God' he means the one, sole, exclusive Trinitarian God and nothing else.

The Jesus of the gospels was now well and truly dead and buried.

CHAPTER TWENTY-ONE

St John's Gospel

(Preliminary Thoughts)

This essay (slightly edited) was an attempt to demonstrate to a friend that I was an unsuitable collaborator for him in a proposed study of St John. I think I persuaded him!

Introduction

B ible studies are now a contentious subject. Five hundred years ago, anyone reading their Bible 'knew' that it was the Word of God, and therefore by definition true and incapable of error. The fact that it contained contradictory statements or incontrovertibly false scientific assertions was irrelevant, though considerable ingenuity was sometimes exercised in explaining away such contradictions. The claim of Archbishop Ussher of Armagh, based on the Julian Calendar and his study of the Torah and ancient Babylonian writings, that the universe was created (on Sunday evening of 23 October) in 4004 BC, is only one of the more notorious examples. In fact it does less than justice to his scholarship, which was considerable for his times, and illustrates rather the fact that as knowledge increases, beliefs change – and always should.

Ever since the Enlightenment, and especially in the last hundred years, there have been enormous advances in scientific knowledge, in archaeological discovery, in the understanding of ancient history, in the literary analysis and interpretation of ancient texts and manuscripts, and in anthropological understanding of the development of religion as one aspect of human evolution. Conservative Christians have always found it difficult to adjust their theology to such new discoveries, and as a result have left their faith vulnerable to a very different view of the world and the cosmos, of which we now know ourselves to be a miniscule and insignificant part.

The Christian churches have failed lamentably to educate their adherents in the implications of such advances in knowledge for the traditional understanding of their faith. Our assumptions have changed radically – and as a consequence so should our beliefs. Agnostic atheism has, as a result, become almost the norm, and certainly entirely respectable, in educated Western society. Even among Christians, few would now insist that Christianity is the best (let alone the only) way for humankind to develop a relationship with God. Religion generally is seen as an aspect of human culture, as varied in its manifestations as any other aspect of social behaviour. All this I regard as progress – and a steady improvement on the past.

But all belief derives from the believer's intellectual assumptions; and if one is to have a meaningful discussion about religion, it is best to declare those assumptions at the outset – otherwise argument will be futile and open-minded discussion impossible. Too much religious discussion consists of two protagonists with incompatible points of view exchanging unprovable prejudices across an unbridgeable divide. Here are some of the assumptions which colour and shape my attitude to any Biblical text I read.

Assumptions (see also Chapter 10)

Is there a God? I don't know. But I find it as likely as not that there is, not as a source of explanation for what is currently inexplicable in the physical universe, but rather as the embodiment or representation of Meaning, Value, and Purpose for all existence throughout the Cosmos.

In fact, I regard the existence of God as a perfectly reasonable hypothesis on which to try to base and organise my own existence. I recognise that it is possible that I am wrong, but I defy even the cleverest person in the world to prove it. Just as every scientific theory is only as good as its current status – it is only true until a better hypothesis comes along - so too with religious belief. It is a temporary working hypothesis for each of us; it may even be that one day I shall find a better one – but so far atheism at least, and its too often aggressive and sometimes unpleasant protagonists, has singularly failed to make its case. Religious faith, therefore, is for me an intellectual decision to act as if its hypothesis is true - and a resolve to shape my life accordingly, however inadequately I may achieve that aim.

If there is a God, we should not perceive that Being as an omniscient, all powerful divinity, sitting up there in heaven waiting to punish the wicked and reward the good, and manipulating every detail of our existence. God is what is – the embodiment of all that was, is, and is to come, and the source of all that ought to be. One can go no further, though I quite like the proposition that 'God is Eternal Mind, expanding ever to elude.'

Prayer: For that reason, prayer in the usual sense of asking for help, guidance, or even favours is pointless; I personally am unable to believe that God can or does 'answer' prayer. But I do believe prayers are often answered, which is a different idea altogether. Prayer as the expression of an individual or communal will or intention, may well bring about its desired end by the very fact of articulating a desire or intention, or by psychological effects upon its object. In that sense, prayer works. If God interferes to answer prayer, then he is profoundly incompetent – far too much that is utterly dreadful happens, despite the prayers of the faithful. The sun shines on the just and the unjust alike.

Revelation: I do not for one moment doubt that for some at least religious revelation is a real and powerful experience. I respect it for its manifest validity for those who receive it, just as I respect those who tell me that modern art is beautiful. My inability to believe it, whether in religion or art appreciation, may well be the product of my own blindness or ignorance. But for myself I cannot accept that such religious experience has any basis in reality, beyond the subjectivity of the individual.

The Bible is not the Word of God, though it is a doubtless well intentioned compliment to speak of it in that way. The claim that it is inerrant is demonstrably false; that God in some way dictated it to the prophets and teachers, if true, is merely a demonstration of God's incompetence; the suggestion that its ethical teaching is infallible is misguided, though of course there is much that is morally admirable in its teaching. The Old Testament Bible is nothing more than a record of one small tribe's remarkable and original insight into the nature of their God, their perception (only at times, perhaps) that there was only one such God, and their struggle to discern their God's purposes and how best to please him.

(Note: see again my comment on gender prejudice in Ch. 1 page 10).

The Bible is an entirely human creation, though it has become for many a sacred text. Its contents, New Testament as well as Old, reflect the outlook and culture of the times in which they were written. The Jewish concept of Midrash ensures that the present is always re-interpreted in the light of the past and its record may well be fictitious, that is to say a creative reinterpretation of what tradition claims to have happened in earlier days. Matthew's Gospel is a good illustration.

The New Testament is the record of one great Jewish religious teacher. His new insights into how mankind should live in relation to God and their fellow human beings proved so alluring to his followers that in the end they felt compelled to follow his vision and to share it with a wider world and to sever their connection with their original tribal parent religion. Old and New Testament alike contain the record of their misunderstandings, follies, and wickedness, as well as their amazing model of human living.

The Church, too, in all its varied manifestations is an entirely human construct. Despite its great achievements, its overall record is sufficiently appalling in too many ways to leave no room for doubt about that. For all its virtues, its leadership has also been at times foolish, arrogant, misguided, wicked, greedy for power, and selfish – as has all human leadership in every corner of the world. For all their admirable and self-sacrificial lives, its devotees have shown similar characteristics as well as being at times indifferent to the needs and suffering of their fellow men. As may be said of all religions, their institutions reflect humanity at its best and at its worst. They tell us little or nothing about God, whose existence and purposes (if any) are beyond all human understanding. But for all that, if God exists, there can be no better purpose for our lives than 'to feel after him and find him' as best we may.

Authors and Authorities: The authors that have particularly informed or influenced my thinking in the last ten years or so will give some indication of the source of my evolving ideas. For some it will doubtless be seen as proof of my invincible ignorance or irredeemable (even heretical) inclinations; for the more thoughtful it may prove helpful as a source of further reading. Most of them have been the authors of several books in my reading list. This list is not comprehensive, but includes, in alphabetical order, Karen Armstrong, John Bowden, David Boulton, Marcus Borg, Dominic Crossan, John Churcher, Charles Freeman, Robin Lane Fox, Robert Funk and the Jesus Seminar, Tom Holland, Richard Holloway, Roy Hoover, Diarmaid MacCullough, Burton Mack, Arthur Peacocke, John Polkinghorne, John Shelby Spong, Geza Vermes. Of these, Borg, Crossan, Vermes, and Spong have been the strongest influences of all.

Which brings me to Jesus and the Gospel of St John.

I regard the teachings of Jesus of Nazareth as a powerful guide to the way in which we should live our lives. In his two great commandments he stated in two lines what many scholars and philosophers have proved unable to express in two million. On the question of whether he was the Son of God or the Incarnation of God I remain ambivalent, because it depends on what you mean by 'God', 'Son' and 'Incarnation'. At best such descriptions may be seen as metaphorical and I feel pretty sure that it would not be any great help to me to think that he was literally any of those things. In the Greek text of St Matthew, the mythical comment of the Centurion, supervising the crucifixion, that 'Truly this was the Son of God' is often mistranslated. In the Greek there is no definite article. What he is actually reported to have said is 'this was a son of God.' Metaphorically, so are we all.

It is worth remembering that the Cult of the Roman emperor was quickly established and popular in the Middle East; Pompey was deified after his pacification and settlement of the area in 63 BC; after the assassination of Julius Caesar, Augustus promoted his deification, and as a result like all his successors, Augustus became *divi filius* – A Son of God or, in Roman terms, Son of a God. Christian myth-making would have had a vested interest in promoting the idea that their own leader was similarly *divi filius*, A Son of God. Nevertheless, I would be perfectly comfortable to be told that Jesus' life can be seen as one revelation (out of many) of the nature of God.

I find it easier, however, to see him simply as a profound religious leader and teacher, with deep, perhaps mystic, insight into the nature of what we call God. So for me whether the stories of his life on earth are literally true or not is a matter of relative unimportance. I assume they have some sort of basis in truth, since I have no doubt that such a person as Jesus existed and was executed by the authorities. That he was resurrected and continued any kind of physical existence after death I find unlikely. There is much to respect in the following passage, drawn from an obituary tribute to Donald Hilton, quoting his account of what he called the 'devastating tension' of the Christian faith for those of a liberal persuasion.

> Liberalism is a call to pilgrimage. Such pilgrimage is not easy. It can be difficult to survive. Certainty is so much less costly; the path is clear and well trodden. But we can survive the pilgrimage that moves between joyous adoration and critical analysis, because when we do so we stand with the Gethsemane Jesus, who longed for the joyous burden of God and hated the consequences of it, but survived through faith; with the searching Jesus, who wrestled in the Lenten wilderness to know God's will; and with the crucified Jesus, who knew God could never disown him, but feared that he had.

After his death it is perfectly possible that his followers, back in their native Galilee after forsaking him and fleeing, had some sort of communal experience, which in metaphorical terms gave them a sense that in themselves and their ideal of community life his spirit was alive. In the language of their time it was perfectly possible to express this as a form of resurrection – revival of an experience that in Jesus' lifetime was overwhelmingly powerful. Those same followers maintained, expanded, recorded, revised, and updated the stories of his life and teaching, much as Plato developed and expanded that of Socrates, while still attributing his teaching to the ideas of his Master.

In the end after some four hundred years Christianity became a world-wide religion, mainly because it formed an unholy alliance with the Roman State and its emperors, who for reasons of *realpolitik* at least as much as of religious conviction saw this new God as someone to be exploited. By then I have no doubt the Christian faith had been so much developed, its structures institutionalised, and its content so adapted to changing historical contexts over centuries, that I doubt if Jesus himself would have recognised it. This can readily be illustrated by the changing ideas about the meaning of Good Friday and the Crucifixion, where emphasis changed from Jewish Paschal Lamb, to Pauline sacrifice for sin, to the mediaeval idea of a debt owed to the slighted honour of a feudal lord, to Renaissance perception of sin and eternal damnation redeemed by the sacrifice of a perfect life.

In fact theological interpretation inevitably reflects the historical context of the interpreter; there is no permanent and absolute meaning. So, to get a deeper appreciation of Jesus' achievement and significance, and the relevance of his teaching today, we must relate it first to the people of his time. For that reason it has become increasingly important to get to know as much as possible about who Jesus 'really' was, what life was like in those times for the people among whom he lived, why his teaching seems to have had such a profound effect upon them, and what it was that seems to have been so totally original about his teaching that it came to be seen as a threat to either or both of the Jewish and Roman authorities, and ultimately became for his Jewish followers a new religion.

But to know who you are, you must know where you came from; or, as Cicero once observed, 'to know only your own time is to remain for ever a child.' The modern presentation of Christianity to the ordinary laity has retained a child-like literalism in its historical understanding of the Bible; it might be less charitable but more accurate to describe it as childish. In those early years there were enormous intellectual struggles between different views of what Jesus taught, who and what he was, and how his church should respond. The early quarrels were particularly acute between the emerging Christian movement and the more traditionalist Jews who made up its first congregations. There can be no infallible or definitive account of Christ's teaching, except in the most doctrinaire and authoritarian kinds of church.

The very early church, the gospel writers, the early fathers, the Gnostics, and the intellectuals of those early days were far less certain, and possibly also less concerned than we would be now, about the literal truth or ultimate meaning of what they taught – in those days there was less distinction between the mythical and the literal, less uniformity of opinion and more debate, more accusations of heresy, and (more desirably) less centralisation of belief. Of the gospel writers, and St Paul whose writings (ca. AD 55-65) preceded theirs, each brings his own agenda to his account, writing in terms appropriate to the time of writing and the community for which he was writing, between roughly AD 70 and 100. There are differences of focus, depending on who their audience were likely to be (and I mean audience, not readers, since it was a largely illiterate society outside the educated elites) – Jews,

Gentiles, Jewish sympathizers, Greeks, Romans etc. There were also many more gospels, most of which failed to be included in the Canon, but all of which were probably expressive of the insights of the particular communities for which they were written. Later, bishops and other leaders seem to have been lords of their own small communities (dioceses), free within reason to propagate their own opinions or interpretations of Jesus' teaching, as it had been transmitted to them.

But then came Constantine, and he (like any soldier or conventional modern industrial manager) decided that there had to be consistency of policy, uniformity of purpose, and that everyone needed to be 'on message' - and on the same message. Various councils of the church were mainly happy to reinforce this edict and so, between say AD 314 and the reign of Theodosius in AD 381 was born the authoritarian, politically powerful, and increasingly centralized and corrupted church that dominated the Middle Ages. Uniformity was enforced at the point of the sword or by torture, the alliance between church and rulers was reinforced because it was mutually advantageous.

There were fierce debates in those early centuries about the divinity of Jesus; there were varied views of the Eucharist; eschatology and apocalypse clearly came to have more than one meaning; Jesus was not necessarily the Lamb of God who died for the sins of the world; he may well originally have been an illiterate and dispossessed peasant leading an anti-imperialist, anti-Roman protest movement, which (though peaceful) was a genuine threat to imperial authority and its quisling Jewish establishment figures; there were a number of other would-be Messiahs in the century or so before the final sack of Jerusalem; Judas may have been a terrorist, a *sicarius* or dagger man, or else he may not even have existed, and was simply the product of Midrash, introduced as an sort of artificial villain of the piece.

Whether all this is true or not is well nigh impossible to say. But the effect of such a possibility is to present Jesus and his mission as a far more credible and solidly historical figure, more an activist, not merely a preacher of good news and good behaviour.

The evolution of Christianity in its first twenty years, from AD 30-50, which we may for convenience call the Oral Period, the years before documentary evidence survives (or perhaps even existed), is a fascinating topic. The early Jewish Christian church was expecting the Second Coming, an eschatological or apocalyptic event, and therefore felt little need to record in any permanent form the sayings and deeds of Jesus. Folk memory, oral tradition, and group reminiscence must have seemed entirely sufficient for the short time remaining before the ending of the world. Yet it is clear that some sort of anthology of Jesus' sayings at least soon began to be recorded. The relatively recently discovered Gospel of Thomas shows the form such an anthology probably took. Oral memory soon added to these, quite naturally, adapting many from conventional Wisdom sayings and ordinary folk proverbs, which Jesus may well have made use of, but did not originate.

Dominic Crossan has shown persuasively that if we take advantage of all the resources of modern academia (textual analysis built on the foundations of anthropology, sociology, archaeology, economic and literary history), we can in fact make reasonable deductions about what first stage documents lay behind the later (second stage) writings which have survived, such as St Paul, writing AD post-50, though his conversion probably dates to circa AD 35, the canonical Gospels (written between AD 70 and 110), and already significantly 'edited' to meet the needs of the developing communities of believers, the extra-canonical gospels, such as the gospels of Thomas and Peter, and other documents such as the *Didache* and *Gospel of Miracles*.

Such first stage documents may be said to exist only in a sort of virtual reality, but the work of many scholars has sought to identify what elements of the record could be described as the 'authentic' words or deeds of Jesus. That the gospels are not the simple records of what actually happened but have, rather, been adapted to the changing circumstances of their authors' times and perceptions, is now beyond question. But that said, the second stage documents represent the best evidence we are likely to be able to lay our hands on, but they must be used judiciously.

Interestingly, The Jesus Seminar, a body of scholars dedicated to an attempt to evaluate in the light of the best of modern scholarship the texts and source materials for the early ministry of Jesus, including some of the non-canonical gospels, have concluded that many of the words attributed to Jesus in the Synoptic Gospels, and none in the Gospel of St John is likely to be genuine. That is not the same as to suggest that not a word of the Gospel is true – but it illustrates the way our understanding of the ancient literary evidence has developed and the new insights that have emerged as a result.

Professor Geza Vermes of Oxford University seems to be thinking along the same lines when, in his *The Authentic Gospel of Jesus*, he states that 'compared with the dynamic religion of Jesus, fully evolved Christianity seems to belong to another world. With its mixture of high philosophical speculation on the triune God, its Johannine Logos mysticism and Pauline Redeemer myth of a dying and risen Son of God, with its sacramental symbolism and ecclesiastical discipline substituted for the extinct eschatological passion, with its cosmopolitan openness combined with a built-in anti-Judaism, it is hard to imagine how the two could have sprung from the same source.'

So can we get back in any meaningful way to the world in which that 'dynamic religion of Jesus' emerged? The combination of a number of authors and works have shaped my view of what might have really happened. The most significant have been, above all, Dominic Crossan (*The Birth of Christianity, The Historical Jesus*), but also Crossan and Reed (*Excavating Jesus*), Marcus Borg (*Jesus*), Charles Freeman (*A New History of Early Christianity*), Geza Vermes (*Christian Beginnings*), John Churcher (*Setting Jesus Free, Dying to Live*), and various books and weekly Internet 'epistles' by Bishop John Shelby Spong. Where I have misinterpreted or misunderstood, the fault is entirely mine. But the following chapter shows, how, broadly speaking, it now looks to me.

CHAPTER TWENTY-TWO

Origins of a Foundation Myth

(The Birth of Christianity – As I Now See It)

An attempt to pull together the threads of my reading in the writings of Dominic Crossan, Marcus Borg, John Shelby Spong, Charles Freeman, The Jesus Seminar, Geza Vermes, Raymond Brown, and others

Part 1: The Situation Round about 4 BC

Background: Judaea had been ruled for most of its history by others. By the Assyrians first, then by Babylon from 581 BC, which destroyed the Temple and deported the leadership; then by the Persians from 538-331 BC; by Greeks when Alexander the Great (331) conquered the Middle East, then by two of his successor dynasties, first the Ptolemies of Egypt (302-198) and then from 198-167 BC by the Seleucids of Syria. Under them a Hellenizing party in the priestly aristocracy tried to convert Jerusalem into a Greek city. This seems to have caused the emergence of the Pharisees as a distinct religious grouping, standing for traditional law and supporting the Maccabaean revolt, which was another reaction to Hellenization. There had already been general disturbances, but the King's response had been to impose a garrison, dedicate the Temple to Olympian Zeus, and attempt to suppress Judaism. This led to the revolt, led by Judas Maccabaeus, a priest of the house of Hasmon, and then by his brothers, which continued until the Seleucid garrison was finally expelled in 142 BC. Simon Maccabaeus was then confirmed as High Priest and for the next eighty years the Jews were independent under the rule of their Hasmonaean high priests.

Under them a programme of territorial conquest developed leading to the acquisition of Samaria, Idumaea, Ituraea, Galilee, Peraea, and a number of Greek cities in Transjordan. But the Hasmonaean dynasty became increasingly secularised and dependent on the aristocratic support of the Sadducees, thus losing popular backing. Then family power struggles developed, until in 63 BC Pompey, who had conquered the Seleucid empire of the Middle East, intervened, stormed Jerusalem, and appointed Hyrcanus High Priest and Ethnarch of Judaea, Samaria, Galilee, and Peraea. After various dynastic and political struggles Herod the Great emerged in 37 BC as Rome's Client King, nominated by Mark Antony, and confirmed later by Augustus, and ruling for the next thirty-three years.

In 4 BC Herod the Great died. Having been installed by Mark Antony, and lacking legitimacy, as an Idumaean and not of the royal Hasmonaean dynasty, he was never popular. But he was able and effective. He built a new seaport at Caesarea and launched the rebuilding of the Temple in Jerusalem on an extravagant scale. Despite five hundred years of foreign imperialism, before Rome arrived there was only one revolt – under extreme provocation from the Seleucids. Under Rome, there were four major revolts (4 BC, AD 66 - 74, AD 115 - 117, AD 132 - 135). After that direct Roman rule was established, the Temple flattened, Egyptian Judaism destroyed, and Jerusalem declared a pagan city, closed to Jews.

Rome's record as an imperial power was a mixed blessing. They brought peace, order, roads, amenities, and commercial development – great blessings for some. But with them came ruthless suppression of disaffection, imposition of a state religion, and the most extortionate exploitation of the resources of the countries they ruled. Until the Romans serious revolts did not occur among the Jews, though low-level unrest was probably commonplace. Josephus' account of Galilee gives no hint of major unrest under Herod. But there was a mood of social disorientation, a feeling that the new rich cared nothing for the ideal of shared community and were destroying Jewish ways of life. But when leaders emerged to exploit this unrest, they were soon arrested and executed – e.g. John the Baptist.

With Herod's death in 4 BC the first of the serious revolts occurred all over the Jewish homeland. Quinctilius Varus, governor of Syria, brought a force of three legions plus auxiliaries to quell it and there were savage reprisals. At Sepphoris, about four miles from Nazareth, a detachment of Varus' army 'routed all who opposed him, captured and burnt the city of Sepphoris, and reduced its inhabitants to slavery.' (Josephus). In Nazareth around the time Jesus was born, men would have been killed, and women and children who did not hide would have been killed, raped, or enslaved. Those who survived would have lost everything. It seems quite likely, that while growing up in Nazareth Jesus would have heard many stories about Roman atrocities. Such talk must have influenced the ideas of the adolescent Jesus and his attitude to Rome, resistance, and violence. After the revolt was suppressed, the Roman emperor, Augustus, carved up the kingdom among the members of Herod's family. Herod Archelaus got the lion's share, Idumaea, Samaria and Judea itself; Herod Antipas got Galilee and Perea; Herod Philip got the North East. It was not till AD 6 that Quirinius, governor of Syria, was sent south to carry out a census, doubtless with a view to more efficient tax gathering. It was local, not world-wide - Luke is simply wrong about the date and the details. If born under Herod, Jesus must have been born at the latest in 4 BC. Antipas, whom Jesus called 'that sly fox' then launched himself on his long and patient strategy of economic development, which would justify, he hoped, his ultimate appointment as King of the Jews. In the end he was exiled, and very briefly Herod Agrippa became King of the Jews in AD 39-43, before finally a Roman Governor was appointed.

Meanwhile the Jews adapted themselves to the new situation: some (notably the Sadducees) cooperated with the Roman authorities, and despite the presence of a Roman governor, the High Priests, of whom Caiaphas was much the most successful, effectively ruled the country. It is a fair deduction that the Pharisees were more nationalist in outlook and better attuned to the feelings of the poor population. There was always tension, the possibility of disorder, and increasing destitution generated despair, itinerancy, lawlessness, brigandage, and messianic hopes of freedom and a new society. Some brigand leaders were not above presenting themselves as new Messiahs. Such was the world in which Jesus grew up.

Jesus himself was probably a child of uncertain parentage, born in Nazareth, a small, poor, but agriculturally self-sufficient village, near Sepphoris, to possibly landless or even dispossessed peasants, possibly illiterate, and growing up with about eight siblings (which can be a problem for some whose beliefs are more fundamentalist than mine). His father, whether real or adoptive, was a labourer rather than necessarily a carpenter, forced perhaps by dispossession or heavy taxation to earn his living in whole or in part from labouring. The development of Sepphoris, and then Tiberias under the economic policy of Herod Antipas, was causing increasing distress to the small peasant land-holders of the time, as well as the fishing community who strove to make a living from the lake. Increasing numbers were being driven into vagrancy, the cities, or lawlessness to survive.

Like other high achievers and mythological heroes, such as Augustus, little is known about Jesus' early years, but in time (as with Augustus) admiration, legend, and mankind's natural mythopoeic tendencies sought to fill the gap. Like Augustus, Alexander the Great, and other heroic figures such as Herakles, Jesus' birth acquired supernatural associations, though not in the gospels of Mark or John, and gradually evolved as the early Jewish movement of Jesus extended into the wider Hellenistic world of the eastern Roman Empire.

It seems reasonable to assume that he was brought up as a conventional Jew and it is perfectly possible that he was what we would now call a 'religious' child, with an unusually deep sense of God. Economic circumstances and natural Jewish piety would have reinforced this tendency, combining also to make him deeply aware of the injustice of imperial exploitation of his homeland, of the utterly wretched circumstances of his fellow rural peasants, and from his presumably regular attendance at synagogue increasingly aware of the long tradition of God's covenant with his people, of the duty to support the poor and fatherless, and of the prophetic denunciation of such injustice upon God's people, perhaps with the added suggestion (typical of priestly castes everywhere) that their sufferings were retribution for their religious shortcomings. He will surely have been aware of the developing concepts within the prophetic tradition of how nation and individual should relate to God, and how the fierce God of Retribution had developed into the loving Father of his people, the defender of Justice to the poor, fatherless, and widow, and how suffering could be interpreted not as punishment for sin but as a sacrificial and creative response to the inevitable cruelty of existence.

Religious influences were more likely from local Pharisees (Rabbis) than the aristocratic and quisling Sadducees (who, be it noted, did not believe in the Resurrection). He will have been familiar with terms such as Son of God, Messiah (Messiah in Greek is Christ = Annointed One), and Son of Man – but he will have been well aware that none of them were unique to any one individual in history, but that they did carry specific historical and religious overtones. He did not think of himself in any of those terms; they were applied to him by others. He would probably have accepted the description of Teacher (Rabbi) or Prophet. Perhaps itinerant sage would be the most accurate, and religiously neutral.

Part 2: Possible Origins of Jesus' Mission

It began when he encountered one of those prophets, John the Baptist, and was baptised by him. The accompanying stories surrounding that baptism we may assume are later, legendary additions, though for Jesus himself it may well have been a profoundly religious moment. But the almost immediate fate of John may have caused him to think carefully about the implications of the politically sensitive role of prophet in the Galilee of his time amid the increasing social problems being caused by Roman exploitation and taxation.

He may have noted the acquisition of ever-increasing landholdings by the rich and the drift of their Roman landlords towards commercial agriculture, which was destroying the smallholdings and livelihoods of rural peasants (for whom ancestral land had a deeply religious meaning), in order to produce more food for the city and profit for their owners. His own family's memories of what happened when the Romans sacked Sepphoris, and the fate of those who had turned to lawlessness, whether out of desperation or desire for gain, probably taught him that violent protest did not pay.

Among his own people a breakdown of traditional family bonds, caused perhaps by the fact that the family small-holding could not support all the children, may have increased itinerancy and the number of vagrants who sought shelter and food from existing householders, who had not enough for their own. He may well have been moved to see how demoralizing it was for such itinerants to have neither hope, nor family ties, nor community support. He may even have been for a time one of these same itinerants, seeking sustenance where he could get it. If not, he certainly chose to adopt their life-style when he launched his mission. He may have associated with the discontented and subversive, or even with those plotting revolution against the occupying power. When in Mark 3.13 he 'goes up the mountain' or, as the NEB puts it, 'he went away into the hill-country' – the reference is to the hilly areas around the Sea of Galilee, an area notoriously frequented by the disaffected and those plotting against the Romans. There, whether fictitiously or significantly, he appoints his twelve disciples, possibly one for each of the twelve tribes of Israel. Is Mark suggesting the idea of uniting the nation against Rome? However peaceful Jesus' mission, it might explain why he was suspected, especially by quisling Temple authorities.

Inconsistencies in the four canonical gospel records, as well as discrepancies in other non-canonical accounts, are due to the long period of time which had elapsed before they were written. If Jesus died ca. AD 30, then forty years probably elapsed before the writing of the first Gospel (St Mark) and possibly as much as eighty years before the last (St John). All four of them will have been influenced by the trauma of the Jewish revolt (AD 66-70), the subsequent destruction of Jerusalem in AD 70, and the consequent Jewish Diaspora. The changing historical circumstances under which they were recorded, and the varied emphases developed by the often differing communities, which sought to reflect the life of their Founder in their individual ways and community values, will all have affected the quality and accuracy of their testimony. The authors were, after all, human, and recent judicial and parliamentary inquiries in this country has shown how innocently unreliable and prone to editorialising is the human memory over even shorter periods of time.

Part 3: The Kingdom of God

This is a kind of shorthand for Jesus' Big Idea. Geza Vermes argues that Jesus' vision was eschatological, in the sense of a prophecy of the world's end, with God/Jesus coming on the clouds to punish the guilty and save the chosen. Internal evidence, he thinks, suggests that Jesus and his disciples did not expect or predict his arrest and crucifixion. Other do not agree. For them Jesus' vision is almost certainly not eschatological; rather, it is an ideal of asceticism, not based on an ideology so much as an acknowledgement of the realities of daily life under Roman exploitation. It made, in fact, a virtue of harsh necessity; it was probably inclusive, indifferent to conventional social values of gender, race, or religion. It was certainly not a movement for violent change in the status quo.

Instead it offered to its adherents a new community of the marginalised and the dispossessed, an expectation of justice restored, but in a new way; a new kind of kingship, which may have seemed to echo that of the emperor; a non-violent means of protest at injustice; a new means of restoring self-respect to those who had lost it; a new way of uniting the community by re-awakening the link between haves and have-nots; a kind of healing (social and psychological more than medical) to the distressed. In short Jesus proclaimed a new manifestation of God's abiding presence in the total-sharing of both possessions and above all of the necessities of life, food and drink, in a new community, whose values were reinforced, re-asserted, re-invigorated by a regular ritual reminder of these values in a shared-meal, which was always a full meal, introduced and concluded by an act of blessing. It challenged accepted ideas of every kind - the current political and religious situation, the conventional values of society at the time, the Roman imperial system, the Jewish faith and above all The Law, the Temple authorities, and popular ideas of Messianic eschatology. But the challenge led to disappointment.

It resulted, inevitably, in execution by crucifixion, probably contrived by the temple authorities, who exploited the Roman authorities' natural anxieties at a time of heightened popular excitement during a major festival, (possibly, though not certainly, the Passover – Spong argues that the details fit an autumn festival better), amid the rumours of a messianic saviour. The death of a troublesome peasant with a small following will have caused no anxieties to the Roman governor. All talk of Pilate's washing his hands and his wife's nightmares are later pro-Roman anti-Jewish 'spin.' The execution probably took place on the Thursday; the body was probably thrown into a common grave or left to the scavenging of dogs and birds of carrion; none of the disciples saw the event – they were terrified and 'all forsook him and fled.'

There was no tomb, and no physical resurrection and the idea that Caiaphas arranged the spiriting away of the body in order to defuse the impetus of the new movement lacks any supporting evidence. News of any such attempted deception would surely have leaked out. There is little doubt that Jesus' followers back in Galilee felt somehow deeply aware of the presence of his Spirit at their subsequent gatherings. But beyond doubt, the Kingdom of God Community survived, revived, and developed.

Part 4: The Post-Resurrection Community

The community survived and developed in two different centres, one rural, the other urban, each emphasising a different aspect of the original teaching. Back in Rural Galilee the movement evolved into a new relationship between itinerants and the householders, which embraced and celebrated the Life Values of their founder, but in time diluted the extreme radical quality of the original Jesus Mission (The *Didache* is an illustration). It continued to be expressed in a mission/ministry of hospitality and healing, hospitality from the haves to the have-nots and healing from the have-nots for the haves. Such healing was not the curing of disease, but the healing of hurt, through the enriching sense of community and communion, dispensed by the have-nots to the haves, and memorably reflected in the words of blessing from the medieval English Rune of Hospitality, *Christ in the Stranger's Guise*. It goes as follows:

> I met a stranger yest'ere'en.
> I put food in the eating place
> Drink in the drinking place,
> Music in the listening place,
> And in the name of the Triune,
> He blessed myself and my house,
> My cattle and my loved ones.
> And the lark sang in His song:
> Often, often, often, goes
> The Christ in the stranger's guise.
> Often, often, often, goes
> The Christ in the stranger's guise.

In the rural tradition emphasis inevitably was laid upon the habits/life-style of Jesus, of which the outward and visible expression was the shared-meal, in which each contributed what he or she could to the common fare, introduced and concluded with a ritual act of remembrance.

In Jerusalem, by contrast, the Kingdom idea found expression in a new community committed to a life of poverty and founded on the eschatological expectation of a second coming. At the same time its followers scoured the OT to find, develop, and express (in typical Midrash procedures) the meaning of what had happened, so as to find a satisfactory explanation for the 'failure' of their Lord. Particular stress was laid on the traditional theme of the Suffering Servant of Isaiah 53, but also on the passages from the Psalms and prophets, which saw in the sufferings of the Jewish people either retribution for their shortcomings, or the vicarious sacrifice of the scapegoat for the sin of the whole community.

This was an urban community, and increasingly Christianity became an urban phenomenon. The leaders of the movement, Peter, James, Paul were all based in large urban centres, Jerusalem first, then Antioch, and ultimately Rome. The emphasis here was on the Death and Resurrection of Jesus, and increasingly on the idea of his sacrificial death for the sin of the world. Here too the outward and visible expression of the community's belief was the shared meal, sometimes a patronal-type shared-meal (which was the basis of Paul's quarrel with the Corinthians), though in other centres (e.g. Roman Ostia) poor communities probably held genuine share-meals of the original kind.

The Record was originally entirely oral. With the expectation of an imminent apocalypse, there was little point in anything else. Doubtless folk memory, especially among simple people, assisted and perhaps inspired by the female lamentation tradition, soon developed a narrative, which was 'improved' over the months and years that followed. Efforts to make sense of what had happened rationalised and developed the details. Memories became recollections became reminiscence became story became legends became myth (idealised versions of what was believed to have happened).

Probably quite soon collections of Jesus' sayings, began to be made, some genuine, many of them simply borrowed from typical Wisdom sayings. The best examples are the (presumed) Q document, and the Gospel of Thomas. The Gospel of Peter, though itself late may well have embedded within it a very early document (the Cross-Gospel) of a similar type. The *Didache* illustrates one particular community rule, which may have sought to balance the needs of itinerants and householders.

The first extant documents are the epistles of Paul, arguably the true founder of the Christian church. A number of them, notably the less liberal ones, are not by Paul; but those that are genuine, are largely based on the Jerusalem/urban tradition. His emphasis is on the meaning of the death and resurrection; little or nothing is said about Jesus' way of life.

The second generation documents, the canonical Gospels, date from AD ca 70 – ca.100. Probably none of the authors knew Jesus and even the Synoptics differ from each other on matters of detail and emphasis. But there were also many other different gospels; each had its own particular agenda and emphasis, whether a target audience (Jews or Gentiles), community interpretation (John), Gnostic insights, or possibly a desire to support the claim to authority of a particular apostle. But all reflect the developing interpretations of Jesus' Life and Death.

There was no uniformity of Christian identity or belief, and much discussion and debate - not least on the nature of God and the divinity of Jesus and the nature of the resurrection. Most texts speak of dissension and discussion, an ambivalence towards Judaism, and the relationship of the new religion to it. Many different concepts of Jesus and different ways of worshipping him developed and this variety persisted until the Councils convened under Constantine in the early 4th century imposed an unhealthy uniformity on The Church, and reinforced an ultimately deeply corrupting association between political rulers and the Church.

The lack of consensus about the nature or divinity of Christ persisted for at least three hundred years, with much acrimonious argument and each side accusing the others of 'heresy.' The word itself gradually lost its original simple Greek meaning of 'choice', <of which philosophical school's teaching you wished to follow>. It became instead a pejorative word for 'unorthodox belief'. Christianity became increasingly intolerant, by marked contrast with the pagan world of the time. Different communities of Christians developed different practices and traditions, many of them influenced by Gnostic ideas and writings. Some were deeply rooted in

Judaism, some derived from the Gentile communities who were already familiar with cultic ritual and initiation ceremonies, some were Docetists, some indifferent to the importance of the Eucharist, others insistent upon it etc.

Greek philosophers, especially Plato and the Stoics, were always influential, and there were many attempts to reconcile their ideas with those of Christianity. Ethical values were also heavily influenced by Jewish tradition. All these were vigorously debated. Sexual continence seems to have been a constant issue and in the West attitudes to the place of women in the church seem to have been more rigidly hostile than in the East. In fact, to quote Geza Vermes, 'compared with the dynamic religion of Jesus, fully evolved Christianity seems to belong to another world. With its mixture of high philosophical speculation on the triune God, its Johannine Logos mysticism and Pauline redeemer myth of a dying and risen Son of God, with its sacramental symbolism and ecclesiastical discipline substituted for the extinct eschatological passion, with its cosmopolitan openness combined with a built-in anti-Judaism, it is hard to imagine how the two could have sprung from the same source.'

Hierarchy began to develop by about AD 100, when we get the first references to Bishops, (Greek: *episkopoi*, = Overseers). In their early councils, the primary concern seems to have been the continuing attractions of both Judaism and Paganism. There were about eighty African bishops in the late third century, each of them ruling an area little more than a village. Rome became home to a 'fragmented Christianity,' where the bishop (there was as yet no Pope, and certainly no authority over the wider Christian world) had real problems asserting his authority, partly because so many church leaders were immigrants, bringing their own culture and theologies. Ignatius' list of bishops of Rome justifying claims to apostolic succession may be dismissed as probably a pious fiction. Allegations of corruption, sleaze, and self-seeking by some bishops soon emerged.

Social status varies – there were rich aristocrats, but many more were of the artisan class; women were never as 'liberated' as Jesus would probably have wished. Slaves were sometimes given their freedom, but probably no more often than was normal in Roman society. A fuller account of the Cult of the Emperor as the binding force of the whole Roman Empire and the source and underpinning 'creed' of the whole imperial domination system could show that there is an argument for suggesting that there developed a conscious parallelism between the way in which Rome promoted its value system and the way in which the early Christians promoted theirs - as a deliberate contrast, critique, and possibly even challenge to Augustan and Imperial propaganda.

It is easy to exaggerate the initial success of early Christianity. By AD 300, Freeman estimates that 90% of the population of the Roman Empire were not Christian, and 'one cannot talk of any real unity in the Church at this time.' Many areas of Asia Minor reveal no evidence of Christianity at all to the archaeologists. The language of the Church remained Greek; Latin does not appear in Church documents and liturgies until about AD 180 and the liturgy itself remained Greek until the 380s.

It was, Freeman argues, the 'boost of support from the emperor Constantine that transformed it into a social and dynamic force.' Until the coming of Constantine and the formal establishment of the institutional church, the pattern of rich variety of belief and interpretation amongst diverse and disparate small Christian communities across the Empire was maintained. A relatively uniform faith and an increasingly powerful and wealthy church was a final legacy of the Roman Empire. For traditional believers this is probably clear evidence of the hand of God at work; for others it is no more than the usual lottery of History, where the victors re-write the records in accordance with their own perception of events.

Part 5: The Community of the Beloved Disciple

Legend has it that Mary, the mother of Jesus, together with Mary of Magdala, retired to or took refuge in Ephesus, perhaps under the protection of the Beloved Disciple, to whose care the dying Jesus had supposedly entrusted his mother. Her house is still a place of pilgrimage, up on the hillside above the Temple of Artemis (Diana of the Ephesians), whose shattered remains still stand (waterlogged at times) in the valley below. In the two Marys' time, the Christian community was probably small, apprehensive, suspected by Jews and pagan Romans alike, and probably kept a low profile in a hostile environment. It was to be some three hundred years before the new faith finally conquered the old, for good or ill – the latter I am inclined to suspect, since the pagan religion always offered to the world a tolerance and generosity of spirit unknown to the adherents of the newer faith. As Swinburne once wrote, in his Hymn to Proserpine:

> Thou hast conquered, O pale Galilean; the world has grown grey from thy breath;
> We have drunken of things Lethean, and fed on the fullness of death.
> Laurel is green for a season, and love is sweet for a day;
> But love grows bitter with treason, and laurel outlives not May.
> Sleep, shall we sleep after all? For the world is not sweet in the end;
> For the old faiths loosen and fall, the new years ruin and rend.
> Fate is a sea without shore, and the soul is a rock that abides;
> But her ears are vexed with the roar and her face with the foam of the tides.

Following the sack of Jerusalem and the destruction of the Temple in AD 70, there is nothing inherently improbable about the legend of Mary of Ephesus. That there was an early Christian community there is clear from the simple fact that St Paul wrote an Epistle to them. It is also clear that the fissiparous tendency of Judaism made it all too likely that different interpretations of the events of Jesus' life and varied interpretations of the meaning and ideals of the Jesus movement developed.

Some would argue that Mary of Magdala was at least as influential in the early movement as any of the Apostles, that she was honoured as an Apostle, and may even have started her own community. But her role was progressively airbrushed out of the record as the various spin-doctors of the time sought to establish the credentials of their particular favourite among the apostolic leadership. But matters of common public knowledge cannot be easily suppressed. What could not be airbrushed away was the fact, clearly acknowledged in the gospels, that she had been very close to Jesus in his lifetime, possibly closer than any of the emerging leaders of the developing religion, and that she was the first to 'see' the risen Lord after his death – whatever may be meant by that expression. This must have given her a particular status in that early community.

Those who wish to pursue the topic in detail should read Brown's *Community of the Beloved Disciple (1979)*, which is alluded to by the Oxford Commentary in its Introduction to John. The editor's conclusion is that such reconstructions as Brown's are 'interesting but difficult to prove; they simply project contradictions in the Johannine literature onto a historical axis.' But, as I have already often suggested, the 'historical axis' is essential for a full understanding of the Jesus mission.

One can only speculate about whether more than one school of thought emerged among the Ephesian Christians and/or the Johannine Community; whether this John was the beloved disciple and, if such he was, whether he founded his own community; whether it amalgamated with another grouping, which with the influx of pagan converts became more anti-Jewish; and whether the two groups together developed a high Christology, which became the basis of this gospel; whether the first John, who had known Jesus, actually wrote the Gospel named after him (unlikely), or whether its author may have sought to record a Johannine interpretation of the Passion story to settle differences developing in the two communities. These are questions to which there can probably be no definitive answer.

It has even been suggested, not entirely implausibly, that the Beloved Disciple is a literary fiction, standing symbolically for any and every convert to the new religion, and that the commission of Jesus from the cross to that disciple to 'behold thy mother' is another literary device, a fictional, and therefore symbolic, acknowledgement attributed to its founder that the new religion is the child of the old Jewish religion, from which it was increasingly becoming differentiated. Objections must include the question of whether Jesus ever intended to found a church and whether he ever saw his movement as anything other than a reforming branch of traditional Judaism. Vermes insists that Jesus' vision never reached beyond a purely Jewish eschatology, perhaps with the hope that after the salvation of the Jews, Gentiles might be encouraged to follow. What almost all scholars will agree about is that the fourth gospel is the latest of the canonical gospels, that it was composed around AD 100, and that its attribution to John is designed to give it the authority of a very significant figure in the Jesus movement, whether he is John the son of Zebedee, his putative disciple known as John the Elder, or John, the unidentified leader of the Johannine community, or John, the nom de plume of an anonymous editor.

It is generally recognised, too, that it is a very different kind of document from the three synoptic gospels; that it is the product of an highly literate writer; that it is interpretive rather than a mere record of events; that Jesus' discourses are lengthy expositions rather than the short pithy sayings and parables of the earlier gospels (there are no parables in St John); that key thematic ideas are developed in a manner that is literary and creative rather than simply historical; and that its primary aim is to declare to the world that Jesus was the Messiah and that he was the incarnation of the Logos of God upon earth.

Part 6: St John's Gospel - Structure, Themes, and Problems

The Oxford Bible Commentary suggests that the structure of the gospel may be seen as falling into a Prologue and two books. The first book, telling how Jesus revealed his glory to the world, lends itself to four geographical groupings (1.19

– 3.21, 3.22 – 5.47, 6.1 – 10.39, 10.40 – 12.50), three ending in Jerusalem and the fourth via Jerusalem back in Galilee. The second book consists simply of a series of narrative episodes, in which 'Jesus reveals the glory of his death and resurrection to his disciples.' It starts with Jesus washing the disciples' feet, includes the three sections of the Farewell Discourse, and the Passion narrative plus resurrection stories.

Viewed thematically, one can recognise a series of ideas or images intended to bring out the evangelist's key assertion – that Jesus is the Messiah and the Son of God. Such themes include contrasts between light and darkness, life and death, truth and falsehood, heaven and earth, while at the centre of the tale stands the Master, the embodiment of the Word of God, the Logos, whose words, encounters, and miracles often have both literal and metaphorical meanings.

Problems that arise include elements which may be due to nothing more than careless editing but are, more likely, due to the author's desire to arrange his materials for emphasis or to express his own ideas about meaning of the Christ. It is, for example, difficult to reconcile details in this gospel with the Synoptics (including the decision to place the cleansing of the Temple at the start of Jesus' ministry and the uncertainty about the day of the crucifixion, the order of chapters 5 and 6, and the source and origin of Chapter 21, the Epilogue, which cannot have been part of the original text).

For traditionalists the absence of a miraculous birth story may be a problem, the absence of any parables (so characteristic of the itinerant teacher of the Synoptics) must be at least a disappointment, and the lengthy discourses that replace the pithy sayings of the synoptic Teacher of Wisdom must surely seem deeply improbable, to all but the most literal-minded. John's account of Jesus' ministry lasts three years; that of the Synoptics one. In John there is no account of Jesus' baptism. But theologically speaking, given the Evangelist's convictions, how could a mere mortal like John be shown to have baptised the sinless Son of God? There is no Last Supper, or at least none as a Passover meal, no agony in the garden, and miracles are presented as 'merely' signs.

Ephesus

Ephesus itself was one of the most significant cities of Roman Asia Minor, a trading entrepot, on which people of many nationalities and diverse religions converged, and its remains are still one of the most remarkable archaeological sites of the ancient world. It lay at the heart of Ionia, an area which six hundred years earlier gave birth to Ionian Science, and had always enjoyed a long history of intellectual speculation and intelligent debate. It was the birthplace of Greek philosophy, whose later exponents included Socrates, Plato, Aristotle, Democritus. Inevitably their influence may be detected in the language and style of this particular Gospel. It may also explain why ever after it remained the most influential source of guidance and inspiration for Christians in the wider world beyond the narrow confines of Judaism, where their faith was born. Greece (along with Jerusalem) has always been seen as the birthplace of Western Christian civilisation.

Conclusion

All in all, it seems clear to this writer at least, that St John's Gospel is not a historical record; it is a profoundly thoughtful literary invention, written long after the events it purports to describe, and designed to reinforce the author's perception of the significance and meaning of Jesus' ministry, primarily if not entirely for the Christian community of his time and place, namely Ephesus around the year AD 100. To understand it, you must understand its historical context.

This inevitably over-simplified account cannot do justice to the work of the scholars from whose ideas it is derived. The Bibliography gives some indication of their numbers and range of interests. For me their work has been a very real source of liberation, since they have helped me to separate the legendary and mythical from the historical, and to derive from those historical elements a fuller and deeper sense of the extraordinary achievement of the Jesus of History, whose memory has been eclipsed by the (for me) far less convincing Jesus Christ of Faith.

CHAPTER TWENTY-THREE

The Birth of Christianity - A Concluding Comment

Where I am Coming From

It is difficult for anyone living in the 21ˢᵗ century to take literally every detail of the Bible's account of events and actions in either the Old or New Testaments. It is even more difficult for anyone who has studied Ancient History, as I have, and understands the nature and workings of oral traditions in the communities of the ancient world. (The Homeric epics are an illustrative case in point – rooted in history, probably, but developed into mythological narrative, yet believed by their communities for centuries afterwards to be historical). For those who have studied social anthropology (which I have not) and understand in detail how ideas develop and how community memory operates in early society, it must be more difficult still to swallow every detail of the Bible accounts. In addition, quite apart from the researches of scholarship, sheer common sense makes some of the events recorded in the New Testament deeply improbable. Of course there is a substratum of accurate record in some, even many, of the biblical accounts, but they are likely to have been 'improved' over the centuries (like Homer).

Nevertheless, I still call myself a Christian; I regard the teachings of Jesus of Nazareth as a powerful guide to the way in which we should live in our modern communities; on the question of whether he was the son of God or the incarnation of God I remain ambivalent, because it depends on what you mean by 'son' and 'incarnation'. But I feel pretty sure that it would not be any great help to me to think that he was. Nevertheless, I would be perfectly comfortable to be told that his life can be seen as one revelation (out of many) of the nature of God.

I find it easier, however, to see him simply as a profound religious leader and teacher, with deep, perhaps mystic, insight into the nature of what we call God. So for me whether the stories of his life on earth are literally true or not is a matter of relative unimportance. I assume they have some sort of basis in truth, since I have no doubt that such a person as Jesus existed and was executed by the authorities. After his death it is clear that his followers maintained, expanded, recorded, revised, and updated his teaching, much as Plato developed and expanded the teaching of Socrates, while still attributing that teaching to the ideas of his Master.

In fact theological interpretation reflects the historical context of the interpreter; there is no permanent and absolute meaning. So, to get a deeper appreciation of Jesus' achievement and significance, and the relevance of his teaching today, we must, I think, relate it first to the people of his time. For that reason it has become increasingly important to me to get to know as much as possible about who Jesus 'really' was, what life was like then for the people among whom he lived, why his teaching seems to have had such a profound effect upon them, and what it was that seems to have been so totally original about his teaching that it came to be seen as a threat to either or both of the Jewish and Roman authorities, and ultimately became for his Jewish followers a new religion.

Reading, past and present

In the course of a long life of reading and thinking about my faith, like many others, I moved in my reading from traditional and conventional commentaries, which reinforced existing prejudices, to modern writers who sought to make Christianity more 'relevant'. C.S. Lewis (Screwtape at one time seemed very advanced!), William Temple, John Robinson (possibly the instigator of the progressive movement at the layman's level at least), Rudolf Bultmann, Harry Williams, Paul Tillich, Alec Vidler, Gerald Priestland, Teilhard de Chardin, Michael Ramsey, Ian Ramsey, Stephen Verney, and so on, and on, and on. Although they and their kind offered meaningful insights into the nature and meaning of their faith, it seems to me now that they spoke to us from their own standpoint in the twentieth century, naturally enough, but were somewhat less concerned, perhaps, with the historical dimension: how things were at the very beginning, and why Christian belief became at first so attractive (and to whom?), and then so totally rigid, inflexible, and increasingly unattractive, for the better part of two thousand years. Gallileo, Newton, Darwin and their like, men who changed the intellectual outlook of most normal modern human beings, were of course reluctantly acknowledged, but the broad truth (or otherwise) of the Bible at the historical level was not a significant part of the agenda of such writers, since they were not primarily concerned with what went on in the first three centuries or so; they wanted a new way of looking at things now; they were less concerned with the historical context of the original Jesus. The modern presentation of Christianity to the ordinary laity has retained a child-like literalism in its historical understanding of the Bible.

It became very clear to me that in those early years there were enormous intellectual struggles between different views of what Jesus taught, who and what he was, and how his church should respond. The early quarrels were particularly acute between the emerging Christian movement and the more traditionalist Jews who made up its first congregations. So I began to move into a second phase of reading, which took me down a much more historical track, with considerable secondary interest in what I might call literary interpretation. My reading moved to the more radical interpreters of Christianity – radical in their understanding of the Bible, their recognition of mythos (as opposed to logos) in the evolution of religion, and the consequences for the body of believers who were prepared to travel with them (whom we can call the Radicals or Progressives, while acknowledging a degree of emotional loading in the terms).

My new reading included Bishops Holloway and John Shelby Spong, Marcus Borg, Dominic Crossan, the Jesus Seminar's edition of *The Five Gospels* (yes, they include Thomas) and *The Acts of Jesus*, Burton Mack (on the Q gospel), Don Cupitt, Rubem Alves, C.H. Dodd (on the historical tradition), Karen Armstrong, Arthur Peacocke, John Polkinghorne, Michael Mayne, Robin Lane Fox, Robert Winston, Keith Ward, Richard Valentine, Geza Vermes, AN Wilson, John Churcher, the Folio Society's collection of the Gnostics (increasingly unreadable I found, but useful for a flavour of the genre), and more recently Ian Hazlitt's *Early Christianity*, Charles Freeman's *AD 381* and *New History of Early Christianity*, and Geza Vermes' *Christian Beginnings*. Not all were immediately relevant to my new focus, but the range of material gave me new perspectives.

One serious difficulty was also apparent: whereas in my younger days I could read, mark, learn and inwardly digest, and above all remember with surprising breadth and accuracy (especially for examinations) what I had read, I now find that I retain far less, and end up too often with broad impressions rather than a detailed grasp of the complexities of an argument or the evidence which supports a thesis. Nevertheless, the new picture that emerged for me can be broadly, if crudely, summarized as follows:

As I came to see it, the very early church, the gospel writers, the early fathers, the Gnostics, and the intellectuals of those early days were far less certain, and possibly also less concerned than we would be now, about the literal truth or ultimate meaning of what they taught – in those days there was less distinction between the mythical and the literal, less uniformity of opinion and more debate, more accusations of heresy, and (more desirably) less centralisation of belief. Of the gospel writers (and St Paul whose writings – AD ca. 55-65 - preceded theirs), each brings his own agenda to his account, writing in terms appropriate to the time of writing and the community for which he was writing, between roughly AD 70 and 100. There were also many more gospels, most of which failed to be included in the Canon, but all of which were probably expressive of the insights of the particular communities for which they were written. Later, bishops and other leaders seem to have been lords of their own small communities (dioceses), free within reason to propagate their own opinions or interpretations of Jesus' teaching, as it had been transmitted to them.

But then came Constantine, and the reign of Theodosius in AD 381, out of which was born the authoritarian, politically powerful, and increasingly centralized and corrupted church that dominated the Middle Ages. Uniformity was enforced at the point of the sword or by torture, the alliance between church and rulers was reinforced because it was mutually advantageous, and that, as Robert Frost was to say in a totally different context, 'has made all the difference.'

To find that, for example, there had been fierce debates in those early centuries about the divinity of Jesus, was liberating to someone who, like me, had once felt that even to voice such an idea was blasphemy. To find that there were varied views of the Eucharist, that eschatology and apocalypse might have more than one meaning, that Jesus was not necessarily the Lamb of God who died for the sins of the world, that he may well have been an illiterate and dispossessed peasant leading an anti-imperialist, anti-Roman protest movement, which though peaceful may well have seemed a genuine threat to imperial authority and its quisling Jewish establishment figures, that there were a number of other would-be Messiahs in the century or so before the final sack of Jerusalem, that Judas may not even have existed, and was simply the product of Midrash as an sort of artificial villain of the piece – all that was both stimulating and intellectually encouraging, in that Jesus and his mission began to appear as a far more credible and solidly historical figure, more an activist, not merely a preacher of good news and good behaviour.

This brought me to Dominic Crossan's *Birth of Christianity*. The title sounded exactly what I wanted – an attempt to uncover, in the words of the publisher's blurb, 'what happened in the years immediately after the execution of Jesus.' It was hard work, not least because he is driven by an academically admirable scrupulousness in establishing and justifying the methodology, assumptions, and intellectual validity of his argument. But I felt it was an important book for my own religious development, and the thrust of his argument was persuasive, while to an ancient historian like myself his methodology seemed 'ethical,' to use his own word. For me it represents essential reading for anyone who wants to try and understand what happened, how, and why.

It is a fascinating book, which attempts to describe (or perhaps we should say deduce) the evolution of Christianity in its first twenty years, from AD 30-50, which we may for convenience call the Oral Period – the years before documentary evidence survives (or perhaps even existed), and when the early Jewish Christian church was expecting the Second Coming, an eschatological or apocalyptic event, and therefore felt little need to record in any permanent form the sayings and deeds of Jesus.

Crossan's basic premise has important implications for all those who seek to present a convincing modern account of an ancient religion to a new generation. He argues that we need to take advantage of all the resources of modern academia: textual analysis built on the foundations of anthropology, sociology, archaeology, economic and literary history. If we do, we can in fact make reasonable deductions about what first stage documents lay behind the later (second stage) writings which have survived, such as St Paul, writing post-AD 50, though his conversion probably dates to circa AD 35, the canonical Gospels (written between AD 70 and 100), the extra-canonical gospels, such as the gospels of Thomas and Peter, and other documents such as the *Didache*. Such first stage documents may be said to exist in a sort of virtual reality.

My purpose has been to try and work out what happened in those very early years, as a way of deciding my own personal approach to the faith of my fathers, which I feel has fallen into disrepair and disrepute. My impression from all that I have read is that until the coming of Constantine and the formal establishment of the institutional church, the pattern of rich variety of belief and interpretation amongst diverse and disparate small Christian communities across the Empire was maintained. A relatively uniform and increasingly powerful, wealthy, and ultimately corrupted church was the final legacy of the Roman Empire.

I am very much aware that I have failed to give a proper account of the Cult of the Emperor as the binding force of the post-republican Roman Empire and the underpinning 'creed' of the whole imperial domination system. This was especially true of the eastern half of the Roman empire, where for most peoples (apart from the Jews) emperor worship fitted easily enough into the prevailing culture. For those interested, Stephen Mitchell's *Anatolia, Volume II, The Rise of the Church*, would make an interesting starting point.

There is a good argument for suggesting that there is a conscious parallelism between the way in which Rome promoted its value system through the imperial cult and the way the early Christians promoted theirs in deliberate contrast to, and as a critique of, the Augustan and imperial propaganda. But this, perhaps, is for another day.

Most recently published of all, and a compelling and fascinating study, has been Geza Vermes' *Christian Beginnings*. It seems to me to give scholarly reinforcement to my own amateur understanding of the origins of my faith. His concluding sentence rings like a clarion call to all people of goodwill and open minds to seek a new basis for the theology which underpins their faith. He says, in reference to the Renaissance, that:

> This revolution first created Protestantism, but subsequently spread over the whole spectrum of the churches. It can be seen that now it has reached, or will soon reach, a stage when a fresh revival will be called for, a new Reformation, zealous to reach back to the pure religious vision and enthusiasm of Jesus, the charismatic messenger of God, and not to the deifying message Paul, John, and the Church attributed to him.

Amen to that.

Section D: Letters and Conversations

Reading maketh a full man; conference a ready man; and writing an exact man
(Francis Bacon – Of Studies)

In the same essay from which the above quotation derives, Bacon also remarks that 'if a man write little, he had need of a great memory; if he confer little, he had need have a present wit (= quick mind); and if he read little, he had need have much cunning, to seem to know that which he doth not.'

My own memory, alas, is not what it was, nor my mind as quick; and I lack sufficient cunning to appear to know what I know not. Only perhaps in writing, rather than speaking, have I striven for some degree of exactness and precision – whether I have achieved it remains for others to decide. But to test what I write against the constructive criticism of friends is a great defence against error, stupidity or arrogant certainty. For all these reasons, I am always grateful to those who are willing to join in the search for truth, whether in discussion or by correspondence, because of one thing at least I am certain, that I lack both knowledge and certainty. Friendly discussion can sometimes help to make good such deficiencies. And as Socrates pointed out to his disciples, to know that you know nothing is perhaps the only true wisdom.

As I said in my Introduction, I have had a number of friends with whom, over many years, I have corresponded on many matters, but often and specifically on matters of faith and belief. I have found such converse immensely valuable, for the stimulus to reading and thought, for the questions asked and the criticisms offered. There is also much comfort to be found in the general sense that we all share a common disappointment in the failure of the traditional churches to offer new and more credible ideas about our faith. Our wish, perhaps somewhat stronger than our hope, is that we may find new ways out of the dilemmas posed by an intellectually deficient church and an intelligently aware laity.

Whether the contents of this section have anything to offer the reader, I cannot say. But it does at least reflect something of our common search. I have deliberately given no indication of the provenance of the correspondence quoted or the identities of those to whom I have written. I have no desire to embarrass anyone who might be challenged to defend a position, which is at best tentative and possibly little more than exploratory. But I am pretty sure that the sources themselves will recognise the ingredients of our conversations.

All I would wish to suggest is that such discussions reflect the broad interest of some educated and thoughtful people (whether Christian or not), who find (as I do) a certain emptiness at the heart of the official presentation of the faith. It may also suggest reasons why the traditional churches have lost some of their more thoughtful adherents, and why, in my opinion, much of the blame lies with the leadership (intellectual and pastoral) of those institutions.

CHAPTER TWENTY-FOUR

'Him that Sent Me'

(An Exercise on John 12.44-6)

AV: 12.44 ff. Jesus cried and said, He that believeth on me, believeth not on me but on him that sent me. 45. And he that seeth me seeth him that sent me. 46. I am come a light into the world that whosoever believeth on me should not abide in darkness.

NEB: So Jesus cried aloud: 'When a man believes in me, he believes in him who sent me rather than in me; 'seeing' me, he 'sees' him who sent me. I have come into the world as light, so that no-one who has faith in me should remain in darkness.'

Moffatt: And Jesus cried aloud, 'He who believes in me believes not in me but in him who sent me, and he who beholds me beholds him who sent me. I have come as light into the world, that no-one who believes in me may remain in the dark.'

The Jesus Seminar: Then Jesus proclaimed aloud: 'Those who believe in me do not believe in me only but in the one who sent me. And those who see me see the one who sent me. I am light come into the world, so all who believe in me need not remain in the dark.'

The Jesus Seminar grade and print this saying in black – which indicates that in their judgement, *Jesus did not say this; it represents the perspective or content of a later or different tradition.* They comment: 'This is another version of John 5.23b. There the author employs the key term honour – whoever does not honour the son does not honour the Father who sent him.' 12.45 is another variation on the same theme and makes use of John's peculiar understanding of the word 'see'. (No-one really 'sees' God, except in the sense of having insight into who God is). In 12.46 John again alludes to Jesus as the 'light of the world', a theme he has employed in 8.12; 9.5; 11.9-10; 12.35-6. The contrast is between those who walk in the light Jesus has brought into the world and those who walk in the world's light, which is real darkness. 12.46 goes back to pick up the theme of the Prologue (1.9) 'Genuine light, the kind that provides light for everyone, was coming into the world.'

Their conclusion is that, *These are all Johannine themes, only distantly related to anything Jesus said.*

William Temple comments (using the AV): There is no note of time attached to the record of this utterance. It is a summary statement of His own claims and of the judgement upon those who reject Him. The vital point is that He is the spokesman and representative of the Father. To trust him is to trust the Father; to observe or contemplate Him is to observe or contemplate the Father. He is come not to give light to the world, but to be the light in the world, so that those who believe in or trust Him are delivered from its darkness. His purpose is not judgement but redemption. But judgement follows the offer of redemption. He who has heard and rejected the Gospel is not in the same position as one who has never heard it. The message which he heard is his accuser. And this is so because the message is not original in the sense of originating in the speaker. It comes through Him, like his glory (1.14) from the Father. The Father gave commandment what the Son should say, and his commandment is eternal life.

JAF Gregg comments (Biog. page 233 citing Expository Times, Aug 1951): 'The Fourth Gospel is commonly treated as that Gospel which more than the others witnesses to the Divinity of Christ. But I think its purpose is primarily to witness to what the Father is, as seen in and through the Son. 'He that hath seen me hath seen the Father.' And I am reminded of the words of a well-known mystical writer (Simone Weil) who passed from our midst only two or three years ago. 'You see,' she writes, 'I came to Christ through God, whereas lots of people come to God through Christ. But I can't show them how to do that – all I know about is the reverse route.' Yes, but what she calls the reverse route, the approach to Christ through God, is the historic Christian order of approach. The disciples learnt of God first, and then learnt more fully of Him in Christ....

Belief in God – belief in the One living and self-revealing God – was possible for many years before ever Christ appeared and is the working faith of the pious Jew today. And as witness to that quite solid fact, we possess this practical consideration, namely, that with all our greater knowledge of God that has come to us in Christ, the Christian church has never outgrown its use of the Psalter, the hymn book of post-exilic Judaism, as its manual of public as well as private devotion.'

My comments on the above: Alas, with the near death of Matins, this undesirable state of affairs has now come to pass – it is one of the many elements of our inheritance that the modern church has betrayed.

My correspondent asks: 'will the Greek text in any way bear the proposition that is implicit in Gregg's assertion that to 'see' Christ (in the Johannine sense of gaining insight to Christ), one must first 'see' the Father.' The unanimity of so many scholars makes one hesitate, but Gregg's change of emphasis at least encourages one to look again.

My translation of 12.44: 'Anyone showing trust in me is not showing trust in me but in the one who sent me.' (Gk. *Pempsanta* – the aorist participle, the once-for-all tense, not the perfect, 'who has sent me).

If someone brings me a message from a friend with whom I have quarrelled to the effect that he will be coming to see me in a few days to seek reconciliation, it tells me nothing about the messenger. But knowing my friend as I do, it may carry credibility because he knows my friend, and it may reinforce my belief in him and his friendship. Christ is the messenger – nothing more. Certainly he is not divine, nor frankly, do I believe he is the second person of the Trinity – a strange primitive theological concept dreamed up by the Council of Nicaea, and lacking any authority prior to the late third century AD. We believe the message Christ brings, because we have some idea already of what my friend (God) is. The messenger may be able to add confirmatory details, and if we like him and trust him, it obviously helps the ultimate frame of mind in which both parties seek reconciliation.

But then the messenger explains how distressed my friend has been; how he has tormented himself with sorrow at our falling out etc. etc. As a result, my faith in our friendship is, perhaps, enhanced, and I look forward more eagerly to that reconciliation.

On the basis of that analogy – and analogies are not arguments or proofs, merely illustrations of what may be a truth – Gregg is right to adjust the emphasis. It is indeed possible that some sort of faith in God is needed to see Christ for what he is – God's messenger. Once we get that far, then richer insights will reach us through Christ's teaching. But God comes first.

I have to confess that this proposition suits my own experience. The Jesus of the Gospels was, in my view, finally airbrushed from history by the Councils of Constantine and Theodosius, and the Jesus of ecclesiastical history holds few attractions; the Ecclesiastical and Institutional Church of Jesus even less.

My translation of 12.45: 'Anyone who contemplates and meditates upon me is in fact contemplating and meditating upon the one who sent me.' (The Greek *theoreo* I translate 'contemplates and meditates') (Gk. *Theoreo* is used of a spectator at the public Games and Religious Festivals, and of the activity of the Mind. (The normal Greek word for seeing is *horao*.) To be a *theoros* is, *inter alia*, to be a state ambassador to an oracle. *Theoreo* has strong overtones of religious activity – it does not just mean 'see'.)

My translation of 12.46: '(Like) the (sun's) light I have entered the world, so that all those who trust me (while still) in the/their darkness may not remain (there).'

English speakers sometimes forget that extraordinary power of an inflected language, such as Greek or Latin, to exploit distorted word order without destroying sense. The location of a word in an emphatic position may be a signal. My idiosyncratic translation attempts to draw attention to one possible effect of word order. The bracketed words show where I have inserted words to achieve the effect I wanted.

The Greek in v.46 starts *ego phos* - ' I <as> light into the world have come' (perfect tense). Whatever else it means, it is unlikely to mean 'as a light **for** the world.'

CHAPTER TWENTY-FIVE

Faith and Ideology

(Letter to a Friend)

I do rather agree with you and Crossan (and Robert Bellah – *Religion in Human Evolution*) that societies need a group ideology/theology. The problem is how to find a replacement belief or value system, once religion (of whatever kind) has lost credibility with ordinary thinking people. It does not terribly matter what a few high-powered intellectuals think - they can be ignored by the rest of us. The trouble begins when their elevated ideas begin to become the stuff of middle level discourse - among ordinary, thoughtful, and reasonably educated people, like you (and me, if you insist!)

It is the mediation of high-falutin' ideas to not so high-falutin' people that is the source of the problem. The agnostics and atheists have managed it; the theologians have abandoned the struggle and betrayed us all. The ordinary middle of the road thoughtful citizen has, I suspect, retained perhaps a residual sense of/desire for a divinity of a kind; but is fed up with the absurdities of theology, ritual, spiritual pretentiousness and the associated hypocrisies of religious leaders. What will replace religion?

Well, we have been here before. The Greeks (what would I do with out them?) of classical fifth century Athens reached pretty well exactly that point. The common herd remained superstitious, god fearing, polytheistic etc. The intellectuals (rich and educated on the whole) had supped at the tables of Ionian science and Socratic dialectic and reached the conclusion that the conventional religion would not do. Witch hunts ensued, stimulated by the media types – for example, Aristophanes with his political comedies, who pilloried Socrates in his *Clouds* - and in one of those witch hunts, resulting from a political crisis caused by military defeat and the need for scapegoats, Socrates was executed for 'corrupting the young.' But, thanks to Plato (= St Paul??) Socrates' teaching lived on and was developed into the philosophy of Plato, Aristotle, and ultimately gave rise to Stoicism, Cynicism, Epicureanism etc. (to give you a simplistic overview).

The practical Romans then gradually converted the intellectual Greek stuff into a more realistic stoicism, which became the dominant 'faith' of the governing classes (Fate = Purpose = meaning = self-control and steadfastness). The leisured affluent classes turned to Epicureanism (atomic theory - no gods - be happy - cultivate your garden). But into the middle of that came Augustus and a new religion - or dimension of religion at least - in the shape of *Roma et Augustus*, Rome as the city of destiny and Augustus, (*divi filius*) son of God (like Jesus?), as the agents of Fate, working in tandem to rule the world. There is purpose and meaning in life; our purpose and duty is to cooperate with it; adherence to duty and a stoic endurance of suffering and setbacks was the mark of nobility. Death had no fears for you and no dominion over you.

'These shall be your arts, O Roman,' says Virgil, (the emperor's poet-laureate and spin-doctor, but rather more original than most of their kind and certainly less devious), 'to impose custom on peace (or: the habit of peace), to show mercy to your subjects, and to war down the proud.' The cult of Augustus developed a complete ecclesiology in the East, but was introduced more cautiously in the West. He had his priests, his temples, compulsory worship for all (very public school), and as long as you did your stuff as and when the state religion required it, you were free to worship who and what you liked otherwise. So the plebs of the common herd had something to admire, found structure to their existence in religion, and a purpose as rulers of the world. The educated classes did not believe a word of it, but went along with it because it made for peace, order and good governance. As Ovid said in a masterly hexameter:

Expedit esse deos, et ut expedit esse putemus.

'It is expedient that there should be gods; and since it is expedient, let us believe in them'

Others could I am sure work the analogies better - or totally refute them. But I find a broad equivalence - death of religion; new ersatz religion for the masses; practical Ethics for the leadership.

CHAPTER TWENTY-SIX

God's Interaction with a Suffering World

Thoughts on a Polkinghorne Essay

An atheist friend wrote: 'I consider that P. is nit-picking. He fails to define the God who is interacting – but only so far as it does not upset P. and his understanding of science.' My reply follows:

I share your dissatisfaction with this. The trouble is that if my mind was ever sharp, it no longer really is, and I find it difficult to nail down what my intuition tells me is the illogicality of P.'s proposition. I have the same problem with sermons I hear and books I read. I often suspect there is something wrong with the argument, but too often fail to identify quite what it is. I did a little philosophy for my Classics degree, but never much enjoyed it, and would have made a mess of Greats had I gone to that other university and had to study logic as well as philosophy.

My overall reaction to P.'s essay was that I cannot differentiate the God who is supposed to be interacting with the world from the finger-pointing divine tyrant whom he dismisses at the start of his talk. The God of Love, who is the flavour of the month at present among the god-talk people, seems to me exactly the same human God whose tyrannical treatment of His (sic) world we now regard as intolerable. The only difference is that he is now Mr Nice instead of Mr Nasty/Mr Indifferent and has a cunning plan to make us all good – if we want to be. The god-talkers would probably reply that Love is the highest and best of which we are capable and therefore it must stand as the best metaphor we have for God.

(Interesting, isn't it, how few words we have in English for the variations of love. If Eskimos have fifty-two words for snow, you might have thought that English could have developed a range of words for love in all its variations. We've never really absorbed the Greek word *agape*, which St Paul uses in 1 Cor 13. Perhaps the English stiff upper lip is responsible.)

To do him justice P. is struggling very hard to produce a better concept of God than the traditional one. But at the start he rightly dismisses both the cosmic tyrant and the god of deism (i.e. an indifferent god who sets it all going and stands back and waits for the (big?) bang), but at the end he is still using the language of personal involvement – God remains a God who 'does indeed act in the world,' but in P.'s description still acts like a human parent, who accepts that he must let his children grow up in their own way. The analogy remains the traditional one – a god who is like us, differing only in scale, degree, and grandeur.

I think that progressive people are trying very hard to 'invent' or 'define' a different sort of god altogether – one who is the totality of all that is and all that we are, while avoiding, unsuccessfully in my view, the accusation of being New Pantheists – though if you call them panentheists, it makes them feel better. I personally am pretty comfortable with pantheism.

There seems an inherent contradiction in P.'s proposition that 'God has made a world in which creatures can make themselves…' That still leaves us with a Genesis 1 & 2-type God, but one who is subtler and more complex than the Babylonians and Jews imagined. I can't really swallow that. In fact the more I think about it, the more I incline in some ways to a) the Unmoved Mover (of Aristotle, I think) or b) Plato's ideal of the Absolute, existing outside of time, and best expressed as Beauty, Goodness, and Truth (add Love if you like) or c) the Pantheistic embodiment of All That Was and Is or d) some sort of Embodiment of All Human Potential, which we recognise and acknowledge by deifying the greatest and best of our kind or e) Something/Someone which/who totally is beyond our conceptual horizons, but which/whom we glimpse or sense from time to time in our better moments or noblest concepts (the cop-out solution?).

The bit of the essay I enjoyed most was the exposition of developing scientific ideas and acknowledgement of its limitations. He has the lucidity of a true scholar, when he is talking about what he really knows about, as opposed to merely speculating about. But having dealt with chaos theory, I wish he had gone on to tell us a bit about String Theory, which I find an interesting idea without understanding what it is.

CHAPTER TWENTY-SEVEN

The Homosexuality Issue

Letter to a Friend

A friend sent me a whole heap of cuttings from local newspapers about a row over a senior Anglican cleric, who had 'come out,' after having had a twenty year partnership with another man. Shock and horror among what one might call 'the usual people' and more threats of schism. The Archbishop asked for time for the house of Bishops to consider their position on the matter – as if the whole Anglican Communion had not been considering it for the last twenty years. Anyhow, I thought to myself that perhaps I would try to think out what I thought on the matter, because I find it quite difficult to separate gut feeling from thoughtful analysis.

Thank you so much for the various missives you sent me. It is interesting to see that these are the same problems as poor Rowan Williams faces across the whole of the Anglican Communion. I do wonder how dear grandfather would have handled the situation. I suppose my way of looking at it is simplistic, but here goes.

The whole homosexuality issue is a bit of a pain and the temptation is to say to the church authorities everywhere – 'it serves you right. It is a problem of your own making. If you had the courage long ago to educate your congregations in the developments of Biblical scholarship and modern scientific understanding, you would not now face difficulties, especially from fundamentalists of the most intolerant kind, in such relatively unimportant issues as homosexuality, women priests, and creationism.'

Those difficulties derive from a failure to teach that the Bible is not in any literal sense the Word of God. Though it may well contain insights into the nature and purposes of God (though even there, no one can tell for sure), it is the product of fallible human thought over the centuries. As a result primitive Jewish values, based on primitive scientific knowledge and particular cultural traditions, have infected (or affected) the modern views of a regrettably ignorant church membership.

Non-scientist though I am, my impression is that the science is now pretty clear: that human sexuality ranges across the whole spectrum of inclinations. If so, then someone needs to say loud and clear that all sexual activity is 'natural' for human beings. Of course 'natural' is not necessarily the same as 'good', but good is not always an absolute – it may be merely a value judgement, and the inclinations of the majority do not necessarily impose obligations on minorities.

Those of us heterosexually inclined, however, are perfectly entitled to count

128

ourselves lucky, or even blessed, in our ability and desire to have children, and even to sympathise with those not so inclined; but to claim a moral superiority or to assert that homosexuals are wrong (or sinners) is not legitimate. If sin is involved, it must lie in infidelity, not sexual preference.

Heterosexuality is inevitably the primary force in all nature, and sexual pleasure (whether homo– or hetero-) is entirely secondary in the animal kingdom at large. Outside the human species, however, and possibly its immediate ancestors (monkeys etc.) procreation for the continuance of the species is of necessity the core and fundamental value. But there seems to be perfectly good evidence of homosexual behaviour even in the 'lower' (sic) orders of animals, though whether for social bonding, population control (e.g. certain species of penguin), or mere pleasure must remain uncertain. They are, by definition, outside the boundaries of moral judgement.

The issue seems to me a matter of cultural values, even within the species of *homo sapiens*. Heterosexuality (and monogamy within it) is not necessarily the only 'natural' activity, but it is reasonable to offer a judgement as to whether any one particular set of values is advantageous for society and preferable for the individual. But the judgement is a moral one, only if moral values are seen as absolutes; if not, the judgement is simply cultural and to an extent subjective.

My own view is that most moral values exist only within a limited culture or nation, and only for a limited period of time, until different ones take their place. What is the best state for the human species generally, and more particularly for our own society, must depend on varying circumstances. If we claim to be of a particular religious grouping, the teaching of the founder of our religion may add an extra dimension to the judgement. But given that even the founder is human and not divine (and I include Jesus in that category) then we are entitled to ask whether the founder was right for all time. I would submit that the answer is 'not necessarily' – since all religious leaders are the product of a culture and a chronological setting. Was Mohammad wrong to allow four wives? Are the *mores* of tribes that we presume to regard as primitive any worse than ours? Is capital punishment right or wrong? And so on.

The Christian churches' condemnation of homosexual activity derives from Leviticus and the Old Testament. Such Jewish cultural tradition has been refined by the Christian insights developed by Jesus, who (it is my impression) did not get very worked up about sexual *mores* of any kind. I doubt if he had homosexual inclinations, as some would contend, since his relationship with the women in his entourage is at least interesting and at best unclear. But I am not aware of Jesus ever saying anything about homosexuality. Paul, not Jesus, is the New Testament problem and his background is Jewish and rooted in the Old Testament. Some would go further, and not entirely implausibly, suggest that the 'thorn in the flesh' from which he suffered may well have been a homosexual inclination with which, in accordance with the culture of his time, he felt compelled to wrestle constantly. After all, ancient society had different values from modern, some of them little more than superstitions and taboos.

My guess then becomes that once a partnership is established, fidelity to the partner seems to work best for both parties, most obviously but not necessarily exclusively, in the case of heterosexuals and their offspring (if any); for that reason it is to be encouraged. (But in ancient Sparta they clearly reached a different judgement, appropriate to their culture, since children were reared by and for the state, and homosexual love seems to have been a useful quality in encouraging mutual loyalty and courage in her soldiery). It is also likely that physical health is best protected by a limited exposure to a variety of sexual partners. Overall, therefore, fidelity is perhaps a more important issue – and value - than the sexual orientation of the partners.

By now, it seems to me, the whole squabble is reduced to cultural values and social and physical advantage – and if others reach different judgements, that is their absolute right. For me the thing that I find regrettable in all the debate on this subject is the intemperate and unforgiving quality of the debate within the churches on one side, and the ostentatious parading of their inclinations by the homosexual fraternity on the other. I fully recognise that minorities feel they need to make their case public. But I think their cause would be much better furthered by a quiet pursuit of their chosen way of life, rather than obtrusive parading of their inclinations. But they could legitimately reply that heterosexuals are no less offensively shameless, and it would be hard to disagree.

It is, of course, not all that needs to be said on the subject. The creative drive of the homosexual fraternity is sometimes channelled wonderfully into the arts and literature, and society too often fails to acknowledge its very real debt to them in that area.

I do acknowledge that the issue will continue to cause difficulties for the churches. But in the end gay priests and women priests are both problems of inherited culture; both derive from the failure of the churches to educate their adherents. I agree with one of Rowan Williams' predecessors, Archbishop Michael Ramsey, who said that there are no reasons in the New Testament against women as priests; what he said about gay priests I do not know – but they have been with us in plenty for centuries and we should rejoice in the fact that there is no longer any need for secrecy in our society at large. It is shameful that the churches are less tolerant than the society they exist to serve and to which they, too often hypocritically, claim to offer an example of goodness, generosity, and love. Since a majority in the church assemblies has reached a decision on both issues, we should simply encourage the objectors to go their own way, and quietly remind ourselves that the church may well be better without them.

This may all be nonsense – I am really trying to think aloud as I write. But thank you so much for provoking me into trying to write an essay on a topic that I usually skirt delicately round, not least because I am uncharacteristically uncertain about what I really think.

CHAPTER TWENTY-EIGHT

Memorable Sayings in an Evolving Legend

(Notes from an unknown source)

Potentially 'factual' (a compelling teacher of wisdom)

1. Let him that is without sin cast he first stone.
2. Inasmuch as ye have done it to the least of these my brethren, ye have done it unto me; and inasmuch as ye have not done it ....
3. The first shall be last; and the last first.
4. The Sabbath was made for man, not man for the Sabbath.
5. Unfairness (recognition that life often is unfair):
   a. The parable of the talents.
   b. Mary praised for not helping with the housework
   c. Prodigal son – my sympathy with the elder brother

The birth of the Legend and The Jesus of Faith, not History

6. On the cross:
   Jesus, remember me when you come into your kingdom (the thief)
   Today you shall be with me in Paradise
   (In the earliest account, by Paul, there is no story of betrayal, no arrest, no trial, no Pilate, no Barabbas, no thieves, no words from the cross, no darkness at noon. Mark does not refer once to eye-witnesses; he creates this narrative in eight 3-hour segments to fit the liturgical pattern of a 24 hour vigil, and to portray Jesus as the expected Jewish Messiah, using midrash to rework Psalm 22 and Isaiah 53. - Spong).

   My God, my God, why hast thou forsaken me – Psalm 22.- did Jesus also doubt? Father forgive them, for they know not what they do mother behold your son; son behold your Mother – Jewish faith as 'mother'? It is finished (Mission complete)

   At the cross:
   Truly, this was a god's son. (the centurion) – issues of translation?

7. He is going on before you into Galilee; there you will see him, as he told you – the earliest element of the tradition?
8. Abide with us, for it is towards evening and the day is far spent (Emmaus).
9. The Artaban story - a modern myth (See Bibliography, Henry Van Dyke, *The Story of the Other Wise Man*)
10. Gospel of St Thomas (a Wisdom teacher - no narrative; just sayings)
    (No. 82) He that is near me is near the fire
    (No. 77) I am all: from me all came forth. Split a piece of wood; I am there. Lift up the stone and you will find me there.
    (No.102) Damn the Pharisees. They are like dogs sleeping in a cattle manger; the dog neither eats nor lets the cattle eat.
    (No. 113) The Kingdom of God <tr: Father's Imperial Rule> will not come by watching for it. It will not be said, 'Look here!' or 'Look there!' Rather the Kingdom of God is spread out upon the earth, and people don't see it.

Commentary says: Jesus posits a kingdom that already exists in the world, but that remains invisible to people in the world. The Kingdom does not function as an apocalyptic vision… but as a state of being congruent with the existent world and present for those capable of seeing it.

CHAPTER TWENTY-NINE

Tradition and Other Matters

(Serendipity – The Fruits of a Chance Encounter)

A chance encounter and a delightful conversation in Norwich Cathedral, which we visited while on holiday, led to an exchange of letters with a complete stranger and my recommendation to him of the writings of Bishop John Shelby Spong.

In the course of one letter he raised a very interesting issue:

Two books by Robert Lee on Norfolk Clergy in the nineteenth century point to a problem. The message of both books seems to be that the Norfolk Clergy in the 19th century… 'by identifying themselves so closely with these mechanisms of social and economic change (Poor Law, Schools etc.)… had become inextricably linked to the great elite project that had made – intentionally or otherwise – the labourers' own past a foreign country.'

I think that Lee makes a very important point that still echoes in rural Norfolk. Lee suggests that earlier generations of clergy had been content to allow customs deeply in the mind of people (maypoles etc.) to live alongside the church. Translating the point to theology and a new view of Jesus' birth and resurrection, it would be very easy for teachers/preachers to leave behind myths and stories which are still bedded deep in people's minds. On a funeral visit recently a young man told me about the need to give a gold coin 'to pay for the ferryman.' Here is somebody trying to talk about resurrection and life after death. This desire remains firmly in the minds of most. So somehow there has to be evolution. This seems a much more worthwhile project than women bishops or the Anglican Covenant.'

I replied:

I am so glad that you found Spong's book (*Eternal Life: A New Vision*) interesting. I share completely your reservations about his final chapters. I have read about eight of his works, and every time I am encouraged and satisfied by his demolition of old shibboleths and some of his new insights into biblical texts. But every time he promises that the next book will attempt to build new structures in their place; and every time he has, to a degree, disappointed. *Eternal Life* was the same – it was a very useful summary of where he has got to in clearing the space from his own 9/11 assault upon the Twin Towers of traditional faith, which served no less devastatingly than Al Qaeda to show up the vulnerability of the old structures. But, like the Americans generally, he is having a real problem in agreeing what to build in their place, and where and how.

I still remember with enormous pleasure our serendipitous encounter on the Crossing of the Cathedral. I am so glad that it proved fruitful in some small way for yourself as it did for us. I am delighted that you have discovered a hidden point of Progressive light amidst the darkness of the Norfolk wastelands. When I was producing a Map of Progressive Churches for the PCN, I seem to remember there was another such just on the other side of the Wash. I suspect that many such groups keep their heads down and quietly get on with the business of exploration without frightening the horses or disturbing the natives. It is where I see the best hope for the future. I think a couple of recent addresses by the PCN Chairman, John Churcher, may have a bearing on your final question, which I am carefully avoiding getting started on, you will have noticed.

All my reading has been somewhat obstructed by the enormous traffic jam created by Diarmid MacCulloch's huge *History of Christianity* (I am at page 250 with another 750 to go). Very good so far, and helping to pull together the threads of all my recent reading into the early history of Christianity, notably Dominic Crossan, Jonathan Reed, Marcus Borg, Charles Freeman, and even Karen Armstrong. But increasingly a declining memory leaves me with broad impressions rather than detailed recollections.

MacCulloch's reaction in a piece for *The Times* to the flight of the bishops into the arms of Rome said all, I felt, that needed to be said. I have once or twice reached for my keyboard to pen a letter to the same newspaper lamenting the childish objections of the traditionalists to women and/or gay bishops, or clergy. But discretion has so far proved the better part of valour. If there is one thing that is absolutely transparent about the Jesus of history, it is that in his efforts to reform or transform Judaism he associated with, and gave a particular welcome to, all those whom conventional contemporary moral and ethical standards found objectionable. Given the track record of some Popes, Bishops, Cardinals and Priests through the ages, their successors have no business casting stones at anyone. Changing times and circumstances require adaptive reaction; Jesus exemplifies this massively.

And so to your question about Tradition

We think we stand upon the shoulders of giants. But what are we to do when we discover that Giants don't exist and are the stuff of folk tales? I notice how easily I lapse into metaphor. What else is there when you are, as if in Francis Thompson's *No Strange Land*, striving to touch the intangible and to view the invisible? The key to it all is to be clear about the value and function of Tradition.

I suppose the Roman Catholic Church is the strongest example and advocate of its importance. Whatever that church has incorporated into the body of its belief and customary practice seems to have become part of The Tradition, and thereby to be fixed forever after as established Truth. After one generation it becomes Practice; after two Custom; after three, Tradition; and soon after, Eternal Truth, which is often indistinguishable from Myth, in the proper sense of the word. Where it changes, as it has occasionally, the fact is ignored or denied. It lends enormous strength to the institution, qua institution.

But there is nothing in the laws of man or God which dictates that tradition is inviolate. It is simply what was done or said in the past; it merits respect; we may learn from it; but once it has outlived its usefulness, that should be an end to it. If we are irrationally tied to tradition, when the earthquake finally comes, all the greater will be the fall thereof, I suspect (like the Berlin Wall).

That said, of course all progress is cumulative and ideas accretive. So inherited belief, practice, tradition have their place, but only insofar as they add to the total effect and do not stultify. As long as we all recognise, and are taught by the church to recognise, that much of the biblical record is a blend of fact, legend, and mythology, and its theology the record simply of the best insights of each generation, and that we must distinguish between those elements in deciding what is important, little harm is done. For me the past of my forebears has as much potential for enrichment of meaning as seduction into error. But it has both.

Christmas is a rather obvious case in point: in the days when religion was more primitive (if one may be so arrogant as to suggest that) the winter solstice and the recovery (new birth) of what Chaucer called the 'yonge sonne' was so hugely important to the agricultural communities of the time, that it must have seemed of paramount significance. The associated religious rituals to bring back the dying sun must have seemed absolutely critical for the community. That, for me, makes the choice of 25 December for the birth of Jesus potentially all the richer, as a festival of renewal and rebirth for the newer church community, as it was for their pre-Christian ancestors. But I don't actually believe it – nor do I need to. The fact that mid-winter is probably the least likely time for shepherds to be out in the fields keeping watch is neither here nor there; it does not diminish the appeal of the Christmas story – one just must not be misled into believing it, because sooner or later, as with children and Father Christmas, we will discover that it isn't true. If we are not prepared for it, the result may be distressing. Yet the tale of Santa Nikolaus is enriching to the totality and may well have a basis in truth.

So too with your maypoles. The fact that they are almost certainly phallic in origin and part of early summer pagan festivals of fertility for (again) agricultural communities makes them admirable community events. I will come back to community in a moment. The church's long standing obsession with the idea that sexual activity is sinful (the legacy of Augustine and his hero, St Paul), and that Eve was the source of man's fall from grace, long ago generated a prudish disapproval of such rural festivities. But they should be seen as nothing more than sources of community coherence and seasonal revelry, than which in any society nothing can be more important. I totally agree with Robert Lee's contention that the church's excessive identification with mechanisms of social and economic change 'made agricultural labourers' own past a foreign country.' With doubtless worthy motives, the church destroyed a valuable element of social cohesion and imaginative enrichment.

Easter is a bit different, because I assume that there the choice of date has been dictated by the association with the Jewish Passover, rather than an agricultural festival, though that may well also be inherent in its Jewish origins. But again, the 'contamination' of the Christian story by Jewish ideas of sacrificial death and the banishment of the scapegoat carrying the sins of the people, has invested the whole event with enhanced religious significance. This has prevented us from seeing Jesus' death as simply a noble act, (which in purely historical terms is all it may be), the expression of supreme self-denial, the very pinnacle of ethical conduct, and thus a moral example to us all, in that (in the Bible account) he dies as perhaps we all should die with a blessing for others on his lips and a concern for others in his heart.

The example of an unjust death endured without malice towards those that inflicted it is sufficient, though of course to any religious believer the religious/theological accretions are important. To find power and meaning in the story, I do not need an overlay of Jewish ideas of sacrifice for sin, though I recognise the force they give to the basic idea. The Jewish overtones do greatly enrich the meaning and power of the whole story. There the power of tradition to enrich is still transparent, though with the passing of centuries it may well cease to be so. Once it outlives its usefulness, it must be left to die. And that goes no less for such religious traditional custom and practice as has acquired the status of something more than mere folklore and festival. If you ask me for examples, I have to confess that I find myself asking what, if anything, in Christian teaching would I die at the stake to preserve. The answer is, I suspect, almost nothing. As Queen Elizabeth I observed, 'True religion is the love (or was it fear?) of God – the rest is argument about trifles'.

It is all a matter of identifying what is important and why it is important and what is the purpose of its preservation or abandonment. Is its value social, mythical, theological, poetic? Is it simply harmless? My own difficulties with the Eucharist place even that central mystery of the faith in a similar category, since for me it is less important than it certainly is to many others.

I remain pretty open-minded about whether Jesus actually told his disciples to 'do this in remembrance'. I don't even think that it matters much. What was really significant was his idea of the shared meal, where all were welcome and each contributed what they could to the common store and (contrary to the custom of the time) all partook alike of the same food, whether feast or famine. But I recognise the accretive power of the tradition to enhance the power of the sacrament for those that accept it, and I fully acknowledge that within a generation or two the tradition/legend of the Last Supper was established and this gives it something of the authority of antiquity. But now for some like me it has become an impediment, though for many it still remains at the very centre of their faith.

I have been attending a course in the Parish called Fresh Expressions – sadly tedious and deeply unconvincing, and manifestly all about getting more people back into the churches, while claiming to be about going out and learning from others 'where they are' - which is very much an in vogue phrase at present. But the unspoken yet obvious intention is to bring them back to true (sic) belief, which rather wrecks the point of going out to people 'where they are!'

In the final talk, given by a profoundly thoughtful priest (a woman) who was a stipendiary vicar and also a long-standing trainer of clergy and spiritual counsellor, there was a wide-ranging survey of where the church is at and how it got there. She made for me a series of very telling propositions. I paraphrase from my notes just to get the thrust of her thesis, which I have quoted in reduced print to make clear what is her insight as opposed to anything of my own – though I largely agree with her.

> There used to be a Christendom: a way of life in Europe where the whole culture, its politics and economic life were rooted in and expressed within Christian activities and images. The church was society; society was the church. Church – as a sociological term - is a religious institution embedded in the whole of society in just that sort of way. In England the Church (ie C of E) was so embedded. Church should be distinguished from Sect. A Sect - in sociological terms - is a religious grouping, which shares a personal choice of religious activity. The C of E in England was once a Church, (in the above sense). It was the embodiment of a national Community. It has turned itself into a Sect.
>
> As an institution that C of E was led by a professional group, often in earlier times the younger sons of gentry. To be a Churchman was to wield power. RCs and Dissenters were excluded. Such professional clergy have an emotional and practical commitment to the institution as it is. They are obstacles to change. Ordinary citizens simply used to follow as they were led. It was impolite to discuss personal faith, but it was OK to indulge in theological discussion, because you were safe in your belonging. So until very recently it was entirely possible to belong to the C of E without believing. It offered uniformity of worship; it required conformity to social expectation, rather than belief.
>
> But now, and increasingly, the institutions of the C of E are separating from the other powers and influences in the nation. The Parish Eucharist movement of the mid-20th century made it less possible (I would say almost impossible) to belong without believing. By contrast with Matins, you have to be confirmed to participate fully, and this implies committed belief. To belong now carries the expectation of belief and commitment in time and money.
>
> In fact, the C of E has now become a Sect, in the sociological definition given above. It no longer displays the key characteristics of a Church which is the embodiment of community. Without the coherent adhesion of the generality of the people and their (?unthinking) assent to its value and creedal systems, the majority of the population have been unchurched. Consequently they feel free to pick and mix their beliefs as suits them – and they do.

These are the factors that, it seems to me, have given rise to the situation described by Robert Lee. It takes, and has taken, time and he clearly sees the process as starting in the 19th century. I feel that the real damage was done in the aftermath of WW2 and then by the liberating effects of the late 1960s/70s. For a sect-church (in the terms defined above) it would be quite impossible to tolerate strange beliefs and customs inherited from a pagan or even merely superstitious past.

If this is right, then the 19th century Norfolk Clergy, who 'made their labourers' own past a foreign country,' were unwittingly part of a far wider movement of change by the church at large. Education through the Enlightenment widened horizons and understanding; growing prosperity from industrialisation increased economic independence and independence of thought as well as action; inevitably, and probably with the best of intentions, Robert Lee's Norfolk clergy identified themselves with the mechanisms of social and economic change and help to assist the process.

But it was the Church at large, which (partly through the self-interested obstructiveness of its professional clergy as described above) lost control of the Community's shared outlook, beliefs and values. The community, so to speak, grew up intellectually; the church did not; and worse, it concealed from what it thought of as its intellectual inferiors in the pews the very ideas, which it was beginning to teach its own clergy. As a result, it lost touch with its clientele. Once it ceased to articulate that communal consensus (I think the word might be *weltanschaung* = world view, but I am not sure), it was ultimately doomed to become a Sect (in the sociological sense above) instead of a Church.

As you say, it would be very easy for teachers/preachers to leave behind myths and stories of Jesus' birth and resurrection. But I see no need to leave them behind. What is essential is to tell the truth about them; then to preach about them and to rejoice in them for what they are – legends and stories from long ago, still almost certainly carrying elements of historical truth (cf. King Arthur), and often still expressive of religious truth, and therefore possessed of power and value. In short, they express profound religious truths at a level deeper than literal or historical truth, in the same way as poetry and drama (especially religious or tragic drama) can do.

I am delighted by your story of the young man feeling the need to offer a gold coin to pay the ferryman: at the most basic it acknowledges the need to pay funeral fees; and at a higher level it acknowledges a truth inherited from the distant past that death is another undiscovered country from whose bourne no traveller returns, and that it would be as well to supply the dead with the wherewithal to pay the fare, whether to Charon or any other divine agent. In illustration, and I put it no more strongly, I enclose a copy of Lord Gorell's poem, *I Go A Journey*. In that spirit, perhaps your young man thought 'it would be wisdom to prepare.'

I also enclose, in case it helps give focus to my rambling exploration of your question, John Churcher's address to a PCN Group on what Progressive Christianity is – as he sees it. He is Chairman of PCN. It addresses your question from a slightly different angle, but I suspect we have actually reached very similar positions. John, it seems to me, is working to redefine Progressive Christianity in a way which avoids some of the wishy-washiness of the past. Not easy, but I feel he is beginning to articulate something meaningful. I commend his Website: permissiontospeak.org.uk. Like Spong, he does a weekly sermon, which is always interesting and sometimes provocative! Thank you so much for spurring me into what passes for thought. I wish I had the mental flexibility of my youth. Socrates once remarked in mild irritation to his very clever pupil, Alkibiades, who had thwarted if not defeated him in argument, that 'when I was younger, I used to argue like that.' To which his disciple quickly replied: 'I wish I had known you when you were younger, Socrates'.

CHAPTER THIRTY

Seeking Truth – A Letter

I like this excerpt from Lecky's *Rise and Influence of Rationalism in Europe*, quoted in a slim volume about John Donne, published 1942.

> The question, What is Truth?, has no prospect of obtaining a speedy answer. But the question, What is the Spirit of Truth? may be discussed with much greater prospect of agreement. By the Spirit of Truth, I mean that frame of mind in which men who acknowledge their own fallibility and who desire above all things to discover what is true, should adjudicate between conflicting arguments. ...The persecutor can never be certain that he is not persecuting truth rather than error, but he may be quite certain that he is suppressing the spirit of truth ... Until the 17th century, every mental disposition which philosophy pronounces to be essential to a legitimate research was almost uniformly branded a sin, and a large proportion of the most deadly vices were deliberately inculcated as virtues. It was a sin to doubt the opinions that had been instilled since childhood before they had been examined. It was sinful to study with equal attention and with an indifferent mind the writings on both sides: sinful to resolve to follow the light of evidence wherever it might lead; sinful to remain poised in doubt between conflicting opinions; sinful even to recognise the moral or intellectual excellence of opponents ... A critical and enquiring spirit was the worst form of vice.

I think that sort of persecutor's mentality is what, to their shame, the traditional churches have been lamentably guilty of. The Spirit of Truth was not a quality that they recognised as desirable. But I am not sure that this answers your question about the place of religious tradition in the quest for truth.

Spong had a good letter in one of his weekly circulars, replying to a question from a Minister in the US deep south. The question posed was: 'I struggle with reconciling my 'personal' experience of God, when I can no longer hold to a personal God. How do you, or would you, help a member of a congregation you are serving to understand the dichotomy of progressive religion?'

Spong replied:

' ....I know the mindset of the state and community in which you live and work and I know the struggle that goes on in many clergy between their integrity and their desire not to offend the common wisdom of the world in which they live.

'The first thing you need to do is recognise that for most people religion is not a search for truth, but a search for security. Security is not well served by opening up questions for which there are no answers. You must begin by accepting people where they are. A good pastor, however, does not leave them there forever, for that means they will never grow.

'I would avoid a frontal assault on religious ignorance from the pulpit. A sermon in church does not offer people time to process or space to disagree. They cannot talk back and so they must absorb, resist, or close their minds.'

(Comment by BW - Ironical, isn't it, that the Latin word *sermo* means 'conversation', not lecture – when did you ever hear a sermon that was a conversation between clergy and people?)

'There are other activities that do not have these shortcomings. Study groups, where the standard is that there is no such thing as a 'dumb' question, allow dialogue and growth to take place. A book study group allows the author of the book to be the one raising the issues and thus allows the minister to facilitate the discussion. In newsletters to their congregations I think clergy should write 'think pieces' that invite dialogue and that say, 'Tell me what you think of these ideas.' People will actually read such pieces and they can be the means for opening up deep conversations and significant personal interaction.

'Of course when we say that God is personal, we are not describing God. We are describing our experience of God. Since we are persons, we can receive the transcendent power of life, love, and being only as 'personal'. There is nothing wrong with that. To move from these to a statement about what God actually is, however, is more than any of us should claim. I have never known an honest and open theological attempt to probe the mystery of God to be destructive.' (Quotation ends).

So, to look again at your questions, let's start by misquoting Donne. 'Each man is an island, of itself entire…' yet every man is also 'part of the continent, part of the main. If a clod be washed away, Europe is the less …etc.' That I suppose is one of the paradoxes of life to which you allude. There are many others, such as: God is, allegedly, good – yet he 'allows' abominable evil to permeate our existence. I fish in my memory for the quotation, 'In Ramah a voice is heard of Rachel wailing for her children.' Massacres of innocents, whether in the first Passover or elsewhere, are common enough in the name of God. The OT God in some ways rather resembles Auden's *Epitaph on a Tyrant*, doesn't he?

> Perfection, of a kind, was what he was after,
> And the poetry he invented was easy to understand;
> He knew human folly like the back of his hand,
> And was greatly interested in armies and fleets;
> When he laughed, respectable senators burst with laughter,
> And when he cried the little children died in the streets.

It is the last line that is the heart of a savage truth, with its variation on Motley's famous epitaph on William of Orange in the *Fall of the Dutch Republic*. 'As long as he lived he was the guiding star of a whole brave nation; and when he died the little children cried in the streets.' (En passant - When did you last hear of a Prime Minister of whom that could be said? I do remember one: Churchill.)

The combination of the two quotations points up again one of life's endless paradoxes. Perhaps like Shelley's Prometheus it is our lot 'to suffer wrongs which hope thinks infinite', and loneliness is part of it, since we are, to some degree at least, and inevitably,

> alone, alone, all, all alone,
> alone on a wide, wide sea.

Whatever our ties of love, family, friends and affections, we must to a degree make our own way and make up our own minds. Come the moment of death and we will stand naked and alone before the judgement seat, though whether of God or Man remains to be seen.

As for the problem of how we of the human race can support each other - we are all to greater or lesser degree surrounded by the help and support of those same family, friends and affections. They can offer us comfort, help, and even hope. And hope is something we all need, even though as the Greek proverb has it, 'Hope is a bad guide – but a good companion on the way.' Which of us would spurn such companionship on a long journey? Religion is one purveyor of hope for us all, however uncertain..

Perhaps the truth of it all is that Life is all Paradox – and perhaps Truth is too. Meanwhile I think Arnold's bleakly beautiful *Dover Beach* offers the only answer - until we find a better.

> Ah, love, let us be true
> To one another! For the world which seems
> To lie before us like a land of dreams,
> So various, so beautiful, so new,
> Hath really neither joy, nor love, nor light,
> Nor certitude, nor peace, nor help for pain;
> And we are here as on a darkling plain
> Swept with confused alarms of struggle and flight,
> Where ignorant armies clash by night.

So in answer to your question I can only reply – as you did to me – that it is to a degree always a private and lonely journey. Perhaps this is part of the power of religion, that it offers us the appearance of comfort and support on the way, while other helpers fail and comforts flee.

CHAPTER THIRTY-ONE

Three Wise Men

A Tribute to Religious Mentors

Cromlyn was the nom-de-plume (and sometimes nom-de-guerre) of Canon John Barry, whose weekly column in the *Church of Ireland Gazette* for some fifty years, never lost sight of one of the basic obligations of the church – to comfort the afflicted, and (even more important) to afflict the comfortable. He was for some years our Rector and always a much loved family friend.

In October 2005 he wrote an article in which he reminisced about Archbishop Michael Ramsey and Archbishop John A.F. Gregg, my grandfather, mentioning en passant both my parents, and making reference also to myself, and my recently published book, *A Faith Unfaithful.*

I wrote to him in acknowledgement of his generous comments, and I include the letter I wrote, as a tribute to him and others too, who in one way or another, have been my sort of unofficial mentors. I hope it also illustrates how important it is that Clergy are seen as intellectually alive and flexible as well as spiritually profound. I have been very lucky in some of the Church of Ireland clergy I have known, especially John Barry himself, Canon Eric Elliott, Robin Eames who, when he was still a humble curate, was the only preacher who regularly impressed our family by alluding to the books he was reading, and Canon John Brown, who was chaplain of my old Cambridge College and later Professor of Pastoral Theology at TCD, and Warden of the Church of Ireland Divinity Hostel.

In the article to which I allude, Cromlyn described Michael Ramsey's glorious reaction to a question put to him by a member of his audience. 'Your Grace, are you not greatly depressed... by the criticisms being directed nowadays against the Church, perhaps even fearful that it might not continue to exist?'

For a full column Cromlyn proceeded to describe at length, and in affectionate and enormously entertaining detail, the physical and facial contortions of the Archbishop's reaction. Anyone who knew him will recognise the symptoms immediately. The climax was perfectly contrived, for John was a literary craftsman to his fingertips. I quote: 'The gathering watched and waited in mixed astonishment and alarm – until, to almost audible sighs of relief on their part, the great man spoke.

Do you really think that the Church as we know it might pass away? The foundations be shaken? And God bring in something entirely new? Oh splendid, splendid! I do hope

142

you are right.

'And the most remarkable thing about it all,' Cromlyn remarked, 'was that this dear, lovable, saintly and clever man meant every word of it.'

In the same article Cromlyn also reported to his readers that my grandfather had expressed similar sentiments to a clerical friend, when he had remarked that, 'it may be that the true mission of the Church is to disappear.'

Cromlyn's final comment says all that needs to be said about the Church and its present predicament:

> Not only Ramsey of Canterbury, but Gregg of Armagh, (two men now estimated to have been giants in both mental and spiritual capacity), had both of them been saying, each in his own way, exactly the same thing. So do you not think we should sit up and pay heed?

I have to say that I see little sign that the church leadership has even begun to rise to the challenge. This was my letter:

Dear John,

My Sister, Audrey, has just sent me the latest Cromlyn article, and it would be less than human of me if I did not confess to a degree of pleasure (or pride?? *Absit omen*, for that would be a cardinal not a merely venial sin) at the kind observations you made about me and my book. You gilded the Wilson lily somewhat, but over the years most of us have suffered the opposite fate rather more often and are grateful for the occasional and much more palatable experience of being gilded rather than plastered with the mud that sticks – and sometimes stinks. So thank you so much for all that you said.

But I really wanted to say what pleasure and interest the main theme of your essay gave me. I had not heard the Ramsey story and it is a wonderful reinforcement of grandfather's 'prophecy'. England is an increasingly pagan place, but in a funny sort of way it remains more civilised than N. Ireland, where religious certainties too often reinforce (but are not the cause of) racial intolerance. But really the church here does seem to most an irrelevance, even though in our own small village I notice that it is the church community that sustains most of the village's activities, secular as well as sacred. But people don't see it until they lose it. And our congregations are growing old. As for our arcane arguments over women priests, forms of worship or whatever, most people could not care less.

I was totally caught by your absolutely delightful description of Michael Ramsey's reaction to the proposition that the church might cease to exist. It was a lovely piece of writing and so beautifully exact and accurately observed that Sara and I both felt a moment of enchanted recognition at the description of the facial spasms and eyebrow elevation and then the sublimely lucid and deceptively simple response. My test of a great mind has always been that he/she writes with such simplicity that you think to yourself 'I could have said that…' until you realise that you couldn't – not in a hundred years. I have to contrast Ramsey's wonderful lucidity in his writings and utterances with the sometimes incomprehensible observations of his present successor.

I thought you would enjoy hearing how closely we were both able to recognise the accuracy of your description of the Ramsey shoulders, face and eyebrows. Forgive a slightly long-winded background – but it helps, and of course my advancing years allow me the privilege of anec-dotage before I lapse into mere dotage. When I was at King's Canterbury the Ramseys used to come down to Canterbury at weekends whenever possible, and to an extent he 'adopted' the boys' boarding house, where I was then house tutor. The boys adored them....

....As a result of a series of other connections as well, (my mother and Joan Ramsey went to the same school), we were occasionally bidden to the Old Palace to lunch with the Ramseys. On one memorable occasion our Anna, aged perhaps 2 or 3, climbed into Michael's chair at the head of the table and sat there quite determined to enjoy her meal from that elevated position. Only someone with your genius for observation could have described the scene, the eyebrows working overtime, the palpable discomfort of not knowing how to handle it, the inability to yield his place to Anna despite Joan saying 'come on Michael, don't be so silly', and then the utter distress on his face when Sara simply removed Anna to her designated seat and the child burst into howls and tears. I am sure the terrible thought ran through sweet Michael's head that 'whosoever shall offend one of these my little ones, it were better that a millstone ......etc'. He was a dear man, a great and holy leader of the church, and we have not seen his like since then – in my opinion. Owen Chadwick's biography does him some justice and gave me great pleasure. But it was lovely to read your description, which caught the true flavour of the man, and your recognition of his greatness.

Back to Hillsborough: What are the things that influence us in our lives? My dear father, perhaps for reasons of health, could not sustain a discussion. When contradicted he turned it instantly into an argument and tended to lose his temper when disagreed with. He thought I spent too much time reading and never really forgave me for becoming a schoolmaster. So the exploration of ideas and the pursuit of truth was not an easy thing when he was around. With mother, who loved an intellectual challenge, it was quite different. She was rational, wonderfully well read, highly intelligent, articulate, blessed with a philosophical cast of mind, and of course cleverer than dad, which he found quite difficult to take.

But non-family role models were, therefore, invaluable in my youth, when I confess to having rather feared my father. It was enormously encouraging to find people who were prepared to argue dispassionately, to relish challenge, and not to take contradiction as a denial of their authority. People like you and John Brown, John Crooks and Eric Elliot, made far more difference to a developing mind that you can ever realise. When heads that are older and wiser than your own are willing to take you seriously, despite your youth, and take the time to explain, expound, argue, explore, it is a huge help to one's development.

So when you wonder whether the grilling you say you sustained from me over the coffee cups helped, I can assure you it did, though I have little doubt that I was sometimes a pain in the neck. I have sat at the feet of a number of Gamaliels and it is remarkable to me how many of them seem to have been ordained ministers, all of them men with flexible minds, whose very flexibility did more for the credibility of the church than the 'certainties' of their (dare I suggest?) rather less able colleagues and alleged superiors.

From quite early on matters theological seem to have engaged my attention and though I have no doubt that many of my more fundamentalist brethren will have long since consigned me to the flames of hell, I have a sure conviction that the Almighty will give some credit for trying very hard to work things out and to use a God-given mind in the effort to do so. I still think that the line in Robert Bolt's *Man for All Seasons* says it all: 'Man was born to serve God in the tangle of his mind.'

Of course intellect is not all – indeed goodness and holiness undoubtedly matter more. But unless the faith is underpinned by intellectual credibility as well, it must be built upon crumbling foundations. And it is my fear that those foundations are currently crumbling and we need to find a new way to express old truths, and within those truths to distinguish between what is metaphor and what literal, and then to have the courage to discard stale or outmoded metaphors, and 'truths' that have become implausible.

It may be that the church's mission is to disappear and though I would not quite have Ramsey's courage and rejoice at it, I have to say that much of what it says and does leads me to concede that if it disappears, it will have got what it deserves. However, like Yeats, I wait for some new revelation and some 'rough beast slouching towards Bethlehem to be born.'

Of one thing at least we can be entirely certain. If there is a God, he must by definition be benevolent and omniscient and, though of this I am less certain, all-powerful, and therefore without doubt he has the matter well in hand and fully understands the agony of those watchmen that wait for the morning.

Thank you again for your generosity and kindness and for our long, long association and friendship.

Ne Oblivisceris (Lest ye forget)

A private tribute to the mentors and friends outside my immediate family who over the years have helped or inspired me in my religious wanderings, some by their friendship, some by question or challenge, whether in letter or discussion, some by example, counsel, or instruction, and some perhaps by a single insight or perceptive comment, which threw a flash of light into darker places.

Those whose books have done me similar service are 'remembered' in the Bibliography. But here I record my private debt and gratitude to many others, not all of whom would have shared my views. But civilised argument and discussion is the best possible agent for evolving thought and ideas. Doubtless with unintended omissions due to a failing memory, I list them in alphabetical order, without style or title....

John Barry, George Biddle, Austin Boggis, John Brown, Jock Burnet, Patrick Carey, John Churcher, Roger Clayton Jones, John Crooks, Hugh Dawes, Raymond Davies, Roy Davies, Eric Elliot, David Erskine, John Evans, Moses Finley, Cathy Horder, Pat Johns, Simon Langdale, Catherine Llewellyn Evans, Godfrey Marshall, Don McClen, Richard Meredith, Francis Miles, Hilary Morrison, Peter Newell, John Nelson, Fraser Old, Robin Pittman, George Quin, S.S. Sopwith (S'pwith), John Southwell, Norman Thompson, Andy Vivian, John Young.

> From quiet homes and first beginning
> Out to the undiscovered ends,
> There's nothing worth the wear of winning
> Save laughter and the love of friends.
>
> G.K. Chesterton

Section E: Explorations - Moving Forward

Life is not hurrying
On to a receding future, nor hankering after
An imagined past. It is the turning
Aside like Moses to the miracle
Of the lit bush, to a brightness
That seemed as transitory as your youth
Once, but is the eternity that awaits you.

R.S. Thomas – *The Bright Field*

The heading for this section is surely self-explanatory. It is all very well to complain about the state of the world – or the Church – as it is. But unless you try to find something better to put in its place, your negativity is self-defeating and ultimately meaningless.

But every journey, whether for pilgrim or traveller, begins with a single step; and to a considerable extent each succeeding step is the point of the whole exercise.

As Constantine Cavafy suggests in his poem, *Ithaka*, meaning is to be found in the journey rather than the destination, and of course in the 'turnings aside' at each encounter with the 'miracle of the lit bush.' Whatever the journey, it must be made in the course of our mortal lives and our search for God must be conducted in terms and concepts appropriate to our contemporary humanity. If there is a life after death, it will be pure bonus. It will, also surely take some form of which we cannot conceive. And so:

> When you set out for Ithaka
> Ask that your way be long,
> Full of adventure, full of instruction....
>
> Have Ithaka always in your mind.
> Your arrival there is what you are destined for.
> But don't in the least hurry the journey.
> Better it last for years,
> so that when you reach the island you are old,
> rich with all that you have gained on the way,
> not expecting Ithaka to give you wealth.
> Ithaka gave you the splendid journey.
> Without her you would not have set out.
> She hasn't anything else to give you.
> And if you find her poor, Ithaka hasn't deceived you.
> So wise have you become, of such experience,
> That already you'll have understood what these Ithakas mean.

The symbolism of *Ithaka* for a Christian would make an excellent subject for any group discussion.

As I have already explained, whatever my doubts about the existence of God, I accept it for the time being as a working hypothesis. His existence – or non-existence – can only be asserted; it can never be proved. It is inevitably a matter of faith. But, the real enemy of Faith is not Doubt but Certainty. Faith is an act of the will, a determination to accept the possibility of God and, whatever one's reservations, to live one's life on that assumption. Doubt is Faith's ultimate supporting weapon – it keeps faith flexible, open to changing circumstances and new ideas. Certainty is Faith's supreme enemy and the source of its inevitable destruction. Hope is Faith's best companion and support. There is a Greek proverb, which says that 'Hope is a bad guide, but a good companion on the way.' Faith needs the companionship of Hope, not Certainty. St Paul said something similar, when he remarked that, 'Faith is the substance of things hoped for; the evidence of things not seen.'

I make no attempt to define or describe the God of my uncertainty, but I suspect that in the work of poets and dramatists we may find a language with which to express our sense of his presence, of our surprised awareness of the numinous, a belief in his abiding love, a means of describing the awe and wonder with which we contemplate the earthly manifestations of divinity, in whatever form they are vouchsafed to us.

Duns Scotus Erigena (fl.850 AD) once described theology as 'a kind of poetry.'

Certainly, it seems to me that, when it seeks to give some account of the Divine Being, theology is more akin to poetry than it is to science. How else can we hope to speak of God other than in the language of metaphor and analogy, beauty and wonder – and such language is surely poets' business? In Section F, which is a sort of Appendix to this volume, I set out my own collection of 'sound bites' which illustrate my ideas on poetry and its signposts to the idea of God - again the analogy of the journey or pilgrimage is apparent.

In a sermon once at Pangbourne College I suggested that the quark may be a useful metaphor for our sense of God. Scientists tell us that the more accurately you try to measure the position of a quark, the less accurately you can measure its speed or energy, because the quantum of light needed to carry out the measurement will disturb the particle it is trying to measure. In plain English, you can tell where a Quark is, or what it is doing, but not both. Which sounds a bit like God. You may know him by his works; you may sense him by his presence. You cannot do both at the same time – and you can never see him, except metaphorically.

Recently a very old friend of the family sent me a copy of the visitor's guide to the church of St Stephen's, Walbrook, in the City of London. In that fascinating small leaflet I found this suggestive passage, which offers another metaphor which may help the pilgrim on his way. Writing of Christopher Wren, the church's architect, the author wrote, that:

> He considered geometry to be the basis of the whole world and the manifestation of its Creator, while light not only made that geometry visible but also represented the gift of Reason, of which geometry for him was the highest expression. Like the solution to a mathematical problem, everything fits into place with apparent simplicity; yet this simplicity itself is mysterious and magical.... Life outside is complicated and chaotic. To enter St Stephen's is not to escape into fantasy; rather it is to submit to the strongest positive assertion of the order of the universe.

Aristotle, I think it was, who had carved above the doorway of his School of philosophy the motto, 'Let no man enter here who knows not his Geometry,' while Thomas Hobbes in his Leviathan remarked that 'Geometry is the only science that it hath pleased God hitherto to bestow on mankind.' Of course these are only metaphors – but metaphor is all we have in our striving to express the inexpressible.

Words always fail us, but then, as Simone Weil once said, 'God can only be present in creation under the form of absence,' an idea that recurs constantly in the poetry of R.S. Thomas. And there is still what the medieval mystics called the Apophatic Way, the way of silence, which may turn out to be the best approach of all. As I think St Augustine is said to have observed, 'God welcomes his children by whatever road they come.' No-one has the right map; no-one knows the secret pathway. All any of us can do is take the first step. What I have called Explorations are my own poor attempts to keep on with the journey. The title is pretentious; the result, limited. But it is a start.

CHAPTER THIRTY-TWO

The Church in Twenty Years' Time?

(Responses to my Vicar's Questions)

First Response:

Your email asked about my vision of what 'the Church' might be in twenty years' time. To that I have no useful answer. What follows is a very tentative idea about what perhaps could happen. But I have to say that twenty years is far too short a time scale for anything much to happen. I was lamenting all this thirty years ago and little has happened since then except Anglican women priests.

So my vision of the institutional church in twenty years time is that it will be much as now, but even less so - with fewer clergy, predominantly women, smaller and even older congregations, existing relatively harmlessly (and therefore tolerated) on the margins of an even more secular society, which will be even more inclined to listen to its pronouncements with mild amusement, but willing enough to respect its individual members not for their faith, but for the way in which their lives are lived.

There will be small pockets of committed Christians struggling, as now, to work out what it is that Jesus has to say to our modern age. Corporate worship will still occur on high days and holy days and moments of short-lived national emotion. It will help people feel a little better about things, or about themselves, but will not be seen to have any further bearing on their everyday lives. Sunday worship will occupy a tiny minority. There will be a (very) few women bishops, who will certainly not dare to bring in the revolution we require, because they must establish their credibility first with the faithful few.

The best hope will be that all the diehard feminists and traditionalist clergy will have defected to Rome and the time may become right for a real revolution, with the purified Anglican church leading the way, under a second generation female archbishop of Canterbury. By then pigs will have learned to fly.

Second response:

As I said, if the issues are difficult, then we may assume there are no easy answers. One needs long conversations to try and tease out the various strands of a deeply complex problem.

Much hangs, too, on where we are coming from. My recent reading of the early history of the faith (pre-church) is partly motivated by exactly the same feeling as yours – ambivalence about the institutional church, as it now is, and which I have been sceptical about for the last thirty years (my initial misprint 'thirsty years' is deeply telling), as is made clear by my various addresses in my previous incarnation to Church of Ireland audiences, including a diocesan study-day for clergy convened by the Bishop.

In my desire to make up my mind about what really mattered, I wanted very much to get some idea of what it was that set the whole thing going – what were the essential elements in those very early activities (30-50 AD, say) that presumably gave the early Christian-Jewish communities the impetus to carry on in the face of apparent disaster. That might help me to decide what ought to be important still in the institutional church that evolved from it.

I discount, not as a piece of gratuitous provocation, I assure you, but simply for the purpose of the argument, any supernatural intervention by a God who wanted to make it all happen and planned it all to turn out as it did: if he really did intervene in this way, he made a shockingly bad fist of it, until an efficient Rome took over under Constantine, with its military power and superior secular administration – and wrecked the whole thing. So my account of it all is not intended as a comment about my belief in a divinity – I am still in fact comfortable with the possibility, difficult though he sometimes makes it.

Crossan has predictably influenced my understanding of the period and indeed modified somewhat my rather optimistic view of the benefits of the Roman empire. His *The Birth of Christianity* and his *The Historical Jesus* both attempt to pull together the insights of modern anthropology, sociology, archaeology, history, as well as religious textual criticism, in his evaluation of the gospel record and of the original story that underlies that record. From all this he tries to give us one (but not the only) coherent account of what may have happened then. I felt it was sufficiently interesting to wish to keep his broad argument in my head and I wrote up a summary of it of some 35 pages, including a 4 page account of what I concluded had probably happened.

I was struck by certain features of his reading of the period, which of course I may have misunderstood or oversimplified. This is how it seemed to me.

1. Jesus' mission was a limited mission - to the destitute and dispossessed, the marginalised, the demoralised and the desperate. It is at least quite likely that he was one of them. In that he spoke also to the comfortable and prosperous, it was to remind them of the ancient Jewish concept of Justice and their obligations to the poor and needy. He had little time for the authorities of the established religious set-up (how very modern !).

2. It was primarily a response to the exploitation by the Roman authorities (Herod Antipas in particular) of the whole area and the effects of increasing Roman taxation on the peasant economy, which had always lived on the margins and was becoming increasingly desperate. (This is a picture common to almost all the Roman empire and indeed peasant economies almost everywhere – cruel exploitation by Roman officials to raise taxes for Rome and large profits for themselves, often to fund a political career and/ or ostentatious life style).

3. It was also a mission to Jews specifically, not gentiles, and to rural Galilee in particular – at least until the final week or so.
4. It is in some ways quite difficult to see what was new about Jesus' ethical teaching, compared to what he would have believed in anyhow as a practising Jew. It also seems to me that Jesus largely articulated a pretty conventional Jewish idea of God, as conceived by the later prophets.
5. In fact in this respect there was little original in his teaching; but he reminded Jews of the best of traditional and prophetic teaching and their nation's absolute commitment to Justice.
6. The originality lay in his living and in the fact that he gave to the expendable class of Jewish society a wholly new sense of their own belonging. (You have to read Crossan to see what I mean by 'expendable class,' but in crude terms those at the very bottom of the ladder).
7. His mission clearly seemed to be a threat to some of the establishment and they contrived, probably without any difficulty, to have him executed as a threat to public order and the Pax Romana.
8. Two centres of activity emerged after his death: the first was in Galilee, promoting through itinerant preachers its ideal of living like Jesus. Inevitably this was asking too much for many and a dialectic emerged between the 'have-nots' (totally dispossessed) and the 'haves' (peasants, poor but still in possession of their small holdings), whereby the 'haves' offered hospitality in return for healing from the 'have-nots', not so much cures for sickness, as a healing of social distress occasioned by economic deprivation and the realisation of a new type of sharing-community.
9. The second centre of activity was in Jerusalem, a group of followers of The Way, rigidly committed to the Jewishness of the new movement, and formed of a small community of the *ptochoi*, the Poor Ones. They lived a communal life, sharing all things along the lines of Qumran and other communities elsewhere, but probably much more purist and fanatical. Their focus was on the expected Second Coming and the meaning of Jesus' Death and his Resurrection. This was led by the original apostles, especially James and Peter and, initially at least, their authority over the whole movement was significant.
10. Other communities evolved elsewhere with their own emphases and rules. The *Didache* illustrates the way in which they adjusted or modified the strict interpretation of the Jesus Code (for want of a better phrase) to the realities of community living.
11. Common to both traditions, therefore, is the idea of community and sharing of possessions, plus some form of shared eucharistic commemorative meal – never just a ritual or symbolic sip of wine or sliver of bread. 'After supper he took the cup' – it always involved a proper shared meal to which all contributed what they could, though in the Roman tradition it could also be a patronal meal provided by a rich benefactor. But it was to be shared by all and equally: that was where the Corinthians went wrong.

What does this suggest to me ?

1. Everyone understood about temples, but the early movement never had any. Churches were (and are ?) unnecessary. Indeed the Jesus community, if we may call it that, was a community of believers as a whole, who were seen to be the new Temple, not made with hands.

Comment: The really vital worshipping community when I lived in Wantage seemed to me to be the Open Church (I can't remember what they called themselves) which met every Sunday in the civic hall. Again, no church. In Norwich last week a cleric we met in the cathedral told us that churches with tiny congregations were a real problem and very difficult to close. 'Fortunately,' he said, 'we are a very rich diocese and we seem to be able to sustain them all.' I think he said there were 600. Perhaps wealth is in the eye of the beholder; never normally acknowledged by the possessor.

Conclusion: Our buildings are an incubus about our necks. We should call the nation's bluff and offer them all over to English Heritage or the National Trust, and if they won't keep them going, we should let them fall down. I exaggerate to make a general point.

2. The early community had no priests initially: Paul earned his living as best he could as a tent maker; others as fishermen, tradesmen or peasant smallholders.

Comment: Priests make religion professional and have a vested interest in keeping as much as possible to themselves. They are an unnecessary encumbrance. Again, this is not personal: some of my best friends are or were priests, and I admire their ministry.

Conclusion: I am exaggerating to make the general point that if there were no priests, we would be thrown back on communal resources which would empower or compel the local communities to find their own way to God.

3. Worship was originally simple and unstructured. A real meal – not a ritual or symbolic activity.

Comment: worship has become standardised and its language unhelpful – or meaningless – to many. The obsession with the Eucharist has emphasised one small supernatural element of the original corporate worship, at the expense of what really mattered – the shared and common meal, with a symbolic act of remembrance at the beginning and/or the end. What mattered was the shared meal. The community eating together. Remember Pliny: 'the sum total of their <the Christians'> guilt or error amounted to this – they met regularly before dawn on a fixed day to chant verses alternately among themselves in honour of Christ, as if to a god, and also to bind themselves by oath, not for any criminal purpose, but to abstain from theft, robbery, and adultery, to commit no breach of trust and not to deny a deposit when called upon to restore it. After this ceremony it had been their custom to disperse and reassemble later to take food of an ordinary harmless kind.'

Conclusion: this sounds to me rather Jewish – integrity in one's daily life plus a reinforcement of the sense of community by eating together. House churches might be similar. It seems much more wholesome than today.

4. The earliest Christians were itinerant dispossessed, mutually supporting each other with whatever meagre resources they could and finding in that sharing a sense of community which gave them hope, meaning, and a sense of God in their midst.

Comment: The early Jesus mission was a mission to the socially and economically marginalised. A modern Servant Church should return to a similar role and leave the main citizen body to the tender mercies of the Welfare State – which is, after all, a very Christian invention.

Conclusion: A Christian life is to be lived out in the community, not within the church. Instead of compelling them to come in, we should be compelling ourselves to get out. Church membership is irrelevant and a good Christian life can and should be lived outside as well as within it.

Third response:

Having written my 'essay', I re-read your e-mail and realised that I had not really addressed your questions, which put the other side of the dilemma, which we share. There is force behind your questions. But because I believe strongly in the dialectic process as a way of struggling towards the truth, let me simply put the other side of the argument. Here goes:

1. You say that, *'If the church was really as rich as people think it is....'*
   It is probably richer – still. It owns huge quantities of real estate in the centres of cities, towns and villages – usually with churches built on top of them. It has vast investments, though in its greed in the 90's it allowed its advisers to squander quite a lot – if I believed in an interventionist deity, I would suspect that he organised the losses to teach the church a much needed lesson. It pays out vast quantities in salaries and pensions, not just to clergy (of whom there are far too many) but to its administrators and for doubtful activities such as running schools. It maintains a ludicrously excessive infrastructure of buildings, palaces etc. No secular company would ever run like that. Your current preoccupation with buildings illustrates my point.
2. You say that, *'Without an Institution, would there be no framework for passing on the faith.'*
   Can you seriously argue that the Institution passed on the Faith? It has constantly reinvented and redefined the Faith, and arguably it has distorted

its essentials in such a way that it is a fair assumption that Jesus, if he returned to earth, would not recognise either himself or the faith he founded. The Roman Catholic branch of Christianity is the worst offender, but then it has been going the longest. It needs a reformation of its own. My own interest in the very early period of Christianity derives from the perception that there may be merit in trying to get back to first principles and ditching the subsequent clutter.

3. You ask whether *'the good done in the name of the church would still happen.'*
    An awful lot of good within communities goes on without any help from the church. Where need arises, it is not just the churches that respond. Sara always cites a local couple as an example of this; their mission and service to the whole community is extraordinary and deeply Christian. But they are not church goers, as far as we know. A neighbour, who devotedly looks after a handicapped wife, is for me 'an ensample of godly life' without any reference to the church. The church has no monopoly of goodness within communities and may well siphon off resources and energies that could be better deployed elsewhere. That said, I acknowledge readily how much good the members of our own church do in and for the community.

4. You ask, *'Would the Christian voice have an influence on the nation?'*
    The blunt reply is to ask, 'should it ?', given its lamentable track record in resisting change and improvement – again I blame the Roman Catholic Church more than the Anglican. Does the church have much influence at the moment ? The sometimes incomprehensible Rowan and the (to me) gimmicky Sentamu have no impact on me whatever!

5. *What difference it would make if the whole church disappeared overnight?*
    My fear is that the honest answer is: much less than you might think.

I do apologise if this again sounds as if I am full of anger. I am not. I am full of sorrow. This is the church I grew up in, and loved, not least for the sake of my beloved Archbishop grandfather. I would dearly love to see things differently and I cannot let it go for all my criticisms. When I wrote to the bishop recently to ask for a mission to the marginalised (like me), he ultimately replied that he saw no need for it. You do try very hard and patiently with me; I am probably beyond salvation.

CHAPTER THIRTY-THREE

Poetry

Deus escreve direito por linhas tortas – God uses crooked lines to write straight

Claudel

My first attempt to set out some of my ideas on the subject was an article in the Quarterly Newsletter of the Progressive Christianity Network (PCN) in March 2009. When in the same year I was asked by my own North Somerset PCN Group to introduce a discussion of poetry, with readings by members of their favourite poems, I suggested the broad theme of 'Poetry as a Pathway to God.' I adapted my original article for my talk to the Group.

The consequences of these two initial forays were, first, an invitation to give a similar talk to the very active, and formidably lively, Exeter PCN Group. There followed an invitation to be one of the speakers at the annual conference of Spectrum, a Methodist organisation dedicated to Study, Prayer, Exploration, Reflection and Theology. The theme of the Conference was 'Beyond Words: Re-imagining Faith,' with the sub-title, 'Theology and the Creative Arts.' Much of the material in this section derives from these events.

Ever since I started my first Commonplace Book at the age of fifteen, I have collected (amongst many other pieces) definitions, descriptions, and observations on Poetry. For my first talk, I circulated to members beforehand a selection of these, as a suggested focus for their choice of poems and a stimulus to discussion. I then used a wider range of the same material as handouts for my Spectrum talks.

I am by profession an ancient historian – in both senses of the word; my disrespectful children would probably say 'very ancient.' But I am by inclination a student of literature, with poetry and drama perhaps my first loves; and low-level theology has always been a hobby. And now I find with mild surprise that in old age these three interests have somehow begun to coalesce.

My increasing problems with traditional Christianity have much to do with an historian's concern for evidence and the absolute impossibility of taking the Bible literally. Even as an undergraduate, I was beginning to find the description of Thucydides as *mythistoricus* (i.e. a 'myth-historian') apposite when applied even to the Gospel writers. Classical studies led me to believe that there was little really new in many of the Bible stories – they were transparently mythical, with a veneer of history over the top. (Jesus' teaching is an entirely different matter). But of course myth is a richer form of truth than mere fact. As Stephen Verney says, 'myth is a story which has universal significance and yields up a deeper meaning at every stage of human history. It is a story which nobody has invented, but which has arisen out of the depths of human experience.'

As one who loved poetry, I have long felt that the poet sees more deeply, more accurately, and far more sensitively into the world around us, and that poetic truth is something rather more profound than so-called literal, historical truth. To be literal-minded is often to be superficial, unimaginative, and dull – albeit at times it is a regrettable necessity. To be poetic is to add whole new dimensions to experience by making, as it were, magical connections. Inevitably in time I reached the obvious conclusion that poetic truth and mythical truth are almost one, and that religious truth is closer to both than to any other mode of expression. For, to quote Sir Philip Sydney, 'myth is a tale which holds children from their play and old men from the chimney corner.'

There was nothing very original in this, except perhaps for one who, like me, was a very conventional believer for his first twenty years of life, until at last I began to think for myself. But in a sense I suspect that intuitively I began to perceive what others had long thought. I have no idea where I found for my commonplace book the quotation from Duns Scotus in the 9th century that 'Theology is a kind of poetry,' but it is gratifying to find that I had at last caught up with the older theologians unaided. Increasingly I find that I have been walking the same pathway as some of the more modern ones also.

Poetry is profoundly metaphorical – you could almost define it as 'truth expressed as metaphor.' Interestingly in his book, '*Reading the Bible Again for the First Time*', Marcus Borg states explicitly that 'the Bible is a combination of history and metaphor,' and that 'the ancient communities which produced the Bible often metaphorized (his word) their history. This is the way they invested their stories with meaning.'

I hope that this preliminary set of observations explains why I suggested that we try to pick poems that express for each of us the thought behind the three thematic ideas: 'Beauty is truth, truth beauty'; 'Poetry is a Greater Truth'; and 'Poetry as a pathway to God.'

Let me now focus on poetry. Ezra Pound once famously remarked that, 'poets are the antennae of the race'. It is not the function of the poet to deal in facts, to record information, nor (usually) to report events. That is the task of the duller species of historian or of the journalist - an altogether humbler trade. But as any insect will tell you, antennae are essential if you want to sense where you are heading and to identify where you want to go and also what opportunities or dangers lurk ahead. Poets are in the business of sensing things for the benefit of all of us.

If a reader seeks to know not so much what happened at any given point in the past, or even why it happened, but rather what it felt like at the time, what were the responses and perceptions of sensitive and articulate contemporaries (the 'antennae people') to the events in which their lives were inextricably entangled, then the poet's value is considerable. Could we, for example, fully understand the enormity of the suffering of the First World War without the War Poets? Or the intensity of the feelings of Irish Nationalism without Yeats? Or the pain of exile for the Jews without the psalms, which are traditionally, but unhistorically, attributed to the much earlier King David.

Poets deal in perceptions, insights, moods, emotions, responses, desires, hopes, fears. Historical and journalistic virtues, such as accuracy, objectivity, comprehensiveness, balance, exactness (save of language) are not for them. The poet's virtues are: ambiguities, suggestiveness, compression to the point of obscurity, image and association, echo and overtone, implication not explication, metaphor, simile, symbol, intensity of feeling. In short his whole task is to make connections – not least connections between the seen and the unseen, between the visible world that we touch and see and the invisible world, which we experience through imagination and express through metaphor, and which believers see through faith – in fact connections between earth and heaven. In essence poetry is metaphorical expression, and in poetry, to quote Ortega y Gasset, 'metaphor is something whose efficacy verges on magic, and it seems a tool for creation which God forgot inside one of his creatures'.

No-one would think of asking a poet to write only what is literally true. So, if the Bible is at least as much myth as history – or as Borg puts it, history metaphorized, - and if myth is, as he also suggests, poetry plus, not factuality minus, then the Bible is arguably more akin to poetry than history, and similarly, theology is arguably a poetic activity, as Duns Scotus suggested. So the message is clear: if you want to think theologically, think poetically; if you want to say anything meaningful about God and religion, speak poetically (i.e. metaphorically). Plato, who was a fine poet as well as a philosopher, said much the same: there comes a time, he argues, when logical argument runs out – and then you must have recourse to myth. And for myth, poetry, or at least poetic language, is the proper mode of expression.

When I was working on a source book for undergraduate and A Level students of the reign of the emperor Augustus, I had no difficulty in persuading my directing editor that we must have a section of material from the Roman poets, even though this was a history book. I included a short essay in defence of poetry as historical source material. But now I find that what I wrote about poetry as source material seems to me surprisingly similar to what Borg says when talking about how we should read the Bible.

He recommends what he calls 'a state of post-critical naivety', reading it metaphorically, hearing it as a series of true stories, even as one knows at the same time that they may not be factually true. It's like the classic schoolboy definition of faith as 'the power to believe what you know isn't true' and reminds one uncomfortably of George Orwell's Double-Think in his novel *1984*, but I can see the point Borg is trying to make.

He goes on to say that 'Israel's primal narrative combines historical memory with metaphorical narrative… but the metaphorical approach needs controls… which are provided in part by the historical approach (that is, as I understand it, an understanding of the historical context) and in part by the discernment of the community to which the interpretation is offered. In short the historical and metaphorical approaches need each other.'

In similar vein in my brief essay, I had suggested that, 'Always we must read with care. We must take the poets in the context of their time - a time in which men had grown tired of civil war and turned to Octavian/Augustus as to a god, in gratitude for the gift of peace and as the source of inspiration for old values restored and new ideals espoused. (As a contemporary parallel, think of the Obama effect, though that is of course so far an expression of hope for the future rather than of gratitude for the past). To such feeling the poets helped to give expression.' Like the prophets and psalmists of the Jews, they were speaking to and for their time, but what they had to say had relevance for all time – as great art always should.

Virgil was regarded as an honorary Christian by the Middle Ages; Dante used him as his escort through the Inferno, and in his fourth Eclogue (40 BC), for example, Virgil tells of the birth of a child who will usher in the Age of Gold, in language that could have come from Isaiah. The coincidence with the approaching birth of Jesus influenced the more simple minded to call it the Messianic Eclogue, while earlier scholars often thought, also wrongly, that it referred to the anticipated birth of a son to the emperor Augustus, even though at that date he was still called Octavian and was little more than a successful revolutionary leader. But the poem speaks, always, of the hope enshrined in every new generation and symbolised (or in Borg-speak, metaphorized) by every new birth - the hope that as a species, a nation, a family, next time we will do better. In that respect its message at least is indeed Messianic. Writing a little later, the poet Horace tells us that Augustus will become a God, and like Julius Caesar, his adoptive father, he will ascend into heaven and be seated at the right hand of Jupiter. That was how they thought then – it was not simply court flattery. Augustus was indeed deified, and like Julius Caesar, Alexander the Great, and Pompey before him, he was widely worshipped as a god in the eastern parts of the Roman Empire. To us, of course, it seems fanciful nonsense; and I doubt very much if the poets really believed it. But it was true, metaphorically, even if they knew it was untrue literally. And it was certainly a true reflection of popular feeling. The poetry gave expression to a genuine and deep feeling of contemporary gratitude.

'So what is truth?' asked jesting Pilate, 'and would not stay for an answer.' Back to Poetry. As Robert Frost says, 'poetry is what gets lost in translation', and it is the poetic dimension, the metaphorical expression, that is so vital to a proper understanding of Biblical texts and the expression of religious thought. Inevitably, if we cannot read metaphorically and hear the Bible poetically, we will miss what Francis Thompson called the 'many splendour'd thing.' Like myth, great poetry 'yields up a deeper meaning at every stage of human history.' And that is what is so miraculous about the King James' Bible. It was of course written to be heard rather than read, but it was written in the language of Shakespeare, which probably above any other period of our native tongue, was wonderfully rich, supremely poetic in its imagery and expression, its cadences and rhythms. The English language came to its finest flowering at the end of the mediaeval era, when in the contemporary mind there was still a close kinship between the literal and the metaphorical way of looking at things. All this made that great translation appropriate to its great original. And since then it has almost taken on a life of its own, enriching our language and inspiring the creative imagination of our greatest writers. But above all it encouraged our capacity for metaphorical and religious thinking, because it had the poetic power to move, 'to arrive at the intellect by way of the heart', as R.S. Thomas puts it.

Contrast that with the dreary language of some modern translations (not all), which we have to listen to in church – pitched in language that sometimes sounds more appropriate to a railway timetable or instructions for assembling a piece of DIY furniture, and sometimes making little more sense than the original passages.

The Oxford Bible Commentary (p 364) on Imagery in the Psalms illustrates my point and says all that is needful – I quote: 'Poetry is always seasick when it is ferried to another country. Translation cannot convey the rhythms, overtones, resonances, sounds, alliteration, and plays on words in the original. Metaphor and simile play a very large part in the appeal of the psalms, and the ultimate horror of the ability of translation to destroy the poetry is seen in the Good News Bible.' Such translations are, doubtless, more up to date and scholastically sound, but possibly also at times the fruits of the inevitable fudges and compromises imposed by a worthy (or even desperate) desire for consensus. But in an age of scientific realism, where we have lost the capacity to think poetically, is it any wonder that we find our faith blighted by fundamentalist biblical literalism, reinforced by unpoetic, literalist translations and liturgies?

Meaning in poetry is not like meaning in prose; poetry is many-faceted, subtle, in-apprehensible. Prose conveys information; poetry indicates connections and suggests response. Poetry is 'what gets lost in translation', theology is poetry; myth is 'poetry plus theology'. George Steiner suggests that all creative artists, 'together with the saints, secular and religious, in some manner ransom mankind.'

Poets and their poetry are what we all need to ransom mankind's religion and make it live again.

EXAMPLES

Some of the poems or prose-poems that in one way or another, in whole or in part, have hinted to me of the numinous, the religious dimension, and the divine

Church Going – Philip Larkin
Morte d'Arthur – Tennyson
To a Grand-daughter – Anon
I Go a Journey – Lord Gorrell
On his Blindness – John Milton
Crossing the Bar – Tennyson
Socrates on Swans' Songs – Plato
Rabbi ben Ezra – Robert Browning
The Nightingale and the Rose – Oscar Wilde
In Church, Kneeling, The Bright Field, A Marriage – R.S. Thomas
God's Grandeur, Glory be to God for Dappled Things, Heaven-Haven – Gerard Manley Hopkins
In No Strange Land, The Hound of Heaven – Francis Thompson
Prayer, the Church's Banquet, Love bade me Welcome – George Herbert
The Passionate Man's Pilgrimage – Sir Walter Raleigh ('Give me my scallop shell..')
Earth's crammed with heaven – Elizabeth Barrett Browning
Because I could not stop for Death – Emily Dickinson
Journey of the Magi – T.S. Eliot
In the Bleak Midwinter – Rosetti
Come O thou Traveller unknown – C. Wesley
The Oxen – Thomas Hardy

Lead kindly Light – Cardinal Newman
Tintern Abbey - Wordsworth ('I have felt...')
Dover Beach – M. Arnold
Batter my heart, three-person'd God – Donne
Christians and Unbelievers – Dietrich Bonhoeffer
No coward soul is mine - Emily Bronte

And in the Bible (inter alia)

Psalms 8, 104, 121, 139 and others
Isaiah 35
God's reply to Job - Chapters 38 (esp.31-36) – 42.6.
II Kings, 5 (Naaman) – not strictly a poem, but read in the AV it has poetic power!!
Genesis 1
St John 1 and 13. 34
Philippians 4.4-8
I Corinthians 13 (of course!)

Hymns?

To these I would add a fair number of hymns, usually from pre-twentieth century collections, whose words seem genuinely poetic, and tunes often inspiring. Some of these older hymns have been spoiled by the distortions caused by an absurd contemporary effort to achieve gender neutrality or political correctness. Most however have survived.

Though the Victorians and their predecessors were entirely capable of producing their fair share of banal versification, modern hymn writers I find more consistently dreary. I fully accept that this may say less about their quality than about my lack of poetic or musical sensibility, but I do find their language too often vacuous, lacking formal structure, metrical discipline, and any serious attempt to express what passes for their thought in the heightened language appropriate to poetry and worship.

CHAPTER THIRTY-FOUR

Poetry as a Pathway to God

Spectrum Conference
Beyond Words; Re-imagining Faith
Theology and the Creative Arts

Part 1

I am rather fond of what may well be a somewhat hackneyed story of the Scottish Minister, called upon at very short notice, to stand in for an absent colleague. He apologised to his congregation for the inadequacies of his address, by explaining that he had so little time to prepare that all he could do was to say whatever words the Good Lord put into this head. 'Next week,' he went on, ominously, 'I shall do much better.'

Alas, I can offer no such excuses for my own inadequacies, but I do rather feel that I am here under false pretences. I am not a natural speaker; I am not a poet; I am not an expert in English literature; I am not greatly enamoured of much of the modern poetry I have encountered. But my interests are literary, in that I read Classics at Cambridge; and linguistic in that I have translated texts for several ancient history source books. But above all, I am not a theologian, though theology has always been an amateur interest since my undergraduate days, when a wise old don told me that theology should be always part of the reading of an educated man.

I suppose it does represent credentials of a kind that for some twenty years I used to broadcast for the BBC on *Thought for the Day*, *Prayer for the Day*, and occasionally on the *World Service*. I also put together some 40-minute Studio Services, which involved selecting poems and music on chosen themes, and then writing the linking material, before finally delivering them live from the studio – always a bit scary.

All of this, together with constant correspondence with agnostic or troubled friends, has at least forced me to re-examine constantly the basis of my beliefs, to try and read my way to some sort of account of my faith, and to articulate it in a manner which is reasonably honest, if not entirely defensible intellectually.

When I was asked recently by my daughter, a non-church goer, but religiously sympathetic, how to explain the idea of God to my nine-year old grand-daughter, I really had very little to offer - and that simply reinforced my long standing dissatisfaction with my Church's teaching and my increasing sense of marginalisation from it. What do we mean by God? Who or what is God? Where is heaven? A friend of mine is currently writing a book in which he asks those very questions of all the clergy in his deanery. He tells me that the questions seem to cause them considerable embarrassment, and their answers border on the incoherent. If so, others as well as I, clearly have a problem. That is why I wondered if poetry, or perhaps more accurately the poetic mind-set, might assist our search.

Another friend of mine to whom I posed the same questions, tells me that forty-seven years ago Michael Ramsey, in an effort to explain what John Robinson was trying to say in his somewhat disturbing new book, *Honest to God*, commented: 'his advice is this. Relinquish the image of God as Beyond. Cease to think of God as a definable, supernatural person. Relinquish definitions of God such as 'God is....' Begin the other way round. Look into the depths of human existence, and discover deep down the ultimate reality, the ultimate meaning of things. This ultimate reality is personal; it is love. Then we can say that love, the ultimate reality, is God.' It illustrates just how timid the church has been since then in embracing that insight offered by one of our great Archbishops. But I do concede that the proposition that God is not Love, but rather Love is God might frighten the horses in my own Anglican stables.

Let me go a little further: the concept of Jesus as God Incarnate I find improbable as literal truth, and unhelpful as metaphor. His remarkable life, his deep experience of God, and his excruciating death all seem to me historical certainties. On that basis I can readily enough accord him the status of a great prophet, profound mystic, or even a saint, though I sometimes feel that the currency of sainthood has been debased over the last fifty years; but not divinity, except a sort of mythical divinity, of the kind which has honoured many mortal men whether in legend or history, as great figures and benefactors of the human race. So the search for God remains for me a deeply important activity, not least because I doubt if it will be many more years before I discover the answer – or perhaps not.

So much then for my lack of credentials. I only hope that your verdict on my thoughts will not be like those of a certain Scottish Lady. Under the impression that she had been reading a modern novel, she once returned an English dictionary to her local Library with the comment: 'Verra interesting – but a wee bit disconnected.'

Part 2 (The problem of Language)

The theme of this Conference is Re-imagining Faith. Perhaps the more media-sensitive term, re-imaging Faith would have been more appropriate. For in the end, along with paradoxes, images – or metaphors – are all we have with which to express what is ultimately inexpressible.

> O world invisible, we view thee,
> O world intangible, we touch thee,
> O world unknowable, we know thee,
> Inapprehensible, we clutch thee.

Always in this sort of discussion we come back to the problem of language. It is the supreme achievement of the human species, the ultimate artefact of our big brain. It has given us the power to control ourselves, each other, and our environment; it is with words that humankind spins a complex web of meaning and purpose above the abyss of eternity in a otherwise meaningless creation. Yet we tend to forget that language never expresses the whole truth; it offers only and always an approximation to the truth. And this inevitably hampers us in our search for God.

So, may I start by offering two basic propositions: the first is that poetry and metaphor are blood-brother and sister, inseparable companions, and willing servants of all religious discourse. Religious language is inevitably profoundly metaphorical and therefore, I would suggest, poetic. It does not state facts; rather, it opens possibilities and suggests insights and connections. It is hardly a very new idea. Duns Scotus, the mediaeval theologian of the mid-ninth century (810-877), said much the same thing, when he observed that 'Theology is a kind of poetry;' or, as one modern author (Rubem Alves in *The Poet, the Warrior, and the Prophet*) puts it, 'Poetic metaphors are rainbows and bridges over things eternally apart.'

Marcus Borg, a contemporary biblical scholar, concurs, suggesting that....

> Like biblical narratives generally, the Pentateuch, Israel's primal narrative, combines historical memory with metaphorical narrative. The Exodus story contains some history remembered, but it is not what we think of as historical reporting; rather it is history turned into metaphor, history metaphorized.

William Barclay agrees: 'Treat everything you read in the Bible as metaphor', he says, 'unless you can be certain that it is not.' Karen Armstrong, makes the same point in her book, *The Battle for God*, commenting that....

> The mythoi of the Bible had never intended to be factual..... Mythical language could not satisfactorily be translated into rational language without losing its raison d'etre. Like poetry, it contained meanings that were too elusive to be expressed in any other way. Once theology tried to turn itself into science, it could only produce a caricature of rational discourse, because these truths are not amenable to scientific demonstration. This spurious religious logos would inevitably bring religion into disrepute.

In the face of such a consensus, it seems to me that the problem with modern thinking about God and religion is that we have progressively lost or abandoned the poetic, or metaphorical, way of looking at the world. Ever since the days of the Enlightenment, the human species has become habituated to the language of prose, the fact-based and therefore conceptually restricted, literalism born of scientific patterns of thought. We are no longer equipped to do God-talk effectively.

As Richard Firth so sensibly suggested in his recent Spectrum article, the idea that the Bible could be called in any meaningful sense the Word of God, except metaphorically, is the by-product of this evolution in our ways of thinking. In fact, the Bible is a human construct, folk-history, metaphorized by folk-memory into a library of man's attempt through the ages to read the Mind of God. Even Stephen Hawking acknowledges this to be a very difficult task.

Predictably enough, therefore, the Bible is full of poetry and memorable metaphors. Everyone will have their favourites; mine include Job chapters thirty-eight - forty-one, surely the longest set of rhetorical questions in literature; or that wondrous psalm 139:

> O Lord, thou has searched me out and known me. Thou knowest my downsitting and mine uprising; thou understandest my thought afar off. ...If I ascend up into heaven thou art there; if I make my bed in hell, behold thou art there. If I take the wings of the

morning and dwell in the uttermost parts of the sea, even there shall thy hand lead me, and thy right hand shall hold me)

But here we must be careful. I wonder whether the power of this psalm and many of its more famous passages owe as much to the translators of the King James' Bible, whose centenary we celebrate this year, as it does to the imagination of the original writers. Poetry does not readily translate into another language, since it is almost impossible to recapture the overtones and associations, which the original had for its contemporaries. I know of no better expression of this problem than the Oxford Bible Commentary (p.364). In his introduction to the Psalms the editor observes that,

> Poetry is always seasick when it is ferried to another country. Translation cannot convey the rhythms, overtones, resonances, sounds, alliteration, and plays on words in the original. Metaphor and simile play a very large part in the appeal of the psalms, and the ultimate horror of the ability of translation to destroy the poetry is seen in the Good News Bible. (And not only that version either, I suspect).

So much for poetry and metaphor as blood-relatives.

My second basic proposition is this: Tradition is a dangerous ally, whether in institutions or in the evolution of ideas. Those who put their faith in tradition are straying onto dangerous quicksands, where time and the tides of knowledge, fashion, and opinion constantly alter their locations, so that you can never know which area will simply swallow you up. What seems safe today may well be fatal tomorrow. All tradition decays; long-standing tradition decays absolutely. In fact, as Bishop Richard Holloway tells us, 'a tradition must be continuously subverted and reinvented, if it is to have an enduring life.' T.S. Eliot said roughly the same thing about poetry, maintaining that it involves the 're-winding of the decaying strands of tradition.' As he puts it in *Little Gidding* (V):

> Every phrase, every sentence is an end and a beginning,
> Every poem an epitaph. And any action
> Is a step to the block, to the fire, down the sea's throat
> Or to an illegible stone.'

Tradition is dangerous, if not deadly – with apologies to the formularies of the Methodist (or Lambeth) Quadrilateral. Even in biblical times this was perfectly well understood. Here is Dionysius, The Areopagite, (mentioned in Acts xvii.34) On Celestial Hierarchy:

> We cannot, as mad people do, profanely visualise these heavenly and godlike intelligences as actually having numerous feet and faces … They do not have the curved beak of the eagle or the wings and features of birds. We must not have pictures of flaming wheels whirling in the skies … The Word of God makes use of poetic imagery when discussing these formless intelligences; but it does not do this for the sake of art, but as a concession to the limitations of our own minds.

Finally, at a slightly more flippant level, just to keep our feet on the ground, and to reinforce my demand for updated imagery, here is a quick word from A.C. Grayling, contemporary philosopher and atheist: 'Apart from what physics tells us, there are all

POETRY AS A PATHWAY TO GOD

sorts of fallacies with religious belief. A God that could be everywhere all the time could even eat itself for breakfast.'

Two thousand years later, it seems to me, we continue to ignore these sensible reservations. God is still up there in the clouds of Heaven, sending down his Son, but also (like any Greek god) begetting him with a mortal woman, and then making him come back from the realms of the dead (like Orpheus, Odysseus, or Aeneas) and appear to his disciples. After that he ascends into heaven, to become (probably to his own uncomprehending surprise) the second person of the Trinity – a concept, which for at least six hundred years afterwards caused endless problems for thinking Christians.

In fact, as the title of this Conference suggests, we must break loose from the shackles of tradition and try to re-imagine and to re-image, our idea of what belief in God means and how Jesus fits into the picture. My own reading over the years has allowed me to abandon with relief the mythological elements (which have long troubled me), or to accept them as what Borg calls 'history metaphorized.'

And if it seems to you that I have reduced an inspired original to mere historical fact, effectively no different from secular and atheistic history, I offer as antidote a brief quotation from Neil MacGregor's recent *History of the World in a Hundred Objects*:

> With objects… we have to add to our normal critical apparatus a considerable **leap of imagination**, returning the artefact to its former life, engaging with it as generously, as **poetically** (his word), as we can, in the hope of winning the insights it may deliver….

Thinking about the past is always about poetic re-creation. We acknowledge the limits of what we can know with certainty, and must then try to find a different kind of knowing, aware that objects must have been made by people essentially like us – so we should be able to puzzle out why they made them …<But> can we ever really understand others? Perhaps only through feats of poetic imagination, combined with knowledge rigorously acquired and ordered.

Jesus is not an artefact but our image of him undoubtedly is - the product of traditions, which the church has modified and transmitted down the centuries. The process by which we should strive to recover the reality and meaning of Jesus' life is surely similar to that of any artefact. It requires constant re-evaluation through rigorous historical research, to which traditional churchmen seem somewhat averse, and poetic re-creation, for which modern Christians seem singularly ill-equipped.

In fact my own reading suggests to me that the early Church from the time of Constantine ceased to try to live out the meaning of the life of Jesus, (their artefact, as it were), and instead concentrated on its exploitation, the uses to which it could be put. Those uses tend to emphasise the pursuit and defence of wealth, status, power and self-interest, both for the institution and its potentates, instead of seeking to follow the teaching of the one who said that 'whosoever shall be great among you shall be your minister; and whosoever will be the chiefest, shall be servant of all.' (Mk.10.43)

No wonder we need all the scientific, literary, and historical expertise we can get, combined with the poetic exercise of our own imaginations, to help us reach what Macgregor calls 'a different kind of knowing,' to get behind and beyond the facts to the ultimate reality, some deeper sense of the meaning of Jesus' life, and through that perhaps to a more compelling idea of what we mean by God.

Part 3 (Back to Basics: the First Commandment)

Jesus, when challenged, was able to encapsulate the whole of his message in a single sentence, containing the two great commandments, which he claimed embodied the Law and the Prophets: 'Love God with all your heart, mind, soul, and strength; and your neighbour as yourself.' The Synoptics - Matthew (22.37), Mark (7.7) and Luke 10.27) - all add Mind to the original quotation from Deuteronomy (6.5), which confined the love of God to heart, soul and strength. I find it encouraging that perhaps Jesus was the first to add rationality to the more traditional implements of religious faith.

In the Exodus version of the commandments comes the warning not to make for ourselves 'any graven image, in the likeness of anything in heaven or earth.' It reminds me of the observation of an early Greek philosopher that 'if horses had gods, they would make them like horses.' At the very least such warnings should encourage us to avoid any sort of fixed or anthropomorphic idea of God, whether in artefact or language, lest our images of God and Jesus become our own graven images. The analogy with great art is obvious: generation after generation we re-examine and re-interpret the great works of music, literature, painting and sculpture. Generation after generation we should do the same in our search for God, whom my mother once, in a memorable phrase, defined for me as 'Eternal Mind, expanding forever to elude.'

Of the two great Commandments, I myself would argue that the church has in a sense already won the battle for the second, the Golden Rule, that we should love our neighbours as ourselves. For all its imperfections modern society has so absorbed its inheritance of Christian values that it barely thinks of them any more as Christian, because those values are now the norm in Western Society. In that sense the churches' mission in this area is accomplished, though of course there is a massive amount of work still to be done. But where, perhaps as a consequence, the Churches have taken their eye off the ball, is in the search for, and the proclamation of, God. Here is A.A. Milne, of Christopher Robin fame, writing in 1948, well before John Robinson's *Honest to God,* describing a Vicar's sermon, in a perceptive but painfully entertaining poem called *The Norman Church*:

> He ambles on, and leaves behind
> The impress of a muffled mind,
> Which overhears itself impart
> A formal message learnt by heart;
> A message asking little more
> Than phrases from a common store,
> Which for the teacher and the taught,
> Become an anodyne for thought,
> And give them painlessly the comfort they have sought.
>
> Oft he had trembled on the brink
> Of thought – but did not dare to think;

And Doubt had come – but not for long,
Since all too clearly Doubt was wrong.
('Retro Satanas!') 'Behind me Satan' was his cry
When Logic called to ask him Why;
And imps of Reason rushed to find
A postern-gate into his mind,
And frightened him, and left uneasiness behind.

But slowly with the passing years
His Faith had covered up his fears,
And left him to his great content
Above all reasoned argument;
So that, convinced that he believes
The doctrine which his flock receives,
He sees no cause to dwell upon
Its doubtful points, but pushes on,
Lest in a pause for thought its value would be gone.

So that, it seems to me, is now the Churches' greater task: to lead their followers towards the fulfilment of the first great commandment by finding a new language with which to guide the lost, the sceptical, and the unbelieving towards a rediscovery of God.

Part 4 (Poets as Seers and See-ers)

Bishop Jack Spong, in his latest book, *Eternal Life, a New Vision*, suggests that theism, (which is the traditional image of God as a supernatural, external father-figure, who comes to our aid,) is dying.... the casualty of an expanded world view. But he insists that he 'does not think God is dying, and so he seeks to go beyond theism, but not beyond God.' For him the primary issue for everyone is this: 'how do we now conceptualise God?' The issue of how we should pray to the God once conceptualised is purely secondary. In this I am sure he is right – I am rather less sure that what he offers us by way of a new conceptualisation is entirely persuasive, but it is a start and a worthwhile attempt.

150 years ago, John Ruskin wrote that 'The greatest thing a human soul ever does in this world is to see something and tell what it saw in a plain way...... To see clearly is poetry, prophecy, and religion – all in one.' I have no doubt that Ruskin was thinking of all kinds of artists, not just poets. But our focus today is on poets, both as see-ers – that is, writers who see (in Ruskin's sense) more clearly into the nature of reality than the rest of us; but also poets as seers, in the conventional sense: those who have the gift of religious or prophetic insight - but also the craftsmanship of language, which enables them to express their thoughts in words which have an inherent power, akin to the spells of ancient magic, and whose effects can have something of the quality of incantations. Like blind Teiresias, poets know what has been, what is, and what is to come. And the best of them compel our attention by the clarity with which they express their vision, and the power of the imagery with which they take us beyond prosaic argumentation.

Intellect and reason can only take you so far. There comes a point where the language of reason breaks down and something more is needed. For Plato, a fine poet well as a philosopher, this was Myth. The climax of the argument in his dialogues is often the telling of a mythical tale, a profound, religious truth, expressed as story – but in language richer and more multi-layered than parable. Here is a short passage from the last of his early dialogues, Socrates' words of encouragement, his 'swansong' so to speak, to his disciples just before his execution.

> Do you think I have less powers of divination than the swans? For they, when they know that they must die, having sung all their lives sing louder than ever, for joy at going home to the god they serve. Men, who themselves fear death, have taken it for lamentation, forgetting that no bird sings in hunger, or cold, or pain. But they are Apollo's own birds, and share his gift of prophecy; therefore they sing because they can foresee the joys of another world. (Plato: *Phaedo*)

Here too is R.S. Thomas, in a fine apology from an educated, rational yet God-haunted man, who has found it hard to move beyond his own belief in rational argument and prosaic exposition of belief to something deeper, and in its primal simplicity more profound. His apology is addressed to Prytherch, a Welsh hill farmer, whom he has long despised and roundly criticised for what he sees as his ignorant refusal to move outside the narrow confines of the simple world view, which shaped his religion.

> It was you who were right the whole time:
> Rich in this: that the day's end
> Finds you, still in the same field
> In which you started, your soul made strong
> By the earth's incense, the wind's song,
> While I have worn my soul bare
> On the world's roads, seeking what lay
> Too close for the mind's lenses to see,
> And come now with the first stars
> Big on my lids westward to find
> With the slow lifting of your hand
> No welcome, only forgiveness.

And here is John Cornwell (author of *Newman's Unquiet Grave*) reviewing Frank Schaeffer's book, *Patience with God*. 'The Christianity of the East,' he says, 'which separated from Rome and western thinking a thousand years back, is marked by imagination, mystery, and non-judgemental love. Eastern thinking does not seek to combat militant atheism with knock-down proofs, but rather with what Pascal calls 'the reasons of the heart.'

Poetry, I would suggest, is certainly one way of 'seeing with the heart what lies too close for the lenses of the mind to see', and these two passages are a useful corrective to those of us who perhaps rely too much on rationality.

Part 5 (The Loss of an Organic World View)

Poetry, I have suggested, is a kind of Theology, and if we need to find new and different ways of thinking about God, it may be one possible pathway towards the answer. It could even turn out that this pathway is a way forward into the past, so that in Eliot's famous lines,

> The end of all our exploring
> Will be to arrive where we started
> And know the place for the first time.
> Through the unknown, remembered gate
> When the last of earth left to discover
> Is that which was the beginning.

(T.S. Eliot – *Little Gidding*)

But it is not so much poetry that offers the pathway, but what one might call the 'poetic' or metaphorical way of looking at things, a way which in some respects is almost mediaeval. In this context, there is a close parallel between religion and tragic drama, because they both depend for their most effective expression upon the power of poetic language and a late mediaeval way of looking at the world. And both have been casualties of the Reformation and the Enlightenment, which between them have given birth to the literal and prosaic modern mind. The result has been to tear religion as well as art loose from its moorings in the thought-world of myth and poetry.

And here, surely, lies the secret of the glory of the 1611 King James' Bible. It owes much, if not everything, to the blessed chance of coming into being at a moment in history when the English language was reaching its first full flowering, when, as George Steiner puts it in his book, *The Death of Tragedy*, the 'Organic World View,' and society's 'Community of Expectation' were not yet lost to the encroaching clouds of modernism.

The power of the printed word was still the preserve of the rich and educated, for whom Latin, and Greek remained familiar second languages, used in educated and scientific discourse; the rules of classical rhetoric still set the accepted norms of style. But for the great majority of the population, it was the spoken word which (in MacLuhan's phrase) was still the medium that carried the message. And in those times spoken English had a richness of vocabulary and a mellifluousness of sound, which perhaps it was never to achieve again. It was the language of Shakespeare and Milton; of a superbly educated and scholarly Queen; and it was also a time of discovery and intellectual excitement, as well as the religious challenge of Reformation and Puritanism.

The translation committees set up by King James combined exact scholarship with practical good sense, and an acute awareness of the importance of the new translation being heard in public, rather than read in the study. Symbolic of this characteristic, perhaps, is the comment of one scholar, recorded in the committee's minutes, who justified the alteration of one particular word by the fact that *semnioteros erit ho logos* – the word will be more solemn, awe-some, sacred, royal, regal, majestic. The Greek word *semnos*, carries all those implications. Somewhere in all that lies the secret of the beauty, the majesty, and inherent poetry of the King James Bible.

Last autumn I attended a course in the Parish called Fresh Expressions – sadly tedious and deeply unconvincing, but redeemed by the final talk, given by a profoundly thoughtful Anglican woman priest. In a wide-ranging survey of where the church is at and how it got there, she made for me a series of very telling propositions. 'There used to be a Christendom:' she said, 'a way of life in Europe where the whole culture, its politics and economic life, were rooted in and expressed within Christian activities and images. In this country the Church of England was 'a religious institution embedded in the whole of society.' Therefore, until very recently 'it was entirely possible to belong to the C of E without believing. It offered uniformity of worship; it required conformity to social expectation, rather than belief. It was impolite to discuss personal faith, but it was OK to indulge in theological discussion, because you were safe in your belonging.'

Increasingly, she argued, the institutions of the C of E have become divorced from the powers and influences in the nation. As a result, she suggested, it was now more like a sect than a church in the old sense. We will never recover the organic world view, which once gave to Greek audiences, or their Shakespearean counterparts, a shared perception of the world portrayed by the actors they were watching. But if religion is to be revived, it must depend on a broadly based revival of the poetic way of looking at things. Without some sort of recovery of the poetic mind-set, the poet's insight born of an intuitive perception of reality, and what Steiner called its mythological, symbolic and ritual points of reference, it is hard to see how religion can ever recover its hold on the human imagination.

We must recover the capacity to look at things poetically, to 'metaphorize our Bible history, treating everything we read as metaphor, unless we can be certain that it is not. For Religion, like Myth, is poetry plus, not science minus.' (Borg).

Part 6 (Reviving the Poetic Way of Looking)

I doubt if there is much point in my simply reading a few poems to you as models of how we should write or speak about God. After all one man's meat is another man's poison and it is impossible to avoid a degree of subjectivity. So although it may seem somewhat abstract, I hope it is more useful to try and explore in a little more detail what we mean by poetry, how it works, and why the poetic mode of thinking might lead us in a 'godward' direction.

Ian Ramsey, the much lamented Bishop of Durham, who until his early death promised to be one of great archbishops that the Church of England never had, in his book *Religious Language* discussed the way in which we should talking about religion. You have to try all sorts of approaches, he says: different analogies, metaphors, examples, illustrations, tones of voice, until suddenly, at different points for different hearers, 'the penny drops' and the message goes home. The old schoolmaster in me can recognise that activity, and that joyous sense of heaven revealed when, suddenly, a pupil says – 'Oh, now I see what you mean.' In the search for religious insight, I am sure it is the only way to go. John Donne illustrates the process admirably:

> On a huge hill,
> Cragged and steep, Truth stands, and he that will
> Reach her, about and about must go
> and what the hill's suddenness resists,
> win so.

Many others, offer similar insights: *Poetry is a raid on the inarticulate* (T.S. Eliot*); God* *uses crooked lines to write straight* (Paul Claudel, quoting an old Portuguese proverb); *The poet's duty is to tell the truth, but tell it slant* (Emily Dickinson); *Poetry is the language of the unspeakable* (Goethe); *Poetry is that which arrives at the intellect by way of the heart'* (R.S. Thomas); *A poem draws the nearer to beauty and truth in so far as its words reveal the unceasing journey of the soul towards its own beauty and truth* (Maeterlinck). Bishop Richard Holloway describes poetry as *the gift of priestly attention;* and in that sense perhaps all poets should be seen as priests, profoundly and attentively focused on the search for God.

I have collected definitions of poetry for fifty years and could offer many more. As ways of talking about God, that poetic combination of paradox and unpredictability (the logic of divinity), truth (the logic of the head), the unspeakable (the language of the angels), love (the logic of the heart), and beauty and truth (the soul's destination and the heart's desire): all these are essential elements in any approach to the idea of God.

Poetry at its best opens up the way to them all. Even Jesus' parables are simply prose metaphors, which come at the same general point from different angles, as if he too realised that God must be approached obliquely.

Part 7 Poetry: the Art of the Oblique

Tell the truth, but tell it slant. Perhaps this is why God may best be approached obliquely, whether in poetry, or any other form of art. Diarmid MacCulloch in his *History of Christianity* (p.413/4), summarises the teaching of Thomas Aquinas' (aka. Thomism) as follows:

> This greatest of scholastic theologians understood that all language about God had to employ the sideways glance, the analogy, the metaphor... and his judgements on Truth are presented as a summary of probabilities, of the balance of arguments – something which those turning to his great work for certainties have not always appreciated.

And of course if we are looking for ways of coming to God slant-wise, with the sideways glance, then metaphor, the key constituent of both poetry and religious language, is obliqueness. Ortega Y Gasset memorably once remarked that 'in poetry, metaphor is something whose efficacy verges on magic; it seems like a tool for creation, which God forgot inside one of his creatures when He made him.'

If, as suggested by Donne and Ian Ramsey, we can train ourselves to go about and about, with quickened imaginations, alert to things that come obliquely to our vision, sensitized to metaphor and the tingle factor inherent in all poetic language, until suddenly the penny drops - if we can do all that, then surely we shall begin to make effective use of that tool for creation which God forgot (or possibly deliberately left behind) when he created us. Then, at unexpected moments like R.S. Thomas, we may suddenly exclaim:

> Life is not hurrying
> on to a receding future, nor hankering after
> an imagined past. It is the turning
> aside like Moses to the miracle
> of the lit bush, to a brightness

that seemed as transitory as your youth
once, but is the eternity that awaits you.

Poetry, surely, more than anything else, offers us a resource by which we can be helped to turn aside for a moment to the 'miracle of the lit bush.' Perhaps the best summary of its effects for me can be found in the introduction to my favourite anthology, called *Spells*, by Frank McEachran.

> A spell, he says, is concentrated poetry, of sound or sense, an incantation whose effects are partly musical, partly expressive of profound feeling or emotion, conveying an idea, whether simple or complex, through powerful images, purity of tone and language, and unity of purpose – everything directed to the single end of conveying an idea as powerfully and expressively as the poet can. Its effect verges on magic.

And yet, to my admittedly prejudiced mind and ear, all we get from our modernised versions of hymns, prayers, translations and liturgies is language drained of all poetic power, endowed with all the richness of a Telephone Directory or the minutes of the proceedings of a House of Commons Committee.

Part 8 (Absence and Emptiness)

Neil MacGregor, again in his *History of the World in a Hundred Objects*, suggests that Art and Language developed in tandem, emerging at very much the same time as a religious sense: a moment in history when artefacts become, not just functional tools but also objects of deliberately created beauty. Often, of course, the purpose must have been magic, a self-interested attempt to manipulate the environment, to extract assistance or gifts from the deity, whether by bribery, flattery, obsequious prayers, or sympathetic magic. But always it was informed by a sense of the numinous, a feeling that the divinity was there to be approached or placated – or paradoxically, was perceived to be there by being absent.

Dionysius the Areopagite, made the same point when he suggested that 'the most godlike knowledge of God is that which is known by unknowing.' This was what the early mystics called the Cloud of Unknowing, the *via negativa* (the apophatic way), by contrast with the *via positiva*, (cataphatic), which has been preferred on the whole by Western Christendom (though it has its mystics also), in what E.M. Forster dismissed as 'poor talkative little Christianity.' R.S. Thomas wrote of the same phenomenon:

> It is this great absence
> That is like a presence, that compels
> Me to address it without hope
> Of a reply. It is a room I enter
> From which someone has just
> Gone, the vestibule for the arrival
> Of one who has not yet come......
> What resource have I
> Other than the emptiness without him of my whole
> Being, a vacuum he may not abhor.

Rubem Alves makes a similar point about the Eucharist,

An empty, silent space for our dreaming, before the Absent One.... It is not the presence which performs the miracle. The miracle is performed by the power of the absence. God is the Absence which saves.

Poetry has always striven to offer ways of expressing that which is unseen as well as seen, implied as well as present, suggested as well as obvious. It makes connections of which the ordinary observer may be unaware. The importance of emptiness, space, the interstices between what is seen; the sense of the numinous, suggested by what has been called 'the thin places of the earth', where the walls between earth and heaven are so thin you can almost see through them – these are all things which poets are better equipped to explore than mere mortals like myself. (Andrew Motion's recent poem on the death of Harry Patch is a fine example of this).

Poetry and metaphor, the tools of the poet's trade, can do this better than any other vehicle, since jointly they are 'a medium of suggestion, a single word pregnant with unpredictable meanings… which leads to infinite horizons', a 'tool for creation', a pathway to God whereby, to quote Boethius, if we have the courage we may conquer earth to reach the stars.

> Ite nunc fortes, u bi celsa magni
> Ducit exempli via. Cur inertes
> Terga nudatis? Superata tellus
> Sidera donat.

> Go now, brave souls, where the high road
> Of great example leads. Why like cowards
> Turn your backs? Once conquered, it is Earth
> that gives the stars.

Part 9 (Plus ça Change)

> The old order changeth, yielding place to new,
> And God fulfils himself in many ways,
> Lest one good custom should corrupt the world.

Was Tennyson's King Arthur right, I wonder? Or is the French proverb closer to the truth? 'Plus ça Change, plus c'est la même chose.' Since earliest times religious ideas, the search for ultimate meaning, has been part of poets' business. The great Greek dramatists were all poets, writing religious poetry, for the drama festivals, which were always religious festivals, in plays which are always theology, dressed in heaven's embroidered clothes.

Aeschylus pondered deeply on the meaning of undeserved suffering and the inadequacy of the gods' dispensation of Justice – so did Job. Sophocles became a god, elevated to divine status as a benevolent local deity by his fellow citizens, because like the sculptor Pheidias, his contemporary, he was thought to have 'added something to the idea of God.' In his play, *Women of Trachis*, in a powerful comment on his father's death and the extremes of human misfortune, Hyllus, the son of Herakles, can declare,

You have seen a terrible death,
and agonies many and strange,
but there is nothing here that is not Zeus.

Euripides infuriated his contemporaries with his sceptical questions about belief. In *Bacchanals*, his greatest play, the product of his old age, the theme concerns the arrival of a new God, a new religion, of particular appeal to women - and therefore typically threatening to male traditionalists. But the moral of the play is that we must recognise any new god's power, welcome it, and respond to it. 'We are here to worship, not to play intellectual games with the idea of god', says the prophet Teiresias to the new god's arch-opponent, King Pentheus (*ouden sophizomestha toisi daimosin*).

Always through the centuries, though religions may differ, the language of religion, whether the visual or verbal, seems strangely familiar, always striving to express similar ideas, whether of creation, eternity, divinity, protection, peace, hope. To illustrate the point, we might compare the Greek Apollo of Claros from the 5th century BC with the pagan atheist Lucretius, and the pagan (but honorary Christian) Virgil (both Roman, and both dead shortly before Jesus was born), with George Herbert in the late 16th century, William Wordsworth and Francis Thompson in the 19th; Larkin and my already much quoted R.S. Thomas in the 20th century.

They are just a few examples of the many we could find, where intimations of divinity may perhaps break through.

Apollo of Claros:

Self-born, untaught, motherless, unshakeable,
Giving place to no name, many named, dwelling in fire,
Such is God. We are a portion of God, his angels.....
To him then look
And pray at dawn looking outward to the east.

(*Oracle* ca.400 BC)

Lucretius:

Mother of Aeneas, joy of all men and gods alike,
Venus, the source of Life: beneath the wheeling stars of heaven
You quicken with life the seas which bear our ships
And the land which brings us all the fruits of the fields.
Through you all living creatures are conceived
And rise to behold the light of day.

Lucretius 94-55 BC (*Invocation to Venus from de Rerum Natura*)

Virgil:

In the beginning, Spirit deep within sustains the heaven and earth
The gleaming plains, moon's shining globe, and Titan's stars,
And Mind moves all material things it permeates.

Virgil 70-19 BC (*The Aeneid*)

George Herbert:

> Prayer, the Church's banquet, Angels' age,
>> God's breath in man returning to his birth,
> The soul in paraphrase, heart in pilgrimage,
>> The Christian plummet, sounding heaven and earth;
> Engine against the Almighty, sinner's tower,
>> Reversed thunder, Christ-side-piercing spear,
> The six-days' world transposing in an hour,
> A kind of tune, which all things hear and fear.
>
> Softness and peace and joy and love and bliss,
>> Exalted manna, gladness of the best,
> Heaven in ordinary, man well drest,
> The milky way, the bird of Paradise,
>> Church bells beyond the stars heard, the soul's blood,
>> The land of spices, something understood.

George Herbert 1593-1633 (Prayer)

Wordsworth:

> For I have learned
> To look on nature, not as in the hour
> Of thoughtless youth; but hearing oftentimes
> The still sad music of humanity,
> Nor harsh, nor grating, though of ample power
> To chasten and subdue. And I have felt
> A presence that disturbs me with the joy
> Of elevated thoughts; a sense sublime
> Of something far more deeply interfused,
> Whose dwelling is the light of setting suns
> And the round ocean and the living air,
> And the blue sky, and in the mind of man:
> A motion and a spirit, that impels
> All thinking things, all objects of all thought,
> And rolls through all things.

Wordsworth 1770-1850 (Tintern Abbey)

Francis Thompson:

> The angels keep their ancient places;
> Turn but a stone and start a wing!
> 'Tis ye, 'tis your estranged faces
> That miss the many-splendoured thing.

Francis Thompson 1859-1907 (In No Strange Land)

Philip Larkin:

> A serious house on serious earth it is,
> In whose blent air all our compulsions meet,
> Are recognised, and robed as destinies.
> And that much never can be obsolete,
> Since someone will forever be surprising
> A hunger in himself to be more serious,
> And gravitating with it to this ground
> Which, he once heard, was proper to grow wise in,
> If only that so many dead lie round.

Philip Larkin 1922-1985 (Church Going)

Religious insight and religious language are always a matter of 'going about and about', as John Donne suggests, until the penny drops; of seeing and hearing between the words, behind the words, beyond the words. It is what is not explicitly said that carries the force; the sense that God's presence is in the absence, in the working of one's own imaginative response to an initial metaphorical stimulus. Rational thought clears the debris and prepares the ground, and even starts the building process. But in the end the building is one not made with hands.

Always it is this capacity to think metaphorically that helps us to articulate our sense of heaven, because metaphor forces us to search behind and between words – and above all to see beyond them. It is the willingness to abandon the thought processes of the scientist and to think like a poet that will give birth, perhaps, to a new mysticism, and open our eyes to the many-splendoured thing, the vision beautiful. And then in time, by some sort of strange alchemy, through poetry, we may find that the God of all truth has arrived at the intellect by way of the heart.

CHAPTER THIRTY-FIVE

Of Time and Place

A Meditation for the Spectrum Conference

When the sweet showers of April have pierced
The drought of March, and pierced it to the root,
And every vein is bathed in that moisture
Whose quickening force will engender the flower;
And when the west wind too with its sweet breath
Has given life in every wood and field
To tender shoots, and when the stripling sun
Has run his half-course in Aries, the Ram,
And when small birds are making melodies,....
Then people long to go on pilgrimages …

Well, it is May, not April, and this is not quite a pilgrimage – but perhaps our situation and our motivations are not entirely different. The pilgrim is a seeker after truth and the divine vision. And so are we. The pilgrim is a traveller – and so are we. And all of us are travellers towards Death, 'that undiscovered country from whose bourne / No traveller returns.' Here is Walter Raleigh on pilgrimage:

Give me my scallop shell of quiet,
My staff of faith to walk upon,
My scrip of joy, immortal diet,
My bottle of salvation;
My gown of glory, hope's true gage,
And thus I'll take my pilgrimage.

Later, in the year 1618, in the Tower and facing execution, he wrote his own epitaph:

Even such is Time, which takes in trust
Our youth, our joys, and all we have,
And pays us but with age and dust;
Who in the dark and silent grave,
When we have wandered all our ways,
Shuts up the story of our days:
And from this earth, and grave, and dust,
The Lord will raise me up I trust.

Pilgrimage and Time are two images I want to look at today. Less than ten years after the writing of the King James Bible and two years after the death of William Shakespeare, at a time when the whole mediaeval outlook was in decline, we hear in the words of a practical man of action, courtier, pirate, adventurer, a reflection of the religious outlook which he would have shared with almost all his fellow countrymen, expressed in language which they would all have understood, a model of clarity and simplicity, whose imagery is precise and vivid and pregnant with extended meaning.

That this is no longer the case in 21st century society is part of the problem confronting all those whose desire is still to follow and proclaim what the early Jesus-People called The Way. How are we to Re-imagine Faith in such a radically changed society, and how are we to express it in a language and with concepts that are vivid, comprehensible and acceptable to our contemporaries?

It is a difficulty explored by T.S. Eliot in his (for me extraordinarily difficult) poem or poems, *Four Quartets*. But I want to use it as the focus for our thoughts, because it is modern, but also because it illustrates, in its very difficulty, how problematical it is for anyone nowadays to express their faith and their ideas about God in language that speaks to modern worshippers and readers.

It is a poem of four movements, written over a number of years and mainly during World War II, around a single theme of Time - past, present and future; a key Idea - that we are all, in a sense, one with Eternity; and a great Hope – that any one of us may, if we have the will and the perceptiveness, be vouchsafed for a moment **in** time, a glimpse of Eternity **outside of** time, a vision of truth and beauty, a blink of heaven. R.S. Thomas' explores a similar idea in *The Bright Field*; but here is Eliot in the third Quartet, *The Dry Salvages*:

> The moments of happiness – not the sense of well-being,
> Fruition, fulfilment, security or affection,
> Or even a very good dinner, but the sudden illumination –
> We had the experience but missed the meaning,
> And approach to the meaning restores the experience
> In a different form, beyond any meaning
> We can assign to happiness.....
> The past experience revived in the meaning
> Is not the experience of one life only
> But of many generations.

'Not the experience of one life only but of many generations.' In 1626, fifteen years after the King James Bible was published, and seven years after Raleigh's death, in a Huntingdonshire village less than fifty miles from here, called Little Gidding, Nicholas Ferrar established a Christian Community of some thirty-five - forty people, of both sexes and all ages, based on the idea, not of an enclosed order, but of a Christian family. They combined regular religious devotion with intellectual and manual labour, and provided a social service for their neighbourhood. Their commitment was to the old, pre-Reformation religion of their fathers, which made them anathema to the Puritans of the new reformed religion.

King Charles I had twice visited the community, but in 1646, he came again in very different circumstances: a fugitive from the battle of Naseby, fought and lost again less than fifty miles from here, and with it the defeat of the Royalist cause. For this crime of succouring one who was in sorrow, trouble, need and every kind of adversity, the house and church were sacked, the community scattered; King Charles and his leading adherents were executed. Nicholas Ferrar was already dead (1637) but like his scattered community, he and his vision were lost and forgotten until the 20th century.

> If I think, again, of this place,
> And of people, not wholly commendable,
> Of no immediate kin or kindness,
> But some of peculiar genius,
> All touched by a common genius,
> United in the strife which divided them;
> If I think of a king at nightfall,
> Of three men, and more, on the scaffold
> And a few who died forgotten
> In other places, here and abroad,
> And of one who died blind and quiet,
> Why should we celebrate
> These dead men more than the dying?

All are dead: or in Eliot's words, 'The houses are all gone under the sea. The dancers are all gone under the hill.' And that includes the soldiers who sacked the place, as well as the members of the sacked and scattered community, and also John Milton, 'the one who died blind and quiet', their arch opponent and one whom we might nowadays call the spin-doctor of the anti-Royalist side. Yet at the time Nicolas Ferrar's community was being destroyed, Milton (1608-1674) was already having to come to terms with the blindness, total within five years, which afflicted him for almost half his life. His own response to this terrible misfortune was a sublime expression of faith in God and patient endurance, in his famous sonnet *On His Blindness*.

> When I consider how my light is spent
> 'Ere half my days in this dark world and wide,
> And that one talent which is death to hide
> Lodged with me useless, though my soul more bent
> To serve therewith my Maker and present
> My true account, lest he returning chide –
> 'Does God exact day labour, light denied,'
> I fondly ask. Yet patience to prevent
> That murmur soon replies, 'God doth not need
> Either man's work or his own gifts. Who best
> Bear his mild yoke, they serve him best. His state
> Is kingly; thousands at his bidding speed
> And post o'er land and ocean without rest.
> They also serve who only stand and wait.'

Waiting patiently upon God is part of the challenge, which confronts the faithful in every age – as the Psalmist reminds us. This is as true for us in an era of disbelief as it was for the scattered community of Little Gidding, and for their opponent, John Milton; for all alike it must have sometimes felt like the end of everything.

But Eliot sees it very differently. On his pilgrimage (whether real or imagined) to Little Gidding in what we would now call 'real time', he receives a rather different intuition, a vision if you like, a hint of heaven, a glimpse of Eternity. At the scene of the martyrdom of Nicolas Ferrar's community, he finds that the past is eternally present, that erstwhile enemies are all equally dead, all gone under the hill, all obedient to what he calls 'the constitution of silence.'

But whereas conventional wisdom suggests that History is always written by the winners, here he finds that whatever record of events we may inherit from those same winners ('the fortunate'), we have taken something much more significant from the defeated - an enduring symbol, perfected in death, teaching us all that under the love of God and in the words of the mediaeval mystic, Julian of Norwich, 'all shall be well and all manner of thing shall be well.' Out of suffering and misfortune, whether of Jesus or his followers, good will come.

Thus the poet's visit to Little Gidding, the pilgrimages, which still take place, the martyrdoms and exiles of its history: all these unite the present/now and the past/then in such a way as to reassert eternal values and the meaning of existence, as part of the Divine Providence, the eternal pattern of ultimate cosmic order. 'All shall be well.'

Such a visionary moment is an Epiphany of History and of England – but also of a God, who operating outside of time yet through time, reveals to us a paradigm of an Eternity, where all are one, united in God's love beneath the everlasting arms.

We cannot revive old factions
We cannot restore old policies
Or follow an antique drum.
These men and those who opposed them
And those whom they opposed
Accept the constitution of silence
And are folded in a single party.
(Whatever we inherit from the fortunate),
We have taken from the defeated
What they had to leave us – a symbol:
A symbol perfected in death.
And all shall be well and
All manner of thing shall be well
By the purification of the motive
In the ground of our beseeching.

Here where history is eternally present, where time intersects with that which is outside of time, Eliot finds in the full, perfect and sufficient sacrifice of the community of Little Gidding, whose end was a new beginning, and whose past suffering unites it for ever with the pilgrims of the present, a perfect symbol of God's love and an insight into the ultimate meaning of Life.

What we call the beginning is often the end
And to make an end is to make a beginning.
The end is where we start from......

Every phrase and every sentence is an end and a beginning,
Every poem an epitaph. And any action
Is a step to the block, to the fire, down the sea's throat
Or to an illegible stone: and that is where we start.....

So for us this Quiet Morning there is time; time to explore our own new beginnings, to find fresh inspiration from art or music or readings, from our prayers or meditations, or from whatever other source we have been given; time, perhaps, to dump a little of the detritus of past certainties (whether of language or even theology) back into the Ocean of Eternity, just as in the *Dry Salvages*, the third of the *Four Quartets*, the River dumps its detritus of human living back into the Ocean to which it too is returning; time perhaps just to be silent inside and outside of time.

We shall not cease from exploration
And the end of all our exploring
Will be to arrive where we started
And know the place for the first time.
Through the unknown, remembered gate
When the last of earth left to discover

Is that which was the beginning. ...

A Celtic Blessing

May the road rise up to meet you;
May the wind be always at your back;
May the sun shine always upon your face,
The rains fall soft upon your fields.
And until we meet again,
May God hold you in the palm of his hand.

CHAPTER THIRTY-SIX

Suggestions for Discussion

(Following Poetry as a Pathway to God)

Part A

What do we mean by God? Heaven? - The impossible question. What is Jesus' status? What do we mean when we say that he is divine, the Son of God? In all such discussions, language is always a problem. It does not express the whole truth; only an approximation. Here are two propositions:

1. Poetry and metaphor are the servants of all religious discourse – 'rainbow bridges over things eternally apart.' Religious language is profoundly metaphorical. Modern people have lost the poetic or metaphorical way of looking at the world – and God – and so they find God-talk increasingly difficult.
2. Tradition is a dangerous ally. Whether in religion or poetry it must be 'continuously subverted and reinvented.' Thinking about the past always involves poetic re-creation. Whether with artefacts or great religious teachers, we acknowledge the limits of what we can know with certainty, and must then try to find 'a different kind of knowing.'

Theism is dead; God is not. 'The primary issue for everyone is this: how do we now conceptualise God?' But there are limits to how far intellect and reason can take us. 'To see clearly is poetry, prophecy, and religion.' (Ruskin). All artists are see-ers and compel our attention by the power of their imagery, which can lift us beyond reason.

But in religion we have lost the poetic or metaphorical way of looking at things. Why? Is there a parallel, perhaps, with the death of Tragedy as an art form? Both depended on a common view of the world, 'a community of expectation', which was fractured by the Reformation and the Enlightenment, which have given birth to the literal and prosaic mind. There used to be a Christendom, a way of life where the whole culture, its politics and economic life, were rooted in and expressed within Christian activities and images. The church was an institution embedded in society; society was the church.

King James' Bible was only just in time. It is the last version of the Bible to retain a truly poetic quality. To revive religion we don't have to revert to the AV. But we must restore the poetic way of looking at things. The process requires all sorts of different approaches.

'On a huge hill,
Cragged and steep,
Truth stands, and he that will
Reach her, about and about must go
And what the hill's suddenness resists
Win so.'

(John Donne).

As Jose Ortega y Gasset reminds us, 'In poetry, metaphor is something whose efficacy verges on magic; it seems like a tool for creation, which God forgot inside one of his creatures when he made him.' We must, therefore, train ourselves to 'go about and about', with quickened imaginations, alert to things that come obliquely to our vision, sensitised to metaphor and the tingle factor in all poetic language, until suddenly revelation breaks through.

Though religions may differ, the language of religion has always seemed familiar, always striving to express similar ideas. Always it is the capacity to think metaphorically and poetically which helps us articulate our sense of heaven. In time, by some strange alchemy, through poetry we may find that the God of all truth has arrived at the intellect by way of the heart.

Possible Discussion Questions

1. Where is Heaven? Where is God? How would you introduce and explain the idea of God or Heaven to a non-church-going 9-year old?
2. Are modern hymns, translations, liturgies an improvement on the past? For hymns, a good tune matters more than good words. (Does it?) Even doggerel will do. (Or will it?)
3. A faith without reason is a house built upon sand. A religion without faith is going nowhere.

Part B

For me there are certain features of poetry that are most compelling – spells and incantations; magic; connections, often inspired by metaphor or the reader's own creative responses; implications, because it is what remains unsaid, what lies in the interstices that matters, in the same way that God can be very powerfully felt even when he is absent.

Perhaps we can speak of two types of impact or effects of poetry. The 'traditional' effect – call it beauty – which once realised remains more or less constant through the centuries, because we can never recapture the immediacy of impact from the time when poets such as Virgil, Shakespeare, Milton, Tennyson, were speaking to their own generation. But the impact of a contemporary poet (such as T.S. Eliot) may be more compelling - not better or worse, but different. When we think of the poetry of the Bible, we confront an additional problem: to what extent does its impact depend on the quality of the translation? And does this in some way invalidate its truth or its quality? As the editor of the Oxford Bible Commentary remarked, 'Poetry is always seasick when it is ferried to another country.'

Poetry changes all the time. But do our ideas of God change? Think of the imagery with which we strive to describe the Divinity: he seems always an omnipotent, omniscient, omnipresent father figure. From beginning to end of the Bible we find limited progress in the imagery of God. Isaiah and Hosea just begin perhaps to introduce new dimensions. The Song of Songs may be a new metaphor for God's love. In the New Testament, even Jesus introduces limited change – God the Father (Abba), mellows a little perhaps, but Jesus' social revolution is much more original than his theological one. In some ways the Gnostics, with their allusive, often peculiar attempts to suggest the unsuggestible come nearer to poetry in the way they ask the reader to discover what lies between and behind the words.

The sense of the numinous has been there ever since homo sapiens emerged. Art and Language, through which humankind learned to express this sense, developed in tandem. Poetry has always tried to explore and express what is unseen as well as seen, what lies in the interstices of material reality, the 'thin' places of the earth. God as Absence as well as Presence has always been an important element among Christian mystics. The unseen, the unspoken, the implied, in fact the metaphorical and poetic, all these will help us towards the sudden revelation of beauty and truth.

So what is it in language that we should be looking for to trigger that sense of the numinous, of the perception that 'a spirit deep within sustains the heaven and earth … and Mind moves all the material things it permeates' (Virgil). Who but a poet can make the necessary connection between earth and heaven? Greek dramatists were profoundly original in their exploration of the nature of divinity and divine purpose; the ancients generally deified natural forces, of course, but also human models, mankind's benefactors (Herakles, Alexander, Augustus), though that concept was corrupted by the later Caesars. But are the saints of the Christian pantheon significantly different? Plato, poet as well as philosopher, achieved a near mystical quality in his thought. The Roman epic poets Virgil and Lucretius perhaps come nearer to originality in their exploration of meaning and purpose in the universe than 'modern' religion?

Is it in the interstices, the empty places, the silences, the 'thin places of the earth' that God is to be found (cf. *The Cloud of Unknowing*)? In Man's yearning for lost bliss (something rather more sublime than Housman's *blue remembered hills*, but of that ilk) and the divine possibilities of emptiness I find the most interesting form of exploration of Divinity. For Plato, all manifestations on earth are pale imitations of ultimate reality. Knowledge, understanding, and wisdom are simply recollections of our soul's once-upon-a-time experience of the eternal; our love of God a longing to return to that ideal world, which once our souls inhabited.

Questions for Discussion

1. If only poetic and metaphorical language can express the idea of God, can God be real?

2. Consider the value and the danger of reliance on tradition whether in art or religion. What kind of imagery might be appropriate nowadays to replace or expand the traditional concepts of Heaven, God the Father, Ascension, Sin and the Fall, Omnipresence, Angels etc.

3. The traditional idea of a Father God derives from the childhood of humanity; ultimately it needs to be abandoned. Most of us cling to it tenaciously because we do not know any other way to envision the holy.

CHAPTER THIRTY-SEVEN

Not Alone

In times of uncertainty and doubt, such as any thinking Christian must find himself in under present circumstances, it is both a surprise and a reassurance to find that others are moving in the same direction. I felt this strongly when I first discovered the existence of the Progressive Christianity Network of Britain (PCN-B); I find it often when old friends, whose opinions I respect, seem to have moved quite independently in the same sort of direction as I have; and above all when from unexpected sources come letters of agreement or support. One such source, wholly unknown to me, wrote unexpectedly from Wales (where the Anglican church seems to be suffering some sort of crisis of identity), supporting my suggestion in a letter to the *Times* nearly six months previously (page 21) that 'what we all need is a new theology that will win the assent of thinking people, who have abandoned traditional churches and their outdated mythologies.'

He wrote enclosing 'some ideas that occur to me with regard to some of the ills of the Anglican church' and suggesting a Plain Man's Guide approach to reinterpreting the Biblical account of the evolution of the Christian religion from its parent Jewish faith. The appeal of his account lay, not only in its brevity and its simplicity, but in the fact that it summarised the story in a style which avoided all the jargon of theological language, which he characterised as 'churchianity', and avoided any reversion to what John Robinson would have called 'mythology.'

He concluded with the observation that 'the poor old Bible has been so misused for so long that its value is not evident, despite modern scholarship. Perhaps it is right and proper to soft pedal those parts of the Bible that are of special interest to the Jewish faith, and recognise that in the OT prophets and the gospels, plus the Acts and letters, we have a record of God wanting to get in touch with us in order that his kingdom may come, and his will may be done.'

My reply went as follows:

I liked your letter very much and have wrestled hard with how best to reply. You say you are 'no theologian.' Nor am I, since I am a retired schoolmaster, a teacher of Latin, Greek, and Ancient History. But that is a profession which can admire and try to use, and to instil in pupils, the habit of simplicity of style and clarity of exposition, such as is exemplified by your 'Plain Man's Guide.' I do not think your approach is in any way 'simplistic,' as you suggest. Most theologians seem to me to be incapable of such clarity – and probably quite often accuse their interlocutors of being 'simplistic', as an excuse for their own obscurity. I wonder if anyone spoke or taught more simply and clearly than Jesus, assuming, as scholars seem to, that St John does not contain any words actually spoken by Jesus.

The best exemplar of a modern approach combined with remarkable clarity of exposition is, I find, Bishop John Shelby Spong. He has done in this generation what I suspect John Robinson did for a previous generation with *Honest to God*. It is quite surprising, but for me the best current 'theological' books are coming out of the USA – allegedly a hotbed of evangelical fundamentalism, yet home also to The Center (sic) for Progressive Christianity (TCPC).

Spong, Dominic Crossan, Marcus Borg, and the Jesus Seminar (a scholars' collective, so to speak) have all produced more interesting and progressive insights into how we might look at the faith in modern terms than anyone I have come across in the UK, except possibly Richard Holloway, former Primus of the Scottish Episcopal Church, and John Churcher, a Methodist minister with a mission from his authorities to evangelise in modern language and with due regard to modern scholarship. He is currently also Chair of PCN-B, the Progressive Christianity Network of Britain, an offshoot of TCPC, and he runs a website called 'Permission to Speak.' I find his sermons helpful.

I think that the difficulty which your approach presents to me is that (for perfectly understandable reasons) it expresses its idea of God anthropomorphically. You suggest, for example, that God 'chose' the Jews as the best tribe to 'rescue his children.' You may reply, of course, How else can we speak of what a God (understood in the traditional way) does, except in human terms? But once you confine your 'vision' to such metaphors, you run the risk illustrated by current church teaching of attributing to this divinity characteristics and wishes that are merely human. The next step is for the church to claim, as it does, to know what he thinks, what his wishes are etc., too often without acknowledging that (by contrast with Stephen Hawking) it cannot in fact 'know the mind of God.' (*Incidentally, though I use the masculine pronoun, I do not of course regard God as of masculine gender; but I prefer to use 'he' as we all do for all sorts of abstractions which are gender free.*)

You are right, of course, to assert then that a 'God of Love, being spirit, needs human hearts and above all hands to do the practical work.' But if so, can a spirit choose? And if he can, are you not attributing to him great incompetence and hopeless failure – in all this time he has made pretty little progress. Is he neither all-powerful, nor all-knowing? Why should he be involving himself in the life of one tiny planet in the vast expanse of the cosmos? Is he only at work on planet earth? And why did he deny insight into himself to all those pre-Christian pagans and all current peoples of non-Christian faiths? It is this sort of problem that, I think, fuels the scepticism of agnostics as well as atheists.

All language about God is metaphor. I suppose at the heart of my letter to the *Times* is my regret at the failure of the Church leadership to guide us towards newer and more effective metaphors, and of course the utter failure of some Christian churches to embrace the inclusiveness for and loving acceptance of all sorts and conditions of humankind, which a Spirit of Love would surely embody. (*I regard the current squabble over women bishops as illustrative of this point*). That is why I find it difficult to accept your idea that the Jews were 'chosen for a special job,' while agreeing entirely with your rejection of the second option that they were chosen as God's 'favourites.' I find their conduct towards their present as well as their past neighbours a travesty of what might be thought of as the wishes of a loving God.

But I do recognise and accept your perception that succeeding generations of prophets represent progress in the evolution of human values and a rejection of the domination culture (almost always masculine), which across the world seems to have become the norm in humankind. The likes of Amos, Hosea, Isaiah clearly represent intellectual (and theological?) advance and must have influenced Jesus. But in other parts of the world others were developing similarly, were they not? I don't understand really what is meant by the 'Axial Age', but it is a fashionable phrase for the period from roughly 1000 BC to AD 1000, when human values, usually expressed in religions, showed marked improvement.

When you see Jesus (along with John the Baptist) as the next step in prophetic development, I am comfortable. I am sure that whatever new vision we evolve for Christianity, it must include a recognition of an entirely human Jesus, as simply another in the line of great prophets – we need to ditch the supernatural dimension to his life and teaching. (*With this my correspondent did not agree, simply failing to see the necessity, as he put it*). This may leave Jesus seeming like a simple ethical philosopher. But if there is a God, then we can surely grant Jesus also a very profound sense of the God-ness of whatever it is God is – and can probably go no further in defining it. But I would then associate Mohammed also with that same line, as the last prophet of the Axial Age. Indeed, I read the other day the assertion that the appeal of Islam for many is that it is genuinely monotheistic, and not complicated by the doctrine of the Trinity. I rather agree.

Finally, I agree totally with your recognition that the vision of the early church seems to have been corrupted by the attractions of power, which can so easily be regarded by those who have the power as God's vindication of their own exercise of it. 'Go, sell all that thou hast.' I do not see much sign of it in the established Anglican Church or the Roman Catholic. The wealth of the Vatican alone would pretty well solve problems of poverty across the world, but it is the likes of Bill Gates and Warren Buffett who are pouring their wealth into world poverty and disease.

I do not regard the Bible as in any literal sense the Word of God, transmitted to his agents on earth by some sort of supernatural dictation. I think you agree. But it is a wonderful work of literature, history, poetry, fiction, which reflects the evolution of Humankind from developed ape to a being ('a little lower than the angels') capable of aspiring to the stars. If this is God 'getting in touch with us,' as you say, then he certainly moves in a very mysterious way his wonders to perform – and is taking an unconscionable time about it. And that is pretty hard on all those who through the centuries have failed to receive or recognise the message.

But all that said, I do find your essay not only clear and moving in its expression, but also a very helpful exposition of how one might present the story of God's relationship with man to those who long for some sort of non-supernatural exposition. In this respect you and I are walking the same path. I would argue that belief in God may be mistaken, but it is a perfectly rational hypothesis on which to base one's view of life, purpose, and the meaning of things. Without such an hypothesis, there can be no discussion, no debate, and belief is pointless. But the addition of supernatural and mythical clutter beyond the God hypothesis is what has become the problem. Richard Holloway has suggested in his latest book, *Leaving Alexandria*, that we should regard the Jesus of Faith as a 'strip tease in reverse.' The original Jesus was simplicity itself; the accretions attached to him over the centuries by the Churches have made him unrecognizable, unreachable, incredible.

A few brief excerpts from my correspondent's reply:

1. I agree that God has made little progress over the last 1900 years, but given human perverseness and Church incompetence, it might be said that significant steps have been taken.
2. It must be wrong to confine God's activity to the Bible, so non-Christian faiths have responded in their own way, e.g. the Buddhist Four Noble Truths.
3. I can't see the need to ditch the supernatural dimension of Jesus' life, given the evidence.
4. The view of the Bible as the literal word of God I find baffling and I lament the confusion it causes. I enclose a few articles written for a local parish magazine, which initially caused almost no interest apart from the rector asking me (very politely) to stop because some of the articles were 'too near the bone'. (*I wonder how many other progressive thinkers have suffered the same fate!*)
5. There is no need for a new theology; the old theology is perfectly sound so long as it is cleansed of the cranky ideas and confusions that the centuries have produced.

I have included this short exchange of letters simply to illustrate my perception that, though he and I may not agree on details, I am sure we are both travelling in similar directions. And I am sure that many others are too. It is so important that wherever possible those of similar outlook should tactfully make their presence felt and their views known, because one day the church leadership may begin to listen. They claim to have 'consulted widely' on women bishops. As an ordinary layman in the parish pew, I have not been aware of any consultation whatever. So I doubt their claim to any sort of wide consultation. But while there is a quiet body of progressive opinion 'out there,' all is not yet lost.

Section F: Soundbites

A poet's duty is to tell the truth, but tell it slant

Emily Dickinson

As I said before, I have kept a series of commonplace books since the age of fifteen, and one of my 'hobbies' has been to collect definitions and description of poetry and its purpose. The quotations which follow are all culled from these books. It is my belief that the metaphorical or 'poetic' way of thought is one of the most fruitful ways of talking and thinking about God. I hope that my attributions are accurate and that these 'definitions' may help to illustrate my point as well as offering food for thought and ideas.

CHAPTER THIRTY-EIGHT

Soundbites I

Poetry: Definitions and Descriptions

- Poets are the antennae of the race.

  Ezra Pound

- Poetry is being, not doing.

  E.E. Cummings

- Poetry is language charged with meaning to the utmost, ultimate degree.

  Ezra Pound

- A poem should be palpable
  and mute
  as a globed fruit
  A poem should be wordless
  As the flight of birds.
  A poem should not mean
  but be...

  Archibald McLeish

- Beauty is Truth, Truth Beauty.

  Keats

- The spontaneous overflow of powerful feelings.

  Wordsworth

- Emotion recollected in tranquillity.

  Wordsworth

- A raid upon the inarticulate.

  T.S. Eliot

- Turning blood into ink: a mug's game.

  T.S. Eliot

- What gets lost in translation.

  Robert Frost

- Poetry is, at bottom, a criticism of life.

  Matthew Arnold

- A profession of private thought, reinforced by craftsmanship of words.

  Robert Graves

- Poetry is the medium of suggestion; prose the medium of statement.

  Jackson Knight

- Art proves nothing, but illuminates everything.

  Anon

- That which arrives at the intellect by way of the heart.

  R.S. Thomas

- A glimpsed alternative.

  Seamus Heaney

- Myth is poetry plus, not science minus.

  Marcus Borg

- The child of epitaph and epigram, poetry is the great disciplinarian of prose.

  Joseph Brodsky

- The gift of priestly attention.

  Richard Holloway

- A poet's duty is to tell the truth, but tell it slant.

  Emily Dickinson

- The poet, described in ideal perfection, brings the whole soul of man into activity.

  Coleridge

- Deus escreve direito por linhas tortas – God uses crooked lines to write straight.

  Claudel

- The language of the unspeakable.

  Goethe

- A desperate attempt to say what cannot be said.

  Rubem Alves

- Poetic metaphors are rainbows and bridges over things eternally apart.

  Rubem Alves

- Treat everything you read in the Bible as metaphor, unless you can be certain that it is not.

  William Barclay

- One single word pregnant with unpredictable meanings.... One word which leads to infinite horizons.

  Rubem Alves

- Poetry is knowledge, salvation, power, abandonment – an operation capable of transforming the world. Poetry reveals this world; and creates another.

  Octavio Paz

- A poem draws the nearer to beauty and truth in so far as its words reveal the unceasing journey of a soul towards its own beauty and truth.

  Maeterlinck

- In poetry, metaphor is something whose efficacy verges on magic, and it seems a tool for creation, which God forgot inside one of his creatures when he made him.

  Ortega y Gasset

- The image does not demand any knowledge. The poetic image is not an echo of the past. It is rather the reverse: by the explosion of the image, a far away past reverberates in the echoes.

  Gaston Bachelard

- Poetry is always seasick when it is ferried to another country... The ultimate horror of the ability of translation to destroy the poetry is seen in the Good News Bible.

  Oxford Bible Commentary

- Poetry complicates the ranges and values of the behaviour of the mind.... By virtue of elision, concentration, obliqueness, and its capacity to sustain a plurality of meanings, poetry gives an image of life which is far denser and more complex than that of prose.   George Steiner

- What in me is dark
  Illumin, what is low raise and support;
  That to the highth of this great Argument
  I may assert Eternal Providence,
  And justifie the wayes of God to men.   John Milton

- Malt does more than Milton can to justify God's ways to man.

  A.E. Housman

- What every poet sets out to do: to see clearly, and to pin down exactly, in memorable, musical words, not only what he sees, but what he feels.

  S.P.B. Mais

- R.S. Thomas fell to talking about never having succeeded in putting over the one thing that is really good poetry – the suggestion, the elusive something that is found, or rather not found, in life, in God – that miraculous suggestion which gives a thrill of the unknown almost.   Byron Rogers

- Poetry gives most pleasure when only generally and not perfectly understood.

  Coleridge

- The poet, described in ideal perfection, brings the whole soul of man into activity. The power and unity of poetry is a fusion of so many opposites, a reconciliation not only of sameness with difference, the general with the concrete... but also a balance of vehement feeling and enthusiasm with understanding and judgement. Through juxtaposition, ideas, concepts, and descriptions are made clear. The more imaginative the juxtaposition is, the more exciting the poem becomes. Everything is there.

  Coleridge

- Homer, like the God Apollo at Delphi, does not say, nor does he conceal – he indicates.   Heracleitus

- A Poem begins with an image, or a memory, or something pregnant with analogy.   S. Heaney

- Music when soft voices die, vibrates in the memory.   Shelley

- Poetic metaphors: visible signs of an invisible grace – this is that.

  Rubem Alves

- Great poetry always consists of ordinary words, transfigured by extraordinary emotion. Aggrieved poets do not write great poetry. The greatest thought, too, however far it may be from the understanding of most men, is always expressed in familiar language. H. Kingsmill

- If poetry comes not as naturally as leaves to a tree, it had better not come at all. John Keats
  (quoted by Neville Coghill in a letter on Why does a poet write poetry?)

- Rumaging into his living, the poet fetches the images out that hurt and connect.
  W.H. Auden

- Poetry makes nothing happen; it survives in the valley of its saying, where executives would never want to tamper; it flows south from ranches of isolation and the busy griefs, raw towns that we believe and die in; it survives, a way of happening, a month.
  W.H. Auden

- Poetry is the supreme form of human locution; poetry is not only the most concise way of conveying human experience; it also offers the highest possible standards for any linguistic operation – especially one on paper… the child of epitaph and epigram, poetry is the great disciplinarian of prose.
  Joseph Brodsky

- I can no more define poetry than a terrier can define a rat, but I think we both recognise the object by the symptoms which it provokes in us. One of these symptoms was described in connexion with another object by Eliphaz, the Temanite: 'A spirit passed before my face: the hair of my flesh stood up.'
  A.E. Housman (ref: Job 4.15)

- In prose we have the word: birds in cages. In poetry the words explode the cage in which they were trapped, and they fly and take us on their wings.
  Rubem Alves

- If I read a book and it makes my whole body so cold no fire can warm me, I know that is poetry. If I feel physically as if the top of my head were taken off, I know that is poetry. These are the only ways to know it. Is there any other way? Emily Dickinson

- The politician and the sergeant major, the banker and the lawyer, are stronger than the poet and the philosopher, the prophet and the saint. The Son of God was crucified. Socrates was poisoned. The prophets were stoned.
  Nicolas Berdyaev

- The greatest thing a human soul ever does in this world is to see something and tell what it saw in a plain way. Hundreds of people can talk for one who can think, but thousands can think for one who can see. To see clearly is poetry, prophecy, and Religion. John Ruskin.

Soundbites II:

Signposts to the Idea of God

Theology is a kind of poetry - Duns Scotus Erigena (fl.850)

Happy the man who can know the causes of things
And beneath his feet who can suppress all fears,
Inexorable fate, and the roaring of greedy Acheron.
But happy too is he that knows the gods of countryside.

Virgil

On a huge hill,
Cragged and steep, Truth stands, and he that will
Reach her, about must and about must go,
And what the hill's suddenness resists, win so.

John Donne

TRUTH

- 'What is Truth?' said jesting Pilate, and would not stay for an answer.

  Francis Bacon

- It is heaven upon earth, to have a man's mind move in charity, rest in providence, and turn upon the poles of truth. Francis Bacon

- All a poet can do today is to warn. That is why a true poet must be truthful. Wilfred Owen

- The truth, my friend, is not eloquent except unspoken; its vast shadow lends eloquence to our sparks of thought as they die into it.

  George Santayana

- A poem is that species of composition which is opposed to works of science by proposing for its immediate object pleasure, not truth; and from all other species (having this object in common with it) it is discriminated by proposing to itself such delight from the whole as is compatible with a distinct gratification from each component part. Coleridge

A GREATER or HIGHER TRUTH?

- Myth is a form of poetry, which transcends poetry in that it proclaims a truth. Myth is poetry plus, not science minus. Myths are metaphorical narratives about the relations between this world and the sacred. Myths are necessary if we are to speak at all about the world's origin and destiny in God. Marcus Borg

- Like biblical narratives generally, Israel's primal narrative (the Pentateuch) combines historical memory with metaphorical narrative. The exodus story contains some history remembered, but it is not what we think of as historical reporting; rather it is history 'metaphorized.'

Marcus Borg

- The metaphorical approach needs controls… which are provided in part by the historical approach (i.e. an understanding of context) and in part by the discernment of the community to which the interpretation is offered. In short the historical and metaphorical approaches need each other.

Marcus Borg

- The mythical past is always present: in the depths of the lake there is no time. The 'once upon a time in a distant land' is a metaphorical way of speaking about present loss.

Rubem Alves

- Myth is a story which has a universal significance, and yields up a deeper meaning at every stage of human history. It is a story which no-one has invented, but which has arisen out of the depth of human experience.

Stephen Verney

- The Poetic Principle itself is, strictly and simply, the human aspiration for supernal beauty; but the manifestation of the Principle is always found in an elevating excitement of the soul, quite independent of that passion which is the intoxication of the heart, or of that truth which is the satisfaction of the reason.

Edgar Allen Poe

- Just as the voice, confined in the narrow channel of a trumpet, comes out sharper and stronger, so in my opinion a thought, compressed in the strict metres of verse, springs out more briskly and strikes with a higher impact.

Montaigne Essays

- (Poetic) Drama is a form of wakefulness, akin to Edward Thomas' sleep into which one goes willing-nilling, to find one's way and lose oneself.

Patric Dickinson

- It is the poet's task to act as a counterweight to the unbalance all about us, to redress the darkness by tilting the scales towards truths which are universal and transcendent.
S. Heaney

- In one of his last essays Bernard Levin, suffering from Alzheimer's, wrote that 'provided we do not try to deny the terrible reality, there is no shame in retreating to the Schubert Quintet, to Shakespeare's Sonnets, to the Rondanini Pieta of Michaelangelo. Whatever Christmas means to us, from nothing to everything, it will last forever. And Love, the beloved republic, may weep but will abide.' For Christians, Levin's 'Beloved Republic' is a monarchy: it is the beloved Kingdom where Christ reigns, with its great and abiding verities: Love, Justice, Mercy, and Truth. And if we desire it enough, they **will** abide.

Michael Mayne

A PATHWAY TO GOD?

If we want to think theologically, we must think poetically; if we want to say something meaningful about God and religion, we must speak poetically (i.e. metaphorically). There comes a time when logical argument runs out – and then you must have recourse to myth. And for myth poetry, or at least poetic language, is the proper mode of expression.

- Self-born, untaught, motherless, unshakeable,
  Giving place to no name, many named, dwelling in fire,
  Such is God. We are a portion of God, his angels.....
  To him then look
  And pray at dawn looking out to the east.

  Apollo of Claros

- In the beginning Spirit deep within sustains the heaven and earth
  The gleaming plains, moon's shining globe, and Titan's stars,
  And Mind moves all the material things it permeates.

  Virgil

- Theology is a kind of poetry; philosophy is the royal road to God.

  Duns Scotus Erigena

- 'Your best god is an idol.' In a comment on this quotation from Fr George Tyrrell (1861-1909) Andrew Pierce points out that Tyrrell was reminding his listeners that we have no approach to the reality of God except through our images of Him, and that no matter how spiritually exalted and/or metaphysically refined our image, it remains precisely that: both ours and an image; we made it and we made it out of something. Idolatry, Tyrrell was warning, is trivialised if we consider it answered by a minimalistic attitude to church décor; we need to attend to our imaginations, because it is there that we confuse - and regularly – image with reality.   (Source uncertain)

- Beowulf – an intelligence schooled by the pains of the world into becoming a soul.   Seamus Heaney

- Theology is – or should be – a species of poetry, which read quickly or in a hubbub of noise makes no sense. You have to open yourself to a poem with a quiet, receptive mind, in the same way as you might listen to a difficult piece of music.... line by line, note by note until it becomes part of you. Like the words of a poem, a religious idea, myth, or doctrine points beyond itself to truths that are elusive, that resist words or conceptualisation.

  Karen Armstrong

- Poetry is the gift of priestly attention… to avoid sentimentality it is important that this prayer of attention should not just be focused on nature; we should look at one another with the same expectation of revelation.

  Richard Holloway

- Psychoanalysis (?like poetry) is 'an attentive hearing of the silence which lies in the interstices of words, in order to hear what is not spoken.'

  Rubem Alves

- This, then, is the end of Tragedy – so to portray life that its tears become a joy forever.   F.L. Lucas

- The power of evil and horror must be granted their full scope; it is only thus we can triumph over them. Only when they have worked their uttermost will do we realise that there remains something in man's soul, which is forever beyond their grasp and has power in its own right to make life beautiful. That is the great revelation, or the great illusion, of tragedy.

  Gilbert Murray

- What I call the auditory imagination is the feeling for syllable and rhythm, penetrating far below the conscious levels of thought and feeling, invigorating every word; sinking to the most primitive and forgotten, returning to the origin and bringing something back, seeking the beginning and the end. It works through meanings, certainly, or not without meanings in the ordinary sense, and fuses the old and obliterated, and the trite, the current, and the new and surprising, the most ancient and the most civilised mentality.

  T.S. Eliot

- Man has been endowed with a threefold life, namely vegetable, animal, and rational. He journeys along a threefold road, for insofar as he is vegetable he seeks for what is useful, wherein he is of like nature with the plants; insofar as he is animal he seeks what is pleasurable, wherein he is of like nature with the brutes; in so far as he is rational, he seeks for what is right – and in this he stands alone, or is a partaker of the nature of the angels.

  Dante

- Though the poet appears to be concerned with the particular, he is actually concerned with that which is everywhere and at all times. From this it arises that sentences, especially of the dramatic poets, even without being general apothegms, find frequent application is real life.

  Arthur Schopenhauer

- Poetry is a mode of communication. What it communicates and how it does so, and the worth of what is communicated from it, is the subject matter of criticism. I.A Richards

- In the midst of the inhumanity and indifference of history, a handful of men and women have been creatively possessed by the compelling splendour of the useless (i.e. the arts). It may be that, together with the saints, secular and religious, they in some manner ransom mankind.

  George Steiner

- Plato was right to say that Eros was the child of Penia and Poros, poverty and plenty, of loss and possession. In Portuguese we have a word to describe this feeling and its seems there is no corresponding word in English: 'Saudades': the feeling which one has when one feels the presence of an absence – the toy of a dead child; an old photograph; the letter which has just arrived; the empty room. 'Saudades' names this feeling of mutilation – I feel that part of my own body has been torn out of me.

  Rubem Alves

- What memory loves is eternal.... One does not live by bread alone, but from words that contain the memory of a lost happiness.... We are what we eat, it is true. But not the whole truth. We are also the food we desire and cannot eat. We are hungry beings eternally.   Rubem Alves

* It is this great absence
  that is like a presence that compels
  me to address it without hope
  of a reply. It is a room I enter
  from which someone has just
  gone, the vestibule for the arrival
  of one who has not yet come.   R.S. Thomas

* Yet let him keep the rest,
  But keep them with repining restlessness;
  Let him be rich and weary, that at least,
  If goodness lead him not, yet weariness
  May toss him to my breast   George Herbert

* O God, thou hast made us for thyself, and our hearts are restless till they
  rest in thee.
                                              St Ignatius

Section G: Building Upon the Ruins

CHAPTER THIRTY-NINE

Issues and Implications -
Where do we go from here?

A: Straws in the Wind

In 1976, almost forty years ago, when Head of Classics and Director of Studies at Eastbourne College, I was asked to write for Didaskalos, the Journal of JACT (Joint Association of Classics Teachers) a review of the new Open University Course, The Roman Empire and the Rise of Christianity.

I am including in this Section a somewhat abbreviated version, because on re-reading it I found to my surprise that already I had a sense of where the whole business of Religious Studies and Christian education seemed to be heading, and was making suggestions for what might be done to halt the trend away from traditional belief. To some extent I think what I said then still holds good. This is what I wrote:

The time is ripe for Classical Studies and Religious Education to establish an alliance in much the same way that an alliance is already being forged between Classical and Literary Studies. Such an alliance must aim to illuminate by fact and reason, not to convert by persuasion based on confessional presuppositions. Christianity did not spring, like Athena, fully armed from the head of Zeus; it emerged gradually from a cultural stewing-pot – and if the claim offends the doctrine of revelation, I am sorry. Among the ingredients of the stewing-pot were Judaism, Mystery religions, Greek philosophy and Roman developments thereof. To 'understand' the religious phenomenon we call Christianity, therefore, it is essential to have some nodding acquaintance with a wide range of topics such as these.

But one must do more. One must also have an understanding of the history (political, social, economic) of the various nations concerned. Roman law, the powers of an imperial procurator, and his methods of implementing the law by means of those powers are clearly relevant to the vexed question of what happened at the trials of Christ and Paul, as Sherwin-White made admirably clear. To find too that the factual elements of the gospel story are so extremely accurate in their detailed representation of the operation of the law may indeed have a bearing on one's attitude to the more 'mythical' elements in their account.

This Second Level OU course aims, accordingly, at breadth not depth. If I understand its intention correctly, it is not for the specialist but offers rather a broad conspectus of the Roman world of the first century AD, and seeks to show how in that world Christianity emerged. It is also extremely careful to emphasize its non-confessional intentions: it is academic, not theological, and thereby forms an excellent basis for the formation of one's own theology.....

....Right at the end of the series we were offered four Units on the Rise of Christianity itself, which sketched for us – again with great clarity – the factors affecting the emergence of the Christian religion from a rather more specifically religious viewpoint. In between we were treated to surveys of philosophy, literature, art, other religions, and social attitudes – all naturally relevant to a general survey of the Roman Empire, but not always, I suspect, justified by the title '**and** the Rise of Christianity.'....

Here then is my first reservation: were the authors clear in their own minds about the aims of the course? Was it a general introduction to the ancient world, designed to stimulate interest (which it did), or was it a course of study directed to an understanding of the evolution of Christianity, as a remarkable but perhaps not unique religious phenomenon? ......

(The central part of my review deals more specifically with the contents of the course itself)

As for the course itself, as a whole: first, it must be good for classicists. For far too long we have studied our subject in its own tidy little Greek and Latin boxes, and probably also within the very limited dates to which we attach the description 'classical.' By this course our horizons are indeed widened and to some extent perspective changed. Sadly, however, here I believe an opportunity was lost. Too much of the material was purveyed from the traditional standpoint of the Roman historian. This is legitimate, I concede, since the course was not a sort of classicist's 'benefit'; but I feel the Rome-centred view is so much the normal one that most would benefit from seeing the history from the viewpoint of the biblical scholar, or indeed of the Roman provincial – just as doubtless biblical scholars benefited by hearing their familiar text dealt with from the viewpoint of a professional Roman historian. To look in more often from the periphery, rather than out from the Roman centre, would be stimulating – to do so more often would improve the balance of the course.

Secondly, the course should also be good from the viewpoint of the student of religion. For far too long Religious Education has been, is now, and probably ever shall be at the present rate of progress, the Cinderella subject of the educational world. One statutory period per week with the padre or RE teacher, or a vague and doubtless well intentioned study of comparative religion ('Come on, Smith: you find out about Buddhism and tell us about it next week') is no way to restore respect for a subject which, in its implications at least, must be the most important any child can study.

If this course shows teachers and students the possibilities of the subject; if it inspires someone to produce a course that is non-confessional, intellectually respectable and stimulating, academically demanding, it will have done the state some service. Certainly it has shown that without religious presuppositions it is possible to study the emergence of a religion as a significant and fascinating cultural phenomenon in its own right. It has revealed a little too of how the religious mind works, the kind of language *homo religiosus* (as opposed to *homo* merely *sapiens*) talks – that too is valuable.

If understanding is conducive to sympathy, perhaps the most significant effect of this course, its real claim to importance, will be that it encourages a sympathetic understanding of the world of Rome and of the Christian – both in rather poor standing at present.

Meanwhile please will some enlightened Examinations Board and some enlightened academics put together an A-level and an O-level course along similar lines. The JACT Ancient History Committee tried, but has failed so far for lack of academic support on the biblical side. Perhaps the course will create some new impetus. It is good enough to do so.

That final plea says something pretty damning, in my view, of the failings of the Church and its leading academics. That we could not find anyone of reasonable academic standing to take on the task of joining the ancient historians in producing a course for A Level, which should have been fascinating, says something of their inertia, or perhaps fear that an intellectually rigorous course might reveal the inadequacies of their approach to explaining and defending their own faith. Given the more recent growth in interest in religion generally, I fear that a great opportunity was missed, since there is still no A Level of the kind I asked for.

B. What do we teach the children?

'The fathers have eaten a sour grape and the children's teeth are set on edge.' If we can no longer communicate our faith persuasively to our children, then that faith is doomed to decay and ultimate destruction. We deserve no less.

At the heart of what follows lies the conviction that we must de-mythologise, de-mystify, de-professionalise, de-sanctify, de-complicate, and de-codify doctrine and worship, not just for children, but for all adherents of the church.

I am less concerned for children of primary school age. Stories are the best medium of instruction and they can handle mythology and legend without anxiety, and have little problem blurring the distinction between fact and fiction. There is still a future for the annual Nativity plays.

My real anxiety is for the next age group – those of secondary school age and immediately beyond in young adulthood. They are naturally sceptical, iconoclastic, and hostile to authority. It is those who were in my mind in the previous article, when I asked for an A Level course that would appeal to the rational side of a student's mind. I am sure that for them a factual, historical, rational, and sceptical approach will be best.

The ethical dimension of Jesus' teaching will surely strike a chord in many, since the young are nothing if not idealistic. But if we then try to tell them that Jesus was the Son of God in any literal sense, we instantly undermine the authority of his teaching. We should seek to treat the whole account as a detective story and try to test what is likely and unlikely, what is 'spin' and why, what is legendary, what is fiction etc. I can think of no better vehicle for this approach than the two books by the Jesus Seminar – *The Five Gospels* and *The Acts of Jesus*. And won't they all enjoy shocking their parents?

Above all, treat Jesus as a normal human being, a great reformer with a mission, like Dr Martin Luther King perhaps, or a religious genius on an equality with the

Buddha, Mohammud, Confucius, Socrates, and other inspirational leaders and teachers, ancient and modern. They will then find less reason to doubt the claims made for his authority.

Re-think the concept of Holy Trinity. The whole idea still puzzles people just as much as it did the ancient Irish, to whom St Patrick tried to explain it by using a shamrock as illustration. Some find it hard to distinguish the idea of three gods in one god from polytheism; indeed, it has been suggested that for some converts the growing appeal of Islam in this country owes much to the uncomplicated appeal of its undiluted monotheism.

Teach the Bible as literature, but not as the literal Word of God, which it manifestly is not, and again we remove another weak link in our chain of argument. That it is a great book, full of profound religious insights and superb poetry, no one need doubt. But it is also the record of a long span of historical development in one particular tribe and as a result in the wider reaches of humankind. As such it contains history, legend, poetry, fiction, contradictory information, some ludicrously outdated rules for moral behaviour, but also values that hold good to this day, horrifying brutality attributed to the god of the Jewish people, visionary nonsense in some of its apocalyptic writings. We should teach the young to relish it for what it is; not for what earlier generations wrongly claimed it was. Only then will its wisdom become credible.

Teach the children that the church and its doctrine is not a divine creation – it is a human artefact, put together by human beings for human beings, and subject to, indeed guilty of, all the weaknesses, shortcomings, limitations, and vices of humankind. But organisations are needed and this is the only organisation we have: use it, improve it, challenge it, respect it, but don't worship it. At its best it is simply a tool; at its worst it is a liability. But we must reform it.

C. Reforming the Institutional Church.

Jesus took on the priests and rulers of the Jewish religion. He himself gathered disciples and encouraged them to spread his ideas. As far as we know he avoided appointing priests; his was a **priesthood of the laity** par excellence. Of course some sort of organisation is needed, even the services of a limited number of professionals, to provide some of the services, which the present churches provide for their adherents. But we must eliminate the mystique of priesthood, which is a legacy from an earlier, more superstitious age. The apostolic succession; the monopoly of Eucharistic celebration; the hierarchy of bishops, priest and deacons – all these are antiquated remnants of the religions of pre-Christian as well as Christian times. They should be allowed to wither on the vine, unless their usefulness is demonstrable. The non-conformist churches need no bishops. Quakers convene under the guidance of the holy spirit and the leadership of ordinary lay people.

Re-think worship. For many the Eucharist may well be central to their spiritual lives. That is absolutely fine, as long as they remember that for some, especially newcomers, it is religious gobbledy-gook. The idea of eating the flesh and drinking the blood of Jesus is primitive and even sacrifice is pretty challenging – a loving God who sacrifices his own son for the sin of the world is hardly morally impressive. Perhaps a memorial service, such as you hold for any dead relative, should be the model, with Bible readings perhaps as eulogies and teaching vehicles. Language and imagery must be changed; but the poetry of the language of worship is essential. But above all, make it special – perhaps by reducing the frequency.

Devise a new routine service for the uncommitted and those who find the Eucharist unhelpful. A modern matins/evensong, with plenty of singing (psalms as well as hymns); bible and other readings; a short sermon treating the congregation as intelligent thinking adults, who want to learn; perhaps offer opportunities for discussion (that is what the original Latin word, *sermo*, means – conversation). Or even simple services of meditation, secular or religious. Bishop Spong, when a vicar, used to run very successful 2-hour Sunday Schools for adults before Sunday worship. I mention it not as a suggestion for immediate action, but as evidence that there are hungry sheep who look up and long to be fed.

Cut Costs Drastically. The church still operates as if it is the fiefdom of the prince bishops of medieval times. It maintains hundreds of large, inefficient, expensive local churches, which are a burden on their communities. If governments want them for tourist attractions, let government pay for them. If they are listed buildings, let the listing authority pay for them and maintain them. Call their bluff. Walk out and let them fall down. Village halls and schools, all have appropriate spaces. Borrow or even rent them. House churches are a promising development. Discussion groups often feel more spiritual than formal worship. Church schools are often very good. But diocesan education officers are another burden on the finances of the church.

Bishops and their staffs need to be reduced. We should re-think the role of the bishop. Every hierarchy contrives to enhance the complexity of its own office, so as to reinforce an impression of importance and indispensability. A bishop is above all Father in God to the Clergy. They may have a leadership role, which extends through the clergy to the faithful generally. They should not be mere administrators in a dog collar.

Why are bishops needed for confirmations, which a parish priest is perfectly capable of carrying out? If bishops have time to sit in the House of Lords, they cannot be over-busy. Start by abolishing all suffragans; then halve the number of bishops. Let parishes run their own affairs in their own way. Vicars should not be looking over their shoulders all the time for fear of offending the bishop. When I look back at the hours and weeks wasted seeking for permission to move one pew or to counter one objection from a single opponent of the wishes of the PCC, the bumbling administration of the diocesan system and its legal framework reminds me of nothing so much as the hierarchies which are usually the symptoms of the final years of collapsing empires.

Disestablishment? – Yes. We need to disestablish the church, let priests and parishes grow up; and let congregations work out to some degree their own salvation.

D. A New Creed?

> No! I am not Prince Hamlet, nor was meant to be;
> Am an attendant lord, one that will do
> To swell a progress, start a scene or two,
> Advise the prince; no doubt, an easy tool,
> Deferential, glad to be of use,
> Politic, cautious, meticulous;
> Full of high sentence, but a bit obtuse;
> At times, indeed, almost ridiculous –
> Almost, at times, the Fool.

T.S. Eliot: The Love Song of J. Alfred Prufrock

But of course, as every lover of Shakespeare knows, the whole function of the Fool is to 'tell the truth, but tell it slant,' which Emily Dickinson tells us is also the duty of the poet. Behind the folly there is the honesty of the licensed buffoon. It is not that the buffoon is necessarily right; but it is always possible that to those who listen to what lies behind the words, there can appear to be a glimmer of good sense, a hint of heaven. I hope so.

What I have written in the preceding section of course may seem to overstate the case and may well convince those who were still inclined to give me the benefit of the doubt that I have indeed tipped over the edge into insanity. But as Pilate observed in a different context, 'what I have written, I have written.'

As a final act of temerity, I set myself to try to work out if there were any bits from the two Creeds (Apostles' and Nicene), which I could continue to say in church in good conscience. Even though I have said them in church for most of my life, over the last decade or so I have found myself no longer able to utter them.

Remnants of two Creeds

I believe in a God, to be found at the heart of all that is, visible and invisible.
This is what I have called 'The God Hypothesis.' No one can prove or disprove God's existence. I am content to accept the possibility as a working hypothesis.
I strive to follow the way of Jesus, son of Mary, also called Christ, who suffered crucifixion under Pontius Pilate, died, and was buried.
I am satisfied that the above statement is historically true. Most of the other claims about Jesus' origins are pious legends.
The memory of his life and death lives on in the hearts of all that follow him.
This is the nearest I can get to 'rose again.' I am sure that something got into the disciples after Jesus' death, which profoundly affected their lives and the way in which they lived as members of a suffering and often persecuted community.
The spirit of his teaching and example sets the standard by which the living and the dead are judged.
That is as my best approximation to the claim that he 'shall come to judge the quick and the dead.'
I call by the name Holy Spirit all that is good and true in those who seek God and strive to live as followers of Jesus' way.

I believe in the possibility of a spirit of goodness, which we catch from others, whether by example or instruction. To some it will seem no more than kindness; the social scientists may call it 'altruism,' and argue that it is no more than a Darwinian factor in the survival of the species. Others may elevate it to a quality of nobility and self-sacrifice. They may all be right. But it is something real and its effect can be compelling. And of course Jesus' Way is not the only way. God welcomes his children by whatever road they come.

I do not, and cannot, believe in the Holy Catholic and Apostolic Church as anything more than a human construct for the propagation of one particular religion at one particular period of human history.

Though I believe that a Church-like organisation is necessary; none is divinely appointed; all are but human constructs; our present one is deeply flawed and needs replacement.

If such a creed were all that remained for the church as a whole, rather than for this somewhat eccentric (Arian?) apostate (as doubtless many would call me), well might historians of church history exclaim, as Shelley did of Ozymandias,

'Look on its works ye Mighty, and despair!'
Nothing beside remains. Round the decay
Of that colossal wreck, boundless and bare
The lone and level sands stretch far away.

Conclusion

We need a new Creed, a new Mission Statement, as modern jargon might express it. It will need to incorporate different ideas and use different language, to convert what is mythological and outdated into words which perhaps by means of poetry express ideas to which modern believers can relate. T.S. Eliot once suggested that all poetry should seek to re-wind the decaying strands of tradition so as to give them new life. So too should religious doctrine. That would be a real Resurrection.

CHAPTER FORTY

Building Upon the Ruins

We are a portion of God, his angels.
To him then pray at dawn, looking out to the east.

Apollo of Claros

In the beginning Spirit deep within sustains the heaven and earth
The gleaming plains, Moon's shining globe, and Titan's stars,
And Mind moves all the material things it permeates.

Virgil, *The Aeneid*

There are more things in heaven and earth, Horatio,
Than are dreamt of in your philosophy.

Shakespeare, *Hamlet*

What rough beast, its hour come at last,
Slouches towards Bethlehem to be born?

Yeats, *Second Coming*

We shall not cease from exploration
And the end of all our exploring
Will be to arrive where we started
And know the place for the first time.

T.S. Eliot, *Little Gidding*

Someone will forever be surprising
A hunger in himself to be more serious.

Philip Larkin, *Church Going*

Science without Religion is lame; Religion without Science is blind.

Albert Einstein

This list of brief quotations ranges from the 6th Century BC to the 20th Century AD. None of them offers answers; all of them suggest ways of looking at the problem of what faith and religion might mean to the people of our day. All of them reflect the fact that humankind has always sought for meaning, and always had a sense of something that is beyond and above itself. In the end, that is what religion does – it offers a way of looking at the world, creation, our lives, and trying to make sense of what we see or fail to see, what we understand and what we find beyond comprehension, and to express that sense of the numinous in our lives which most of us have experienced at some time or other, and which many may call 'God.'

The problem for all those who, like me, profess themselves dissatisfied with what religion (of whatever kind) currently offers, is that we find it easy to demolish its ideas and structures, but very difficult to suggest what form the replacement edifice should take. In this I am entirely typical. I have no tidy answers.

But I am very sure that demolition is needed, and unavoidable if we are to rebuild. I am no less sure that religions need to think in centuries, if not millennia, as they have always done; that they always start as minority perceptions; that they are always modified by the prophets of succeeding generations; and that, being human constructs, their current status quo is challenged by radicals and resolutely, if not savagely, defended by those who have vested interests or status in it, are comfortable with it, or find profit and advantage from it. All that those who seek to re-build can do is to suggest where they think the raw materials of construction may be found. They will often be wrong. If they are right, it will take a century or two to bring the necessary changes to some sort of fulfilment.

I try to remember always that the real enemy of faith is not doubt, but certainty. Where there is certainty, faith flies out the window. Where there is doubt, faith stands close at hand as a trusty ally. Where faith is confident, doubt plays the role of Loyal Opposition.

As one who professes and calls himself Christian, three hypotheses form the starting point of what I will call for convenience 'my faith.' I call them hypotheses, first of all because they are not certainties, and secondly because all scientists start by offering an hypothesis, when they seek to explain something hitherto inexplicable. They submit their hypothesis to peer-group evaluation, and accept criticism, modification, improvement, and even disproof, because to any good scientist truth matters more than winning an argument. Religions, by contrast, usually refuse to submit their hypotheses to any sort of evaluation, and will often punish, even by death, those who challenge them. They bitterly resist all kinds of modification.

I totally accept that there may be more things in heaven and earth than are dreamed of in the philosophies of scientists, and that faith and religion, like poetry, do not lend themselves to scientific evaluation. But if one seeks truth, the scientific method – hypothesis, antithesis, synthesis (which becomes the new hypothesis) - is the way to make a start. It was developed by Socrates around 450 BC, has stood the test of time, and is the best tool for thought available.

Three hypotheses

First, I accept that what I call the 'God Hypothesis' is fundamental to my argument. It is as legitimate as any hypothesis, possibly valid, certainly essential, if the rest of any search for truth and meaning is to have any point at all. The GOD of my hypothesis IS, and is by definition good.

Second, Jesus, the founder of my religion, was an inspired prophet, possessed of a deep relationship with what he called his God (and metaphorically his Father), but he was as human as every other member of humankind, though blessed with spiritual gifts that were certainly unusual, but equally certainly not necessarily unique.

The fact that the gospels record that he addressed God as 'Father' does seem to me to make it pretty clear that he had no illusions about his 'equality' with God, let alone that he had any illusions about being the Second Person of the Trinity. Such ideas are the product of later ecclesiastical imaginations.

Third, all religions and their related structures of organisation, offices, and doctrine are human inventions which, at their best, seek to facilitate religious activities, but too often strive above all else to preserve their own system from all forms of challenge. Their concern is not truth but survival.

Those who find these three hypotheses unacceptable will rightly see little point in continuing the debate. It is not that I am certain I am right. But unless debate begins from agreed assumptions (hypotheses), the protagonists will simply end up in a dialogue of the deaf, generating heat without light, words without meaning, and hostility without end.

So how do we begin?

One of the wisest and most distinguished of all my friends, over the last dozen years or so, has also been my most constant correspondent on all sorts of matters, from the trivial to the sublime. The breadth of his reading is remarkable; and he is blessed with one of the sharpest analytical minds I have come across. He can extract the essence of a book and examine the quality of its argument with a precision and clarity that I find formidable. In the final chapter of his own latest book, he has offered a statement of what he calls his Credo. Predictably, as an expression of faith, it has left me with feelings of inadequacy, since I felt that I had little more to say. It expressed, far better and more learnedly than anything I am capable of, the basis of his own faith, how it has developed, and what he has found possible to abandon. We seem to have travelled very similar roads and reached almost identical conclusions. After a wide-ranging survey, he concludes as follows:

> I believe there is a spiritual impulse in most of us, but one which is ultimately indefinable other than through the laws of love. The primary purpose of any religion is surely to help us to release this spirituality, something which lies outside our own egos in a way which will lead to a better understanding of ourselves, a deeper humility in how we relate to the world around us and everything in it, and an awareness of our practical responsibilities to those, especially our own children, who come after us. Otherwise, or so it seems to me, allegedly God-driven religion has no value at all, other than a way of exercising power and control over people's lives in its own self-interest.
>
> I believe we are all individually responsible and accountable for what we do in this life. There can be no hiding behind anyone else. Each one of us always, has a choice, whoever we are, whatever we believe. And I believe that the 'grace of God', however that is understood, is exercised through our consciences. In short I am attracted to the proposition that Jesus' teachings were more about what humanity should be rather than what divinity is. And I doubt that he would have had much difficulty in accepting the humanist version of the Ten Commandments, as set out in Professor A.C Grayling's *The Good Book – a Secular Bible*. **Love well; seek the good in all things; harm no others; help the needy; think for yourself; take responsibility; respect nature; do your utmost; be informed; be courageous.**
>
> In conclusion, I return, without embarrassment, to Aldous Huxley's answer, at the end

of his life, about what he had discovered during his spiritual journey:
It is embarrassing to tell you this, but it seems to come down mostly to just learning to be kind.

As if by some almost divine coincidence, as I worked on my final revision of this text, I heard the acceptance speech of Aung San Suu Kyi, the Burmese Opposition leader and 1991 Nobel Peace Prize winner, delivered some twenty-one years after the award itself. In it she spoke most movingly of the importance and essential need for kindness in human society, in words which must have resonated powerfully in all who heard her, and softened the hearts even of those who in Yeats' words had so far found that 'too long a sacrifice can make a stone of the heart.'

In fact, almost all discussion returns somehow or other to The Golden Rule, 'Do unto others what you would they should do unto you', or more negatively but no less cogently, 'Do not unto others what you would not that they should do unto you.' It speaks to all religions and none; to all ethical systems; to all communities of humankind. Strip religion of its supernatural accoutrements, and I suspect that its teaching boils down to very much the same thing.

My own approach may, perhaps, be different. But my dark suspicion is that I can hardly improve upon the above. However, here goes.

We surely have to start by recognising the truth of Einstein's statement, quoted above, that Science without Religion may well be lame; but Religion without Science is most certainly blind. Taking Science in this context as effectively synonymous with Reason, we must recognise that a Religion whose doctrines are contradicted by Science or manifestly contrary to Reason, cannot convince, and must ultimately fail, however long it may endure. Of course Reason alone can never be sufficient, but that is because even Reason (like Science) has its limitations. In matters of religion Reason is not so much wrong as simply inadequate, not the whole story, or as Einstein has it, 'lame.' But if Religion challenges Science, it will always lose in the end.

Then, as St Augustine I think observed, we have to acknowledge that 'God welcomes his children by whatever road they come.' John Donne makes a similar point, that Truth stands upon a huge hill, cragged and steep, and 'he that will reach her about and about must go' and, however steep the hill, win through by perseverance. There are as many pathways to God as there are pilgrims struggling along the way. All alike may benefit from the experiences of those who have gone before, but all need the basic confidence, which is the legacy of Reason.

In earlier chapters, perhaps prematurely and at some length, I suggested that Poetry could be seen as one of the possible pathways up Donne's hill of Truth to God. Similarly, a sense of Beauty, whether in nature or in art, may well lead the heart's gaze in a God-ward direction. Keats, for example, suggested that 'Beauty is Truth, Truth Beauty, that is all ye know on earth and all ye need to know.' Much depends on how we define Beauty – and if it lies simply in the eye of the beholder, I am not sure it is likely to prove a very helpful indication of Truth. I wonder if it is more helpful to think in terms of manifestations of God-ness – not godliness, which is an admirable if somewhat pedestrian quality, nor goodness, which is an admirable but merely human quality. God-ness, I suggest, is something more, something suggestive of divinity.

Wordsworth's 'sense sublime of something far more deeply interfused' comes somewhat closer to what I mean. Cynical rationalists will legitimately argue that such feelings are entirely subjective, mere sensation, as likely to be the products of a sound digestion as of a divine manifestation. They may well be right. Yet even the fellowship of a meal shared long ago became in the Eucharist one of the more important features of at least one religion, and was clearly felt to be more than just the product of companionship and good digestion.

For some it is the very sense of community (whether in church for worship, or in any shared activity that brings people closer together) which is the only purpose in going to church. By giving visible expression to one's belief in the value of community, we also gain a feeling of being brought closer to God. The quality of the worship of course and the beauty of the music may also lift the spirit closer to an experience of the sublime.

Then there is our sense of Wonder, the sublimation of mere sensual delight into something spiritual by the capacity of almost any sensed experience to be enjoyed not just for the satisfaction it affords to appetite, but as a source of joy and delight to the very depths and essence of our being, which in convenient shorthand we sometimes call the 'soul'. It lifts that enjoyment into a realm that seems to transcend what is earthly and we are, to quote Wordsworth again, 'surprised by Joy.'

Wonder may seem so overwhelming that our response trembles on the brink of awe, which is so closely akin to blind terror that in a very different context Stormin' Norman Schwarzkopf used it in conjunction with 'shock' - a relatively feeble word - to describe the effect of the allies' aerial bombardment to expel Iraqi troops from Kuwait in 1991 in Operation Desert Storm. But awe, properly used, is suggestive rather of reverence, which itself is not far removed from love, a recognition of superhuman power allied to a certainty that it will not be deployed for evil purposes against us. And that reminds us of the words of the Psalmist, who declared that 'the fear of the Lord is the beginning of wisdom,' or the 'beginning of knowledge' according to the book of Proverbs, or as Job himself suggests more directly, 'the fear of the Lord is wisdom.' Awe is more than reverence; it is not fear, but rather a trembling recognition of our own insignificance in the face of overwhelming majesty.

The contemplation of the wonders of the natural world may often induce such feelings in us. Indeed early religions owe much to the combination of awe and wonder, fear and incomprehension, felt by early mankind in the contemplation of natural phenomena. Now that Science has told us that our world is a tiny speck in a middle-sized galaxy, which itself contains billions of suns and is itself but one among billions of galaxies, shock and awe, wonder and reverence, all continue to seem appropriate. They are in no way proof of God; they may facilitate a sense of God.

But beyond that there lie the questions which science cannot yet answer: Why? What is it all for? Is there a purpose? Does it all make sense? Faced with the inability of science to offer an answer, we are reduced to the same sense of utter perplexity, which once faced our early ancestors when they were confronted by natural phenomena for which we now have explanations. They called them 'God.' We may sometimes use the same term for the source of what we now know to be a vastly greater universe than was conceived of by our ancestors.

Attributing divinity to that which we cannot comprehend has a very respectable pedigree, even though at every stage of our development it is clear that we were wrong to do so. We shall certainly be wrong again. But in a sense, though our earlier gods have been diminished or obliterated by our expanding knowledge, the replacement God which our current ignorance creates has become far more extensive, complex, and elaborate. We no longer think of cosmic phenomena as Gods; but many believers are pretty comfortable with declaring in the Creed that we believe in God the Father, Maker of heaven and earth, and of all things, visible and invisible. All these sensations are conditioning factors which facilitate belief. They tell us nothing of what God is like, what he is, or what he requires of us. If we see or feel that God lies behind or within such phenomena, we may or may not be right. But such a perception is no proof that we are wrong.

And still we have no answer to the question of what it is all for. My mother once described God as 'Eternal Mind, expanding ever to elude.' For Plato he was the Good, and all forms of virtue and beauty partake of the essence of the Good. For Aristotle he was the Unmoved Mover – an idea which Dylan Thomas could have been seeking to express, when he referred to 'the force that through the green fuse drives the flower,' though I suspect that his outlook was more negative than that. But this idea of God as some sort of primal force echoes down the ages, expressive of some inarticulate feeling in humankind that he lies at the heart of all that is.

God asked Job, 'Can't thou bind the sweet influences of the Pleiades? Declare if thou hast understanding', and Job feels compelled to confess his ignorance and repent in dust and ashes. The Psalmist declares that 'if I ascend up into heaven, thou art there; if I make my bed in hell, behold thou art there. If I take the wings of the morning and dwell in the uttermost parts of the sea, even there shall thy hand lead me, and thy right hand shall hold me.' Virgil, whom Dante elevated to the status of honorary Christian, offered the same idea of God as Spirit permeating all that is. Walter de la Mare asked 'Who calls even the starry lichen to climb by agelong inches endless Time?' The extraordinary fact of creativity, the fashioning of something out of nothing, which is the activity of Nature, at one level, and of every kind of artist at another, similarly offers us a metaphor for the possibility of God.

I have never found it hard to imagine myself a pantheist, because I find in Nature such wonder and beauty and complexity that it still offers a powerful metaphor for the God I cannot imagine. Those who reject pantheism but strive to rescue the perception by translating it into panentheism are I suspect singing from the same hymn sheet, and might as well start counting up the number of angels dancing on the heads of a pin. I am sure we are all acknowledging a similar perception.

But how many more dimensions of cosmic eternity have we yet to penetrate? Is it not possible that we are not the climax of creation, as we arrogantly suppose, but still part of its earliest development? May there not yet be far more to know than we have yet discovered? To ask such questions is not to offer even the beginning of an answer; but it may help us to develop an appropriate mindset. But however we now see God, he cannot be a royal king sitting in heaven on a golden throne, dispensing justice to the kingdoms of the earth. He has become far more – a God of infinite possibility. Or as Emily Bronte wrote, in the last lines she ever penned:

Though earth and man were gone,
And suns and universes ceased to be,
And thou were left alone,
Every existence would exist in thee.
There is not room for Death,
Nor atom that his might could render void:
Thou – thou art Being and Breath,
And what thou art may never be destroyed.

And what about Love? The word, sadly, is now so tarnished and cheapened by excessive use and carnal associations that it has lost the purity and beauty that was once its glory. How strange it is that English, arguably the richest language in the world, has so few words for love, when Eskimos can conjure up some fifty-two different words for snow. But for them, of course, snow is the inescapable and abiding reality – no wonder they seek to express their perceptions of it by every sort and kind of subtle variation. Should we not be trying to do the same with our perception of God, if he too is for us the inescapable and abiding reality.

Love that is all-giving, unselfish, sacrificial, utterly generous, all-embracing, all-creative, all-affirming, all-anything-you-like, remains the ultimate metaphor for God. *Agape*, the Greek word for what we might call Spiritual Love, has never caught on, though preachers use it sometimes in a desperate attempt to escape from the modern associations of its all-purpose generic equivalent, though to me it always sounds an affectation. Yet *Agape* is what St Paul called it in his immortal First Epistle to the Corinthians, asserting that in the end three things remain, Faith, Hope, and *Agape* – and the greatest of these is *Agape* (Spiritual Love).

And if Love is our best metaphor for God, Science surely must fall silent: for *Agape* has nothing to do with the sex-drive, the desire to procreate, the selfish gene, or mere carnal pleasure. To love is to be true to yourself by finding your true self in the love for another, and for all others, and in the very joy of it all to experience the prefiguring glimpse of heaven which, if all is well, awaits us in another place and in another time, when we too shall become part of all that was, and is, and is to come – which some call God.

Section H: Bibliography

And ye shall know the truth, and the truth shall make you free

John *8.32*

Truth is not circumscribed by rationality, but it needs rationality to know itself as truth
Archbishop John Habgood

An Apologia

This book has never been intended to be an academic treatise; it is at best the record of a journey. A large bibliography, therefore, might seem to be unnecessary, an excuse perhaps for showing off, but little more. But what I hope this list offers is some sort of evidence for my claim to have thought and read about my faith for a long time. I hope it also acknowledges the sources of my own ever-changing ideas, which have evolved over a lifetime. I may well have distorted, unintentionally misunderstood, or misquoted those sources, or even extrapolated from them ideas that are beyond the intentions of their authors. For all such shortcomings in this respect I can only apologise. For those who wish to pursue the quest further, it may be a useful source of further reading.

I once said to a Cambridge don, who had collected a vast library, whose books occupied innumerable shelves all over a fairly capacious house, 'Have you read all these books?' His reply was very precise. 'No. But I have used them all.' All of the books in this list are in my shelves; most of them have been marked or annotated, whether in whole or in part. I believe I have read the majority, though with a declining memory, I could most certainly not report their contents now. I am sure that, like my mentor, I have used almost all of them. Not all of their contents accord with my own ideas – some have done little more than confirm my own perception of their authors' limitations; others I have read without absorbing them into my own thinking. I include them for interest, comprehensiveness and balance.

I am sure at least that I am a child of my time, in that I went up to Cambridge in 1957 at a time when intellectual excitement was in the air – scientifically with the discovery of the structure of DNA; theologically with John Robinson's *Honest to God*, Alec Vidler's *Soundings*, and Harry Williams as another enfant terrible of the religious anti-establishment. Mervyn Stockwood's tenure as vicar of Great St Mary's, the university church, found me listening with great excitement to interesting national figures like Nye Bevan and Malcolm Muggeridge, as well as Mervyn himself, arguing passionately on issues of the day. My own final year academic supervisor was the great Sir Moses Finley, one of the most exciting lecturers in the university, whose courses were widely attended even by those who were not studying his subject. He was bringing challenging new approaches to the study of ancient history. It was a great time to be a student and inevitable that, however belatedly, I would sooner or later find myself, like my seniors, challenging the accepted wisdom of authority.

I hope, at the very least, I have not suggested that my ideas, which are largely

216

derivative, owe anything to my own genius or original research. The contents of my essays are nothing more than the exercises of a reasonably well-read student, older perhaps but no cleverer than any well-intentioned undergraduate, putting together what he has learned from others. I am not an original thinker or a learned scholar, but I have always been an ordinary, interested man-in-the-pew, full of admiration for those who find faith easier than I do, grateful to many clergy who have listened to me with a patience that does great credit to their calling, but dismayed by the failure of the leaders of my own faith to lead me to pastures less barren than those to which I have sadly had to grow accustomed.

The list, therefore, may offer ideas for further reading to anyone who is surprised, interested, or even outraged by what I have written. I hope I have indicated in the main text my debt to a few authors who have become central to my ideas, and whose openness to new thinking has helped to set me free from the chains of outmoded theology in my own faith community. Some books I read many years ago, but where they have (I believe) shaped my ideas, even by proving uncompelling, I include them. One or two are works of fiction, there is one long poem, but most are conventionally theological, many at a popular level – but we need good popular writers to mediate difficult ideas to ordinary people.

Section 1 contains the books that have remained most strongly in my memory as having caught my imagination or shaped my thinking at the time I read them. Section 2 contains a much wider list of books, which I have read with interest, admiration, or despair over a lifetime.

Reading List 1

Alves, Rubem	The Poet, The Warrior, The Prophet (SCM)
Ardrey, Robert	African Genesis (Collins)
	The Territorial Imperative (Collins)
Armstrong, Karen	A Short History of Myth (Cannongate)
	The Great Transformation (Atlantic Books)
	The Spiral Staircase (Harper)
Barton M. & Muddiman, J. (Edd.)	The Oxford Bible Commentary (Oxford)
Bellah, Robert N.	Religion in Human Evolution (Harvard)
Borg, Marcus J.	Jesus (Harper One)
	Meeting Jesus Again for the First Time (Harper One)
	The God We Never Knew (Harper)
	Reading the Bible Again for the First Time (Harper One)
Borg and Crossan	The Last Week (Harper)
Boulton, David	Who on Earth was Jesus? (O Books)
Bowden, John	Jesus, The Unanswered Questions (SCM)
Brown, Raymond	The Community of the Beloved Disciple (Paulist Press)
Churcher, John	Setting Jesus Free (Circle Books)
	Dying to Live (Circle Books)
Crossan, John Dominic	The Birth of Christianity (T&T Clark)
	The Historical Jesus - Life of a Mediterranean Jewish Peasant (Harper)
	A Long Way From Tipperary (Harper)
	God and Empire (Harper One)
	The Greatest Prayer (SPCK)

Crossan J.D. & Reed, J.L.	Excavating Jesus - Beneath the Stones, Behind the Texts (Harper)
	In Search of Paul (Harper One)
De Chardin, Teilhard	The Phenomenon of Man (Collins)
Dodds, E.R.	The Greeks and the Irrational (University Press)
Durant, Will & Ariel	The Lessons of History (Simon & Schuster)
Fox, Robin Lane	Pagans and Christians (Penguin)
	The Unauthorized Version – Truth & Fiction in the Bible (Viking)
Frazer, Sir James	The Golden Bough (Macmillan)
Freeman, Charles	A New History of Early Christianity (Yale)
	AD 381 – Heretics, Pagans, and the Christian State (Pimlico)
Funk R. & Hoover R. (Edd.) (The Jesus Seminar)	The Five Gospels (Harper One)
	The Acts of Jesus (Harper)
Gregg, John A.F.	The Primitive Faith and Roman Catholic Developments (APCK)
	The Decian Persecutions (Blackwood and then Legacy Reprints)
Harrison, Jane	Prolegomena to the Study of Greek Religion (Meridien)
Hick, John (Ed.)	The Myth of God Incarnate (SCM)
Holland, Tom	In the Shadow of the Sword (Little, Brown)
Holloway, Richard	Doubts and Loves – What is Left of Christianity (Canongate)
	Looking in the Distance (Canongate)
	Leaving Alexandria (Canongate)
MacCulloch, Diarmaid	A History of Christianity (Allen Lane)
Mack, Burton L.	The Lost Gospel – Q, the Book of Christian Origins (Element)
McGrath, Alister	Christian Theology (Blackwell)
	Mere Theology (SPCK)
Murray, Gilbert	Five Stages of Greek Religion (Thinkers Library)
Plato	The Apology
	The Phaedo

	The Symposium
	The Republic
Ramsey, Ian T.	Religious Language (SCM)
	On Being Sure in Religion (Athlone)
Robinson, John A.T.	Honest to God (SCM)
Rogers, Byron	The Man Who Went into the West - A life of R.S. Thomas (Aurum)
Russell, Bertrand	The Problems of Philosophy (Oxford)
Seaver, George	John Allen Fitzgerald Gregg, Archbishop (The Faith Press)
Sedlacek, Tomas	Economics of Good and Evil (Oxford)
Spong, John Shelby	Resurrection – Myth or Reality (Harper)
	Born of Woman (Harper Collins)
	The Sins of Scripture (Harper)
	Reclaiming the Bible for a Non Religious World (Harper One)
	Jesus for the Non Religious (Harper)
	Liberating the Gospels (Harper)
	This Hebrew Lord (Harper Collins)
	Why Christianity Must Change or Die (Harper)
	Eternal Life: A New Vision (Harper One)
Taylor, John V.	The Go Between God (SCVM)
Tillich, Paul	The Courage to Be (Fontana)
	The Shaking of the Foundations (Pelican)
Valantasis, Richard	The Gospel of Thomas (Routledge)
Van Dyke, Henry	The Story of the Other Wise Man (Harper)
Vermes, Geza	Christian Beginnings (Allen Lane)
	The Authentic Gospel of Jesus (Allen Lane)
	The Passion (Penguin)
Vidler, A.R. (Ed.)	Soundings (CUP)
Ward, Keith	Re-thinking Christianity (One World)
Weiner, Jonathan	The Beak of the Finch – Evolution in Real Time (Cape)
White, Patrick	Riders in the Chariot (E & S)
Wilson, John	Thinking with Concepts (CUP)
	The Truth of Religion (SPCK)
	Language and the Pursuit of Truth (CUP)

Reading List 2

Wider Reading

Alker, Adrian (ed.)	Together in Hope (St Marks CRC Press)
Anonymous	The Cloud of Unknowing (Ed.Clifton Wolters – Penguin)
Armstrong, Karen	A History of God (Vintage)
	The Case for God (Bodley Head)
	The Bible (Atlantic Books)
Bach, Richard	Jonathan Livingston Seagull (Turnstone)
Baker, John Austin	The Foolishness of God (DLT)
Barker, Margaret	The Hidden Tradition of the Kingdom of God (SPCK)
Bomford, Rodney	The Symmetry of God (Free Association Books)
Bonhoeffer, Dietrich	Letters and Papers from Prison (Fontana)
Booth, Roger P.	Contrasts – Gospel Evidence (Paget Press)
	The Trouble with God (O Books)
Bragg, Melvyn	Credo (Sceptre)
Bronowski, J.	The Ascent of Man (BBC)
Brown, David	Tradition and Imagination – Revelation & Change (Oxford)
Bultmann, Rudolf	The History of the Synoptic Tradition (Blackwell)
Chadwick, Owen	Michael Ramsey – A Life (SCM)
Clarke, Richard	A Whisper of God (Columba Press)
Cupitt, Don	The Long Legged Fly (SCM)
	The Sea of Faith (BBC)
	The Last Philosophy (SCM)
Davies, Paul	The Mind of God - Science & the Search for Meaning (Simon & Schuster)

Davies, Philip R. et al   The Complete World of the Dead Sea Scrolls (Thames and Hudson)

Dawkins, Richard   The Blind Watchmaker (Longman)

De Chardin, Teilhard   Hymn of the Universe (Fontana)

Le Milieu Divin (Fontana)

The Future of Man (Fontana)

The Making of a Mind (Collins)

Dodd, C.H.   The Bible Today (Cambridge)

The Interpretation of the Fourth Gospel (CUP)

Historical Tradition in the Fourth Gospel (CUP)

Drummond, Henry   The Greatest Thing in the World (Methuen)

Emmet, E.R.   Learning to Philosophize (Penguin)

Evans, J.J.   Guard our Unbelief (Oxford)

Ferguson, Richard   Listen to the Gospels (Memoir Club)

Fortey, Richard   Life (Folio)

Freke T. & Gandy P.   The Jesus Mysteries (Thorsons)

Fuller, R.H.   The Foundations of New Testament Christology (Fontana)

Gardner, Helen   Religion and Literature (Faber & Faber)

Garnsey, Peter & Saller, Richard   The Roman Empire - Economy, Society and Culture (Duckworth)

Gascoigne, Bamber   The Christians (Cape)

Gibran, Kahlil   The Prophet (Heinemann)

Golding, William   The Double Tongue (Faber)

Grayling, A.C.   The Good Book – A Secular Bible (Bloomsbury)

Gregg, John A.F.   The Epistle of St Clement (SPCK)

The Wisdom of Solomon (CUP)

Guillaumont et al   The Gospel According to Thomas – the Coptic Text (Leiden)

Habgood, John   Making Sense (SPCK)

Religion and Science (Mills & Boon)

Hallam, Elizabeth   Chronicles of the Crusades (Guild Publishing)

Handy, Charles   The Hungry Spirit (Hutchinson)

Hawking, Stephen   A Brief History of Time (Bantam)

The Universe in a Nutshell (Bantam)

Hitchens, Christopher   God is not Great (Atlantic Books)

Hobson, Theo	Milton's Vision - The Birth of Christian Liberty (Continuum)
Holloway, Richard	Godless Morality (Canongate)
	Let God Arise (Mowbray)
Holmes, Finlay	Our Irish Presbyterian Heritage (Presbyterian Church in Ireland)
Hoover, Roy (Ed.)	Profiles of Jesus (Polebridge)
Hume, Basil	To Be a Pilgrim (SPCK)
Jenkins, David	God, Miracle, and the Church of England (SCM)
	The Calling of a Cuckoo (Continuum)
Kazantzakis, Nikos	The Last Temptation of Christ (Bantam)
Kirschner M. & Gerhart J.	The Plausibility of Life (Yale)
Lewis, C.S.	Surprised by Joy (Fontana)
	Reflections on the Psalms (Fontana)
	The Problem of Pain (Fontana)
	The Screwtape Letters (Fontana)
Lorenz, Konrad	Here am I – Where Are You? (Harper)
Macgregor, Neil	Seeing Salvation (BBC)
McClen, Don	A Gallimaufry (privately published)
	The Heart of Things (privately published)
Marxsen, Willi	The Resurrection of Jesus of Nazareth (SCM)
Mayne, Michael	The Enduring Melody (Darton, Longman and Todd
Mehta, Ved	The New Theologians (Weidenfeld & Nicolson)
Meyer, Marvin	The Gnostic Gospels (Folio Society)
Micklem, Nathaniel	A Religion for Agnostics (SCM)
Milne, A.A.	The Norman Church (Methuen)
Mitchell, Stephen	Anatolia - Vol I and Vol II (Oxford)
Momen, Moojan	The Bahai Faith (One World)
Morris, Desmond	The Naked Ape (Cape)
Moorhead, Alan	Darwin and the Beagle (Hamish Hamilton)
Mott, Sir Nevill	Can Scientists Believe? (James & James)
Neil, William	The Rediscovery of the Bible (Hodder & Stoughton)
Oldham, J.H.	Life is Commitment (SCM)
Pannenberg, Wolfhart	Jesus, God and Man (SCM)
Paton Walsh, Jill	Knowledge of Angels (Black Swan)
Peacocke, Arthur	Paths from Science Towards God (One World)

Phillips, J.B.	Ring of Truth (Hodder & Stoughton)
Pinkler, Steven	The Blank Slate – the Modern Denial of Human Nature (Allen Lane)
Polkinghorne, John	Science and Providence (SPCK)
Pope Benedict XVI	Jesus of Nazareth (Bloomsbury)
Powell, Enoch	The Evolution of the Gospel (Yale)
Priestland, Gerald	Something Understood (Arrow)
	Priestland's Progress (BBC)
	The Case Against God (Collins)
Price, S.R.F.	Rituals and Power – The Roman Imperial Cult (Cambridge)
Proctor, W.C.G.	The Study of Theology over 50 Years in the Church of Ireland (Weyland)
Pullman, Philip	The Good Man Jesus and the Scoundrel Christ (Canongate)
Ramsey, Michael	The Resurrection of Christ (Fontana)
	The Christian Priest Today (SPCK)
	Be Still and Know (Fount)
Rees, Martin	Before the Beginning – Our Universe and Others (Simon & Schuster)
Ridley, Matt	The Origins of Virtue (Viking)
Runciman, Steven	History of the Crusades (Penguin)
Salmon, George	The Infallibility of the Church (John Murray)
Schumacher, E.F.	Guide for the Perplexed (Abacus)
Simms, George Otto	In my Understanding (Gill and MacMillan)
Smith, Riley	Oxford Illustrated History of the Crusades (Oxford)
Stockwood, Mervyn	Cambridge Sermons (Faith Press)
Temple, William	Readings in St John (St Martins)
Verney, Stephen	Fire in Coventry (Hodder & Stoughton)
	Into the New Age ((Fount)
	Water into Wine (Fount)
Vanstone, W.H.	Love's Endeavour, Love's Expense
Vernon, Mark	Science, Religion and the Pursuit of Truth (Palgrave)
Watson, S.J.	A Dinner of Herbs (Watson Books)
Waugh, Alexander	God (Headline)
Weatherhead, Leslie	The Christian Agnostic (Hodder & Stoughton)
Weinberg, Steven	The First Three Minutes (Deutsch)

Williams, H.A.	Jesus and the Resurrection (Mowbrays)
	The True Wilderness (Constable)
Williams, Rowan	Anglican Identities (D.L.T)
	Faith in the Public Square (Bloomsbury)
Wilson, A.N.	Jesus (Weidenfeld & Nicolson)
	Paul – The Mind of the Apostle (Sinclair-Stevenson)
	God's Funeral (John Murray)
Wilson, Brian W.J.G.	A Faith Unfaithful (Author House)
Wilson, Ian	Jesus, The Evidence (Weidenfeld & Nicolson)
Winston, Robert	The Story of God (Bantam)
Yadin, Yigael	Masada – the Zealots' Last Stand (BCA)

I could have added a fair number of poets to these lists. But they are well covered at (perhaps excessive) length in Chapters 33-35.